STUPIDITY
IN ACTION

STUPIDITY
IN ACTION

LESSONS LEARNED IN
LEADERSHIP THE HARD WAY

CLARK HUFF

*To Mom and Dad for all they provided me,
and their tolerance as they tried to teach me life's lessons*

*To Rudy Higgins for teaching me that the boss doesn't have to
know everything and should listen to and consider others' ideas;
and for his efforts in advancing my career*

TABLE OF CONTENTS

How Did I Get Here?

Never judge a book by its cover or a boy by his stupidity

As my last day on the job ends, I pull my car out of the executive garage and stop in the parking lot to look at my old office building. It is February 29, 2012. I have been working for almost 39 years and wonder if retiring is a mistake. I feel very conflicted. On the one hand, my parents are having health issues and need assistance. Since I am the oldest of their children, it's my duty to take care of them. On the other hand, I am leaving behind a job I really enjoy and people who are like my extended family—friends that I know I'll really miss.

Being the Vice President of Capital and Technology for the last eight years of my career had been my dream job. I got to spend the company's money to build new facilities and improve existing ones. I was always looking for opportunities that provided the company a strategic advantage. It was an adult version of the board game Monopoly, one where I spent roughly $300 million each year to beat out the competition.

How did I get here? I had been a difficult child who didn't show the proper respect to adults, especially those in authority. Because of this, most adults didn't think I'd ever amount to much. My first grade teacher even predicted I would either be dead or in jail before I graduated from high school. She was almost right. But, fortunately, I was lucky enough to spend my childhood in the right town.

I was born in Spanish Fork, Utah, a small farming town about 45 miles south of Salt Lake City. Spanish Fork was a Mormon community where my dad's family had lived for five generations. Although they had been farmers, my dad decided to do something different and became an electrician. My mother had grown up in Moab, Utah, and later moved to Spanish Fork where she met my dad. After dating for several months, they were married in 1949. I was born almost exactly a year later. Since my birthday was one day before my parents' anniversary, as a child I told people I was born the day before they were married. I couldn't understand why this upset my mother.

I was the oldest of four children and thought my siblings' role in life was to be my scientific guinea pigs. Fortunately, none of them were seriously hurt. It turned out that the one receiving the most serious injury from one of my experiments was me. It was not the first nor last explosion I'd be responsible for. But as a child I didn't really think I could be seriously injured. Nor did I think I needed to follow my parents' instructions, particularly if they weren't around. As a consequence, I was always getting into mischief and doing things that were stupid and often dangerous.

As a ten-year-old, I managed to infuriate my mother to the point that I never spent another summer at home until I graduated from high school. Instead, I worked on my uncle and cousin's mink ranches. It wasn't much fun but I did learn a lot about life. As a teenager, I became well known around town for my shenanigans and willful disregard for the law. I borrowed the skeleton, Igor, from the high school biology lab and took it for a joy ride. I thought it would like to see the town for a change. On another occasion my friends and I took live turkeys to the junior prom. To me, nothing seemed to be out of bounds. Consequently, I got to know the local police officers, including the chief of police, on a first-name basis.

As I sit in the company parking lot thinking about my childhood, I can't believe how lucky I'd been to go from being that troublesome boy who disregarded the rules to becoming a senior executive for a company, an executive who controlled millions of dollars. How in the world had I been able to do it? Looking back, I could see that some of my worst mistakes ended up teaching me the most crucial lessons. Unfortunately, I would sometimes have to make the same mistake multiple times before I truly appreciated the lesson. But I did gradually learn and was able to change my behavior. Over time, these changes accumulated and resulted in a different person, a person who was able to gradually advance toward a brighter future. Yet, it took quite a few lessons to achieve this. Oddly enough, one of the first lessons was the result of eight-year-old me getting a BB gun for Christmas.

CHAPTER 1

The BB Gun War

The quest for excitement often leads to stupidity

Much to my parents' dismay, I was not an obedient child. And, unfortunately, they couldn't change that. They reasoned with me, punished me for bad behavior, bribed me with gifts and fishing trips to be good. Nothing worked. I didn't want to be bad. I just wanted excitement. And even though I knew I shouldn't do something, it didn't stop me. In fact, doing something I shouldn't just added to the excitement. My parents tried spanking me but it only hurt for a little while. No big deal. If I was grounded to my bedroom, I always found something to play with or take apart.

Growing up in Spanish Fork, Utah, in the 1950s meant my interest in guns was inevitable. Hunting was a way of life there; it was the main topic of discussion among Dad's friends in the fall. All of them owned rifles and they regularly debated which rifle was best for the deer hunt after debating where to go to shoot that deer. As a boy, I loved hiking in the mountains while hunting deer with dad and his friends, but I couldn't be "one of the boys" since I didn't own a rifle. It would be so exciting to use a gun to blow things apart. I was thrilled when Dad let me fire one of his rifles, under very close supervision. When the opportunity presented itself, and none of my tattletale siblings were nearby, I would sneak out Dad's rifle and pretend I was shooting a deer or defending myself from a bear. As my eighth birthday approached, a rifle seemed like a reasonable request for a birthday present. But despite my crusade to get a rifle, I was seriously disappointed. I only got new school clothes. Whoopee. I couldn't believe it.

Then I had a second chance. My birthday and Christmas were only a month apart. Maybe I could get one from Santa. I pestered my parents nonstop, but based on their stunned reaction when I'd first asked, a deer rifle was apparently out of the question. However, a .22 caliber rifle would be a reasonable compromise since it was the least powerful rifle that used gunpowder to propel a bullet but would still punch holes in wood boards and kill birds and rodents. It seemed like a realistic gift for a boy my age.

Eight-year-old me and my BB gun

As Christmas approached, I vigorously campaigned for my rifle. At this point I had finally overcome most of my shyness and now had several neighborhood friends. They all had BB guns and teased me about not having one. This was ironic to me since a BB gun was just a toy. It used a spring to propel a BB rather than gunpowder. If I got a .22, the shoe would be on the other foot. My friends would be jealous and I could look down my nose and sneer at them and their lowly BB guns.

Christmas Day proved to be a disappointment. Santa left me a BB gun! I couldn't believe it. A BB gun! As an eight-year-old "young man," I'd received a baby's toy. What an embarrassment! And to make matters worse, I'd received a pump action model. To cock it, you pulled a handle down the barrel like a pump shotgun. All my friends had lever action BB guns. They cocked their guns using a lever behind the trigger just like *The Rifleman* on TV. Since my rifle was different my playmates would certainly tease me.

None of us wanted to be different since we knew that meant we would be tormented.

After some thought, I decided to discuss this predicament with Dad. I found him peering in the refrigerator looking for something to eat. Dad had black hair and stood a little under 6 feet tall which tended to intimidate me. He had just speared a piece of Christmas ham with a fork and was closing the refrigerator door when I approached.

"How come I didn't get a .22 for Christmas?" I asked.

"Because you can't be trusted to follow the rules," he said.

He might have had a point. His knitted eyebrows as he scowled at me made me think he wasn't happy about this discussion.

Dad continued. "For example, I told you not to torment your sister, yet you put grasshoppers in her bedroom while she was asleep. You knew she is terrified of them. And despite my warning, you talked your brother into climbing into an empty 55-gallon drum, then rolled him down a hill and he hit a tree. Need I go on?"

This conversation wasn't going where I'd hoped.

"And another thing," Dad said. "You can only shoot your BB gun outside in our back yard."

I couldn't think of a good reason not to shoot it in the house, but I didn't think this was the time to bring it up. Experience told me that when the volume of Dad's voice went up it was time to back off.

I decided to put on my coat and head outside to try out my new weapon. Our Christmas that year was cold and snowy, but I didn't feel any holiday cheer thanks to my new gun's lousy performance. It didn't blast holes in things the way a deer rifle did. Rather, the BBs barely penetrated a board or sometimes just bounced off the wood. If I happened to spot a bird and shoot it, the BB didn't do much damage unless it was really close. Otherwise, it just annoyed the bird.

As the day dragged on, I became bored—not a good sign since mischief usually followed. That evening, my parents took my youngest brother, Brad, to visit friends a few houses away. This was the chance I'd been waiting for. I could now experiment with more interesting targets, those of which my parents might not approve.

I set up a few toys on my bedroom floor and shot them. The BBs just bounced off. Darn. I headed back upstairs. While sitting on the couch thinking, I noticed the glass bulbs on the Christmas tree. I knew that when I dropped one while decorating the tree it broke with a pop. Since my other siblings were playing in a bedroom, I decided to give it a try.

I took aim at a large blue bulb on the Christmas tree and pulled the trigger. It exploded with a satisfying pop. This was exciting. I could pretend that I had a super destructive, high-powered weapon. The ornaments made excellent targets, as long as I didn't get caught. I shot a few more bulbs but didn't want to press my luck too far. I cleaned up the mess the best I could without making any noise and alerting my siblings. Later, I discovered that some BBs had become embedded in the sheet rock wall behind the tree. I hadn't realized this would happen when I missed a bulb. However, since they weren't very visible, I wasn't too worried. However, I was worried my parents would notice the bulbs missing from the front of the tree. I hurriedly moved bulbs from the back of the tree to fill in the blank spaces. I figured no one looked at the back of the tree anyway.

Target practicing on the Christmas tree bulbs continued for the next few days when no one was around. I would only shoot a few bulbs at a time so any change wouldn't be too noticeable. I was having a lot of fun and my aim improved. I was eventually able to hit a bulb from all the way back of the kitchen, over 40 feet away.

Unfortunately, my mother eventually noticed the Christmas tree looking kind of bare. Upon further investigation, she found fragments of broken bulbs under the tree. She wondered what had happened. Then she noticed the occasional BB embedded in the wall. I was doomed. She found me in my bedroom and told me what she had discovered and said I was going to get it when Dad got home from work.

With a sense of pending doom, I waited for Dad. Finally, he trudged through the door. His slow walk told me that he hadn't had a good day at the steel mill. Mom's revelation didn't help his attitude.

"It looks like you've been at it again," he said. "Now do you see why you couldn't have a rifle?"

I didn't know what to say to that.

"I'm confiscating your BB gun for six months, plus you need to clean up the mess you've made."

You'd think I'd have learned something from this. I didn't.

Always remember to watch your back

Finally, toward the end of the school year, I got my BB gun back. Although Mom was not convinced I could be trusted, Dad finally gave in. He was tired of hearing me whine. As he handed me the gun he made me promise to obey the rules. And as an afterthought he told me I'd better not shoot my siblings.

Shooting in the backyard resumed as well as going on some hunting expeditions. My friends were a collection of boys who lived within a few blocks of me. Unlike today, we seldom watched TV since most of the shows on the three commercial channels were for adults and of little interest to us kids. Thus, we spent most of our time playing outside. And since I now had my BB gun back, we walked around the neighborhood looking for unsuspecting birds in the trees that lined the streets. Unfortunately, the birds quickly caught on and flew off as soon as they saw one of us raise our rifles. Since shooting targets wasn't much fun, we needed to come up with somewhere new to shoot where the animals weren't so leery of us.

One of my friends suggested a place on the south side of town called the River Bottoms about the size of a city block and covered with a dense forest of trees, shrubs, and grass. Being fairly secluded, birds and small animals used it as a refuge. There were trails meandering through it and a stream ran along one side. It was about a mile from my house so we could get there on our bikes without much trouble.

Initially, we found the River Bottoms an ideal place to hunt the unsuspecting animals with our BB guns. After a while, however, even this started to lose its appeal. The birds and animals once again started to hide as soon as they saw us coming. We searched for other options but couldn't find any place better. As I thought about the situation, I came up with an exciting idea. I was always ingenious if there was an opportunity for adventure. Why not use the River Bottoms to stage a war? There were plenty of places to hide and ambush someone. And from experience I knew that getting hit with a BB only left a bruise. Sure, it hurt a little, but there was no serious damage. We would be like soldiers we'd seen in the movies fighting in the forests of Europe during the Second World War. We could divide into teams and use our BB guns to attack each other. This seemed like a lot of fun.

As I discussed the plan with my friends, an obstacle raised its ugly head. We had all been warned about the danger of being hit in the eye with a BB. None of us wanted to end up blind. Although we made a rule that we had to aim below a person's shoulders, there was still a chance someone would get hit in an eye.

I was stymied by the problem initially, but then had an inspiration. We could use safety glasses. I knew about them because Dad had to wear them to work at U.S. Steel's Geneva plant and sometimes he inadvertently brought a pair home. When I asked about them, he explained that they were strong enough to protect his eyes from stray metal fragments while pounding on things with a hammer. The glasses also had side shields to further protect his eyes. Since he sometimes forgot to take them back to work, he had accumulated several pairs over the years. And, I knew where he kept them in the bedroom drawer.

Since several of my friends' dads worked at the same plant, they also had access to spare safety glasses. I spoke to them and we were able to round up enough glasses to equip the entire army. To provide extra protection, we would still adhere to the rule of aiming below the shoulders. We also solemnly promised that we would keep our new game a secret. We suspected that even with the safety precautions our parents wouldn't approve. However, the potential thrill of the adventure convinced us it was worth the risk.

On the day of our first battle we stuffed our gear in a couple of backpacks, climbed on our bikes, and vigorously pedaled to the

River Bottoms. It was a bright, summer morning and we were kept cool by the breeze blowing from Spanish Fork Canyon as we made our way through town.

When we arrived, we parked our bikes in the bushes on the perimeter of our play area. It took a few seconds for our eyes to adjust to the dark as we walked under the tall trees, whose shade significantly lowered the outside temperature. Then we followed a meandering trail around the fallen trees and other obstacles to the center of our battleground. In some places we had to climb over large logs where old trees had fallen. I saw bushes and other vegetation intermingled with the trees and made a mental note that they would provide good cover for an ambush.

Upon reaching the center of our play area, the ten of us selected two team leaders. For the first battle, Marty Cole and I were elected team captains. Marty was considerably taller and larger than the rest of us and tended to also be a leader. Marty and I took turns choosing team members. After reviewing the rules, we walked to opposite sides of the battleground. The goal was to eliminate the opposing team. Anyone shot three times was out of the game. We counted to a hundred and the war was on. We began to sneak through the jungle looking for an opponent to shoot.

We weren't smart enough to stick together as a team to defend each other. Instead, we each headed off on our own. During the first round, while sneaking along a trail, I came up behind Marty. He was crouched down behind a log cautiously peering over it to see whom he could ambush. Since his back was turned, I very quietly snuck up behind him. When I got within six feet, I took careful aim and shot him in the butt. He let out a scream, jumped over the log and took off running down the trail. I chased after him. Turned out the pump action gun my friends ridiculed came in handy. I could pump the handle to cock the gun and pull the trigger while I continued to chase Marty. After a few seconds of me shooting and him screaming, I started laughing so hard I had to sit down on the side of the trail to catch my breath. While I was thus incapacitated, he walked back and shot me in the leg three times.

The pump action of my BB gun had turned out to be more useful than anticipated. Now the kids who had sneered at my pump action rifle all wanted one. To rub it in I was very smug about my gun's superiority.

After the fun of our first battle, we headed to the River Bottoms once or twice a week for another war. This was a lot more fun than hunting birds. Since we were all learning from our mistakes, every battle was different. We couldn't use the same strategy too many times before the others figured out a way around it. We also learned the advantage of sticking together so we could help each other out.

Unfortunately, all good things must come to an end. Especially those that are forbidden. After six weeks of exciting battles, one of the warriors was telling a friend about our game and his parents overheard him. A few phone calls later and all our parents knew. Predictably, they were not happy. Unfortunately, to try to save themselves, a couple of my friends ratted me out. They said it was all my idea and they were just following along. I pointed out my foresight in using safety glasses. It didn't help. I was grounded for a month and the BB gun confiscated for another six months. I kind of lost interest in the BB gun after that because there wasn't anything fun I could think of to do with it. Or at least nothing that wouldn't get me in trouble.

Not surprisingly, I was 12 before I got a .22 rifle and nearly 16 before Dad finally gave me a deer rifle. The sweetest part was that when I got the deer rifle I was one of the guys when we went hunting and no longer a junior member of the gang.

There were many valuable lessons I should have learned from this experience. Foremost among these was that obeying my parents and their rules would keep me safe. Unfortunately, I thought I was invulnerable, so this lesson would have to wait for another day. What I did learn was to never trust anyone with a secret and to always watch my back. Particularly if I was bent over and he had a BB gun.

CHAPTER 2

A Hike, Some Fishing, and a Spanking

Just when you think you're rescued, you get a surprise

As a child I was a major pain in the ass. It drove my parents crazy. They knew I did things that were dangerous and stupid, and constantly warned me about how it might end. But I liked the excitement and the risks didn't worry me. I never really believed my adventures would kill me or anyone else. I figured since I was generally the one at risk, it seemed reasonable I could do what I wanted. One of the more memorable examples of this stupidity occurred in the fall of 1960 when I was nine years old and spending a weekend at our cabin in the Wasatch Mountains.

The family cabin was a little less than a two-hour drive east of our house in Spanish Fork. Due to the mountains, the drive meandered quite a bit but was worth it. The cabin was situated in a small, wooded valley that led down to Strawberry Reservoir. My dad and uncle had been building the cabin for almost two years, but their progress was hampered because they could only work on it during summer weekends. I was glad when they finally had the outside walls and roof finished so I could sleep inside. I was tired of sleeping outside with the bugs, rodents, and snakes.

On the morning of the misadventure, I gradually awoke to the smell of cooking bacon. Knowing that breakfast was approaching, I hustled to get dressed and made a quick trip to the outhouse. I didn't like using it due to the flies and bees, but my parents insisted that I couldn't just go behind a tree. The outhouse was necessary since we didn't yet have running water. As I was eating the bacon and eggs, I started to develop a plan to convince Dad to take me fishing in his boat on the reservoir.

The family cabin

I knew he wanted to work on the cabin so I suspected it would be difficult. But after spending the week in school, I wanted to do something fun and I liked to fish. We were within 15 minutes of the lake, so maybe Dad would give in.

"Dad, I don't want to just hang around the cabin all day. Can't we go fishing?"

"Not this morning," Dad said. "You know I need to finish framing the bedroom walls."

It seemed like there was always work to do at the cabin. His current project was to complete the interior walls so that everyone could have a little privacy.

"But I'm tired of hanging around here. Let's just fish for a little while. Then you can come back and work on the cabin."

Dad scowled at me.

"If you think I'm having fun building the cabin you're kidding yourself. But I need to get this done. Now, go play outside and quit bothering me."

"If you won't go fishing, why don't you take me to the lake and leave me there to fish?"

"I'm not about to turn you loose at the lake. If you keep this up you'll be the guest of honor at a butt-kicking contest."

Apparently, he didn't think it was a good idea to have nine-year-old me wandering around the lake unsupervised.

He looked at me for a few seconds and then said, "Why don't you and your brother take your poles and walk down to the beaver ponds to fish. You can be there in fifteen minutes."

I had hoped to avoid this option. Although it was easy getting to the beaver ponds, we almost never caught any fish. Generally, I really enjoyed my brother's company. Although he was two years younger than me, Stan was a good athlete and able to keep up. We had a lot of fun playing together when at home and would often go hiking or fishing when at the cabin. Today, however, I suspected my parents wanted him along in the hope of keeping me out of trouble since he always told the truth and sometimes tattled on me if I was up to any shenanigans.

While Dad stood towering over me with a frown on his face, I decided I'd better not press my luck. Thus, at 10 a.m., Stan and I gathered up our fishing poles and a small tackle box and headed down the dirt road.

As we were leaving, Dad yelled, "Make sure you follow the road and stay by the beaver ponds." Then as an afterthought he yelled, "AND STICK TOGETHER!"

When we were out of sight of the cabin, I decided to take a shortcut rather than follow the road. By heading straight downhill, we would have to negotiate our way through the quaking aspens but the distance would be much shorter. Stan reluctantly followed along after reminding me we'd been told to follow the road.

Although it took longer than expected, we finally reached the beaver ponds. I found a lure in my tacklebox, hooked it to my line, and started fishing. We wandered around the ponds keeping an eye out for any danger. Most of the animals were not a problem, but we had to watch out for badgers since they tended to be aggressive.

As expected, the fishing sucked. We didn't get so much as a nibble. To pile on the aggravation every time we stopped to fish, the mosquitoes swarmed around us. If we were in the boat on the lake we wouldn't have this problem. The mosquitoes wouldn't normally follow us very far offshore. It didn't take long before I'd had enough. Yesterday, while fishing from the boat, we'd had our first bite in 10 minutes. I knew the boat was there just ready to go because after fishing yesterday Dad had rented a space at the dock and left the boat tied up there. I told my brother my plans.

Stan looked alarmed. "Dad told us to stay by the beaver ponds."

"We'll get back before they know we're missing. It's just a 15-minute drive to the marina."

"Even if we walk to the lake, we'll have to fish from shore. You don't know how to run the boat."

"I know all about the boat," I said, indignant. *He* was the one who didn't know how to run it. After all, he was two years younger than me. "Dad has let me sit on his lap and drive it several times. Plus, I know where he hides the key."

Stan stared at me skeptically. I'd show him.

"All we have to do," I explained, "is untie it from the dock, start the engine, and we'll be fishing in no time."

"You're going to get us in trouble!"

If he kept this up, he was getting abandoned again.

"I'm going," I said. "You'd better come along, you big sissy, or you'll be the one that's in trouble. Dad said we had to stick together."

With that, I grabbed my pole and tackle box and headed down the dirt road leading to the highway. Stan watched for a few seconds then reluctantly picked up his pole and followed. He didn't want to be a sissy.

As we headed down the valley, we dropped below the tree line into a sagebrush flat. Any time a car approached we scurried to the upwind side of the road to keep from getting pelted with dust. Although it took longer than expected, we finally reached the paved highway. I was happy to be away from all the dust but surprised by how long it had taken us to get this far. And we still had a long way to go. Maybe I'd underestimated how long it would take. However, I would never give up on something once I'd started.

We trudged along the highway for a while but it didn't seem like we were making much progress. We were also starting to get tired. I decided we should take another shortcut. I knew that the marina was off to our right, just over a low ridge. Since we were walking, what difference did it make if we were hiking through sagebrush or walking along the road? I told Stan of my plan and, although he was reluctant, he followed along.

Initially it wasn't too bad. As long as we kept moving, the bugs weren't bothering us. However, without any water, we were becoming very thirsty. Our faces, necks, and exposed skin were also getting sunburnt. There were several small hills we had to cross that I hadn't considered. They weren't too tall, but still added to our effort. We quit talking. It was all we could do to put one foot ahead of the other.

I could tell by the sun's position that it was starting to get late in the day. It seemed like we had been hiking forever and were becoming very tired and very, very thirsty. We were starting to reach our limit. We could only walk for a few minutes before our legs became so tired that they wouldn't work and would cramp up. We'd sit down and rest but it was hard to get up and start moving again. I felt like just lying down and taking a nap but was afraid I wouldn't wake up until night. As an adult, I now realize we were starting to suffer the symptoms of heat exhaustion. Through my stupidity I had unknowingly put us in serious danger.

After what seemed like an eternity, we finally made it to the marina. I could see Dad's red and white boat tied up near the end of the dock. Although it had a 100-horsepower outboard motor, you controlled it from the front of the boat with the steering wheel, throttle, and ignition switch. We climbed onboard and found a jug of warm, stale water, which we fought over. I won but as soon as I stopped for a breath, Stan pulled it away. There were also some snacks from the previous day. After we had recovered a little we discussed what to do. Since we had put so much effort into getting to the boat, it would be a shame if we didn't go out fishing. Plus, it would give us some time to recover while we figured out how to get back to the cabin.

I found the boat's key in the cubbyhole, untied the boat, and started the motor. As I backed away from the dock, several nearby adults watched us curiously. They apparently hadn't seen a nine-year-old and seven-year-old take a boat out alone before. We pulled a couple of hundred feet offshore and dropped anchor. I didn't want to get too far from the marina since it would get dark soon and I didn't want to get lost on the lake. We unwound while we fished, bug-free, in the welcome shade of the boat's canopy.

Sitting in the boat, I started to reconsider my decision. After all this effort the fish weren't biting. Also, we wouldn't be able to fish long before the sun set. I had no idea how we were going to get back to the cabin. Even with the cool nighttime temperatures, I didn't think we had enough stamina left to hike that far. I felt uneasy about asking a stranger at the marina to give us a ride back to the cabin. Although my parents would probably be a little upset, I hoped Dad would come looking for us and give us a ride.

No matter how much trouble you're in, you can always make it worse

As it turned out, my parents were more than just a little upset. Their nightmare started a couple of hours after we'd left the cabin. As lunchtime approached, Dad jumped in the car to go pick us up. When he arrived at the beaver ponds, he couldn't find us. He decided we might have hiked back to the cabin using a different route so he drove back to the cabin. We weren't there. He and Mom decided we might have headed to the lake to fish so they loaded my other two siblings in the car and drove to the marina. We weren't there either. Instead we were on our cross-country hike through the sagebrush. Unfortunately, they couldn't see us from the road and we didn't see them.

By now my parents were worried and growing more scared by

the minute because two of their children were missing. As an adult, I can certainly understand that. But as a kid, it didn't seem like a big thing. In any case, they drove back to the beaver ponds but we still weren't there. Next, they headed down to the highway and turned south to the ranger station. The ranger hadn't heard any reports of kids wandering around but would watch out for us. He told my parents that if they hadn't found us in a couple of hours, he would arrange a search party.

My parents were now really upset, particularly Mom. They drove around the roads looking for us and checked with the people they met. No one had seen us. They started to wonder if we had drowned in a beaver pond or if someone had kidnapped us. They checked the ponds again but still couldn't see any sign of us. Our parents decided to enlist the help of some of the other cabin owners to look for us. They worked out a search plan and headed out. By now my parents were frantic. The sun would be setting soon. They decided to make one more trip to the marina just in case we were there.

As they pulled into the marina, they saw their boat out in the lake and knew they'd found us. Mom and Dad were initially relieved. Then they became very, very mad. Based on past experience, they suspected I'd caused the fiasco. Pulling up to the dock, they saw us stand up in the boat and wave to them. I was happy that the problem of getting back to the cabin had been resolved. My euphoria, however, was short-lived. As I watched Dad jump out of the car and hurry down to the end of the dock I became worried. His quick stride and bunched up eyebrows made me suspect he was mad. Dad confirmed my suspicions when he yelled, "Clark, get the goddamn boat over here right now!"

Oh, shit. I was in for it now. I decided to put off the punishment as long as possible.

I yelled back, "No!"

This did not help Dad cool down. People around the marina gathered to watch the show. Having an audience was not helping my situation.

Dad yelled back, "What the hell do you mean 'no?' Haul in the damn anchor and bring the boat back to the dock NOW!"

"No. If I do, you're going to punish me."

"You're damned right you're going to get punished, and the longer you stay out there the worse it's going to get."

"Then I'm not coming back."

"Like hell you're not. Don't make me borrow a boat to come and get you. You won't like the outcome."

About this time Stan spoke up.

"We had better go back," he said. "We can't stay here forever and the longer we stay, the worse it's going to get."

It killed me that my younger brother was right, once again. We pulled up the anchor, started the motor, and headed to the dock. When we arrived, there was a small cheer from the crowd, which based on Dad glaring at them, further pissed him off. I knew I was in serious trouble since Dad didn't talk as he tied up the boat. Slowly the crowd dispersed.

While we walked down the pier toward the car, Dad stopped us.

"We are not going to discuss this until we get back to the cabin," he said. "But when you get in the car, you'd better apologize to your mother. She has been worried sick about you. She'd started to think you were both dead. You've put your mother through hell."

When I got in the car, Mom wouldn't even look at me. I told her I was sorry and that we hadn't meant to worry her. She didn't speak. She just shook her head and wiped tears from her face.

As we drove back to the cabin, Dad let the search parties know we were safe. He thanked them but kept the conversation short. I think he was embarrassed by the fiasco. At the cabin, he took Stan and me off to the side. He said that we had done a foolish thing. Not only had we disobeyed his strict instructions, we had put ourselves in danger. On top of all that since they couldn't find us for hours, Mom thought we might be dead. Stan felt compelled to point out that it was all my idea. This just confirmed Dad's suspicion.

I got whipped with a tree branch of my choosing; actually, the second branch of my choosing. Dad rejected the first one as being too small. In addition, I was grounded indefinitely for the Strawberry Fishing Incident, which meant no more fishing on this trip. I had to stay near the cabin. The worst thing was that Mom would only speak to me when she had to. She was really upset with me.

It was difficult for Mom to forgive me for the incident. For the first few weeks, she seldom spoke to me except to give me instructions. At the time, I couldn't understand why she was so upset. I'd known we were all right and although we'd done something we shouldn't, it didn't seem like a big deal. As a parent, I can appreciate how upset I'd be if one of my kids had done this. I now recognize I'd put Stan's and my life in serious jeopardy by setting out on a long hike without water. Unfortunately, I didn't learn the lessons I should have from this ordeal. It would take a few more years before I started to wise up. And, regrettably, Mom didn't forget what I'd done. I didn't realize there would be additional repercussions in the near future. Like everything I did as a kid, things never turned out the way I expected.

CHAPTER 3

Never Cross Your Mom

The quickest route to stupidity is anger

My first memories as a baby are of me sitting next to Mom on the piano bench. She was playing the piano and singing songs to me like "Rock-A-Bye Baby" and "Lullaby and Goodnight." She would play games with me in the front yard and spent most of her time with me. I felt I was special. And I was since I was her first child.

Then along came Stan. Mom pushed me aside and spent all of her time feeding and caring for him. She sang him the same songs she'd sung to me. I felt very sad and neglected. I couldn't understand what I'd done to cause her to ignore me and favor Stan. What made him so special? To make matters worse, as we grew up, Stan was honest and obeyed Mom. She constantly held him up as an example of how I should behave. This guaranteed I'd envy Stan's favored position with Mom while I became more of a problem for her. As I gradually became more rebellious, Mom became very frustrated with me.

Matters came to a head six months after the Strawberry Fishing Incident in what turned out to be a pivotal day in my life. It was early spring, 1961, and as usual Stan and I were playing outside. The day started innocently enough. Stan and I were enjoying the cool morning air while competing in a rock throwing contest. We'd had rock throwing contests before and been told not to do it, but since this time we weren't throwing rocks at each other, I thought it would be all right. The contest was to see who could throw a rock into the newspaper tube first.

Standing on the edge of the road facing our house, we could see our target. It was a horizontal, red metal tube nailed to a post on the left corner of our property that the paper boy used to deliver the *Daily Herald*. Also running along the left edge of the property was the double wide driveway. As usual, the boat and trailer were parked on the side of the driveway next to the property line. The boat faced the street so Dad could easily back up the car and hook it to the trailer hitch. The boat was his prized possession. Not many people in town had one. We not only used it for fishing but also for waterskiing and exploring the scenic canyons of Lake Powell.

As a mature ten-year-old, I thought it would be easy to beat my eight-year-old brother. We were standing on the edge of the street that ran past our house. Although the road was paved, there wasn't yet a curb or gutter. The rocks strewn in the dirt along the edge of the pavement provided our ammunition.

Playing outside was not unusual for us kids, especially considering the limited content on TV and the stifling heat indoors since we didn't have air-conditioning back then. Weekends when Stan and I were outside and our friends weren't available, we often played with each other. Although I was two years older, Stan was generally able to hold his own in our various competitions. We started our rock throwing contest 15 feet from the target using small, marble-sized rocks, taking turns to see who could get a rock in the red metal tube first. Much to my dismay, Stan won. I decided that the contest wasn't challenging enough. We moved back to the edge of the road and started using larger rocks. Occasionally a rock bounced off the tube and hit the boat trailer or the boat's underside. But since the rocks weren't very big and we were relatively close, we didn't have to throw them very hard. Thus, they weren't doing any damage. Again, Stan was the first to put a rock in the tube.

I couldn't tolerate having Stan beat me in a competition. I

would never hear the end of it. Maybe an even longer throw would improve my chances. We moved across the street. Since our target was now almost 75 feet away, we found that the small rocks didn't work very well. We quit taking turns. Instead, we would throw a rock at the tube as soon as we found one big enough. In our rush to get off the next shot, we started settling for whatever we could find; even the large flat rocks as long as we thought they would fit in the newspaper tube. This made the game much more challenging. Few of the rocks were even getting close to going in. Our errant throws would pass by the tube and generally bounce off the driveway or occasionally hit the underside of the boat. Fortunately, the boat was tough and took the punishment without much damage.

Recent picture of the house I grew up in—the newspaper tube (not shown) was on the left edge of the driveway

Finally, on one throw, Stan almost got a large rock into the tube. But at the last second it skipped off the upper lip of the metal tube. Much to our dismay, it bounced up and smacked the boat's windshield with a loud crack. Stan and I just stood there in wide-eyed shock. We couldn't believe what had just happened. We didn't know what to do. After a few seconds, we looked at each other then raced across the road to inspect the damage. Several cracks radiated out from the impact site. The boat was Dad's favorite toy. I started to hyperventilate. There was going to be hell to pay. I was just glad that I hadn't thrown the rock.

From inside the house, Mom heard the sound of breaking glass and dashed out onto the front porch to see what had happened. Stan and I looked up when we heard the door open. At 5 feet, 5 inches tall with a petite build, Mom didn't normally cast an imposing presence. However, this time I was worried. Mom stood on the porch with her hands on her hips and a scowl on her face. She meant business. Which usually meant trouble for me.

"What did you break this time?" she asked in a loud voice.

Initially there was just silence.

"Well?" she asked.

I waited for Stan to confess so I could see him catch hell for once. Maybe then Mom would realize Stan wasn't perfect. However, there was just silence. After several seconds, I couldn't stand it any longer.

"Stan threw a rock and it bounced and cracked the boat's windshield," I said.

"Stan did WHAT?!" She dashed over to the boat and inspected the windshield. Then she turned around and glared at Stan.

Stan stuttered a little and then said, "It wasn't me. It was Clark!"

I was speechless. Stan never lied. I couldn't believe he had resorted to my tactics. But apparently Mom's scowl and tone of voice convinced him there were going to be serious consequences. I was surprised and outraged by Stan's response. Finally, I said, "Mom, I didn't do it. Stan threw the rock."

"I did not! It was Clark!"

Mom glared at me for a few seconds.

"Dammit, Clark. I am tired of your lies. You're going to get it this time."

She dashed in the house and came back a few seconds later with a steel pancake turner she often used to spank me. Glaring, she said, "Get over here right now."

I walked slowly in her direction while maintaining my innocence. But by the look on Mom's face, I could tell I was screwed. It infuriated me to think that even when Stan did something wrong, I was the one who got punished. Mom reached out and grabbed my arm to spin me around so she could whack me on the butt.

At this point, I did something extraordinarily stupid. As Mom grabbed me, I grabbed her arm that held the pancake turner. Although I couldn't get free of her grip, she couldn't really spank me. I was able to impede her swings while dodging out of the way. We danced around on the porch for several seconds, but I was able to avoid getting whacked. Finally, Mom gave up and stormed into the house.

I stood there thinking about what had just happened. I suspected I was in serious trouble. A few seconds later, she came back to the front door and confirmed it.

"Clark, don't you come in this house. You can sit outside and think about what you've done until your dad gets home from work. Then you're really going to get it."

With that, she went back in the house and slammed the door.

As my indignation started to dissipate, I realized I should have let her spank me. It would have only hurt for a few minutes and eventually she'd find out what really happened and I would be off the hook. However, my rage at being punished for something Stan did got in the way of any rational thinking. I did something stupid at the spur of the moment. Now I was exiled from the house. Unfortunately, while she waited for Dad to come home, her anger didn't subside. Instead, it grew as she thought about what I'd done. As a father, I can now understand her anger and frustration at being outmaneuvered by her son. I'm lucky she only exiled me from the house.

Mom didn't speak to me for the rest of the day except to tell me to get out when she caught me sneaking back in the house. As I sat in the shade of the apple tree, I thought about my situation. I suspected I was doomed. My relationship with Mom had never fully recovered from the fiasco at Strawberry Reservoir. It had been difficult for Mom to get over me taking off with Stan. During the winter, she seldom spoke to me and mostly ignored me. I had placed our lives in serious jeopardy due to my disobedience. I think she was continually worried that I might do it again.

In the late afternoon, I moved to the front porch to be in the shade as I waited for Dad. Finally, he drove up in his Oldsmobile. I ran over to him as he parked the car in the driveway.

"Dad, I didn't do it," I said.

Dad looked puzzled.

"Do what?" he asked.

"I didn't throw the rock that cracked the boat's windshield. Stan did it!"

"Ah, shit." Dad walked over and shook his head as he looked at the windshield. About this time, Stan came out of the house.

"Dad," Stan said, "I cracked the windshield. I'm sorry I lied about it and got Clark in trouble."

Now Stan decided to tell the truth!

Dad let out a long sigh. He wasn't happy about coming home to this mess. He told us to stay outside as he headed in the house to talk to Mom. While Stan and I sat outside, Mom and Dad had a long and sometimes loud discussion. At one point I heard Mom shout, "Either he goes or I do."

Eventually, Dad came out of the house and called us over. From his ashen face, I could tell he wasn't very happy. He told me that I was grounded indefinitely and would be helping Mom with chores around the house. I also had to go inside and apologize to her. When I did, she wouldn't speak or look at me. Stan was also punished by being grounded for two weeks. I thought his punishment should have matched mine since he'd precipitated the problem. But I kept my opinion to myself.

I hoped that this was the end of the fiasco. It wasn't. What Dad didn't tell me was that he and Mom had reached a compromise. Mom had finally agreed that I could live at home during the school year, but only if I behaved. However, in return, Dad agreed that he would find some place for me to stay when school was out in the summer. I didn't know it, but I wouldn't spend another summer in Spanish Fork until I was nineteen. Obviously, I needed to learn not to act out when I was upset. Unfortunately, it would take a few more incidents before the lesson would sink in.

CHAPTER 4

The Mink Ranch

If you ever see a mink, don't pick it up

Walking into the mink shed on the first day at my summer job, I was startled. The mink began to screech and bite their wire cages. It seemed like they wanted to get out and attack me. Apparently, they didn't like me. The feeling was mutual. I wasn't happy being there. It was June 5, 1961, and I was ten years old and two hours away from home working on my uncle's mink ranch. My first task was to drag 100 feet of hose up and down the mink sheds to fill the mink's metal water cups. As I trudged along, I tried to understand why my uncle needed me, a ten-year-old, to do this. It didn't seem very tricky. I thought about my family fishing, water skiing, and hiking through the woods at the cabin having a grand time without me. My friends back in Spanish Fork would be playing Little League baseball and swimming while I slaved away in the hot sun.

Dragging the hose along the shed, I looked at the mink and their cages. The adult mink were about the size of a small cat but had pointed noses and webbed feet. Peering into their nesting boxes, I could see the baby mink known as kits. They were about the size of mice and didn't yet have much fur or any teeth and some hadn't even opened their eyes yet. My uncle had mink of various colors including pearl mink which were white, pastels which were brown, and black mink which were, you guessed it, black. I wondered if the mink seemed so aggressive because they were penned up or if it was just their nature.

When I finished the watering, I returned to the shop and the foreman, Dick Wilkes, told me my next job would be scraping. "What's that?" I asked. Dick said, "You clean the old feed from the metal plates." He then pointed me to the breeder pens where I'd be helping Steve, one of the other boys, who would show me how to do it. Steve had me get a pair of heavy leather gloves, a paint scraper, and a metal slide which was a thin sheet of metal about 14 inches long and 7 inches wide with a handle on one end.

Adult mink in their cages

As we walked to the first shed, Steve explained that since the kits couldn't yet climb the metal mesh of the cage, the mink feed was placed on a metal plate on the bottom of the pen. Looking in the first pen, the old uneaten mink feed appeared to be ground up pieces of some type of flesh. Although the remnants had aged and rotted some, I could identify fragments of eyes and ears that were in the mix. It was disgusting. Steve told me it was primarily horse and whale meat and any other meat scraps the mink rancher's co-op could round up. The co-op prepared the feed each morning by grinding up the meat and mixing it with other material needed in the mink's diet. It was then trucked to the various mink ranches so the mink could be fed. Not surprisingly, it didn't take long in the summer heat for the meat to become rancid and stink, which is what Steve and I got to handle.

Steve showed me how to get the mother mink in her nesting box and then push the slide down the slot to block the box's exit. I could then reach in and scrape the metal plate to remove the old feed and throw it in the bucket. We wore leather gloves in case the mother got past the slide and tried to bite us. When the bucket was full, we trudged down the aisle of the shed to a wheelbarrow where we emptied our buckets. When the wheelbarrow was full, we wheeled it to a temporary storage area and dumped it. It didn't take long before I realized this was another boring job followed in the late afternoon by another round of watering. All and all not very exciting.

This drudgery continued on through my first week. As I was watering the mink on Friday afternoon, I thought about all I'd learned during the week. I'd found I needed to be careful around the mink. If I sat against a cage they would bite me on the butt. If I reached in a cage, I had to wear heavy leather welding gloves to protect my hands from attack. I was finding that working eight-hour days in the hot sheds around smelly mink wasn't much fun. In my highly biased opinion, I didn't think a ten-year-old boy should be forced by his parents to work in such conditions. But I was diligently trying to learn my job and help my uncle.

Over time, I did find the mink interesting. During my first days on the mink ranch, I asked a lot of questions. I wondered why the mink were kept in individual cages. Dick Wilkes told me that the adult mink would get in fights and scar each other up if given the opportunity. I was surprised. I thought they would only attack other animals. To prevent them from damaging each other's fur, they were kept in small cages made of a stiff, square wire mesh. A typical breeder pen was 16 inches wide by 30 inches long and 12 inches tall. The bottom of the cage was also made of wire mesh and raised a couple of feet above the ground. This allowed the mink manure and other debris to fall through to the ground so that the pens stayed fairly clean. Since the valuable mink always wanted to escape, the cages were housed in sheds 200 feet long and 10 feet wide. This way, if a mink got out of its cage it was still contained in the shed. Walking down the aisle in the center of the shed, the mink in the cages on either side would watch for an opportunity to escape. Uncle Dick had 23 sheds each containing hundreds of screeching mink.

But despite all I was learning, I felt sad about being away from my parents, siblings, and friends. I just couldn't understand why it was so important that I help my uncle out. What I didn't know was that this was the solution to a problem that had vexed Dad. I had seriously aggravated and stressed my mother out with craziness like the Strawberry fishing episode and the rock throwing incident when I restrained her from punishing me. Because of these and other troubling activities, she had initially insisted that I had to go. Finally, she compromised which meant Dad had to find someplace for me to spend the summer. I had no idea I was in that much trouble. For me, any incident, no matter how bad, was forgotten the next day. I would play with my friends and torment my siblings as if nothing had happened. Not Mom. My various escapades just keep pushing her concern and outrage higher and higher. Thus, Mom had to take a breather to regain her composure.

Since most of Dad's friends lived near us, they were too close to be of much help. And it wouldn't be good for me to just sit around someplace. I'd already proven that when I was idle I came up with stupid things to do for entertainment. Finally, Dad had an inspiration. He talked my uncle into letting me work on his mink ranch. Normally, Uncle Dick hired a couple of kids to help out during the summer months. Even though I was a little young for the job, he agreed to help out his sister, my mother. Since the mink ranch was a two-hour drive from Spanish Fork, Dad thought this would provide sufficient separation between Mom and me. It also explained why they seldom came to see me while I was working on the ranch.

Dad's next problem was how to tell me. He didn't want me

to have bad feelings towards Mom. To keep me from worrying about my upcoming exile for too long, Dad didn't tell me about it until a few days before school let out. Then he sprang his trap. He explained that Uncle Dick had called and really needed my help to take care of the mink during the busy summer. It should have dawned on me that if Uncle Dick was in a bind, he could easily hire someone more capable than a fourth grader. But, Dad's explanation played on my ego. I was proud to think that my uncle believed I was such a valuable worker. It was years later before I found out what was really going on.

As soon as school let out in 1961, my suitcase and I were on our way to West Jordan, Utah. Despite my burnished ego, I was not happy. Normally, summer was a time that I got to swim and play baseball with my friends. Since my grandmother's house was next door to Uncle Dick's, I got to room with her and her youngest son, Uncle Russell. Russell was only six years older than me and was living with Grandma while he finished high school. However, he occupied the second bedroom in Grandma's two-bedroom house and didn't want any company. This meant that I spent my nights in a sleeping bag in the backyard unless it rained. Then I would sleep on the front room floor.

The area around the mink ranch was surrounded by fields of wheat, corn, and alfalfa with only a few houses nearby. There were few streetlights, and with low humidity the night skies were lit up by brilliant stars and the moon. However, the darkness also added to my fear of sleeping outside alone. Fortunately, Uncle Russ's dog, Albert, slept outside with me. Albert stood a little over 2 feet high and looked like a golden retriever except his fur was a dark brown. He would attack anything or anybody that trespassed. This helped me to cope with my fear. Albert and I soon became good friends.

I found there were advantages in being outside. Advantages like cooling off quicker than in the non-air-conditioned house. I found it refreshing to lie on my back looking up at the stars. Sometimes, I would see a shooting star flash by overhead and wonder if it was a satellite crashing to earth.

Although I could relax at night, it was hard work during the day. The kits were born in the spring. Typically, there were four kits per litter. The kits lived with and were nourished by their mother for the first few months of their lives. They quickly grew fur and teeth and were far from harmless after a couple of months.

When I arrived in June most of the work was in the sheds with breeder pens. At the start of the summer, the kits lived there with their mother. About mid-summer, the kits were vaccinated. Near the end of summer, they were weaned from their mother and isolated in individual cages. By the time I left for school, the kits were almost fully grown.

My uncle didn't participate in the normal day-to-day work. Instead, he managed the overall business from his house. He had a vast knowledge of mink and judged mink shows internationally. Mink pelts from his ranch were known for their high quality. Uncle Dick's foreman handled day-to-day operations and kept us "troops" in line. When I first started on the mink ranch, the foreman was Dick Wilkes. He was a tough, macho individual who looked after things. I quickly learned that he didn't tolerate nonsense. He gave us our daily orders and made sure things were being taken care of. My uncles Blake and Russ worked on the ranch along with one or two other adults and a couple of kids. During most of the time I was there, one of the kids was Dick Wilkes' son, Ricky. He was a year younger than me and liked to get into mischief. Thus, we became good friends.

Learning the art of shenanigans

Much to my chagrin, I soon found I wasn't the only one who liked to pull pranks. As the new kid, I was the target of several practical jokes. During my second week on the job, one of the older kids tricked me into going into the large, walk-in freezer. The freezer was used to store wheelbarrows full of mink feed to keep it from spoiling. As I walked into the freezer, the door slammed with a loud bang. I jerked around and found that the door was closed and locked from the outside. Then the lights went out. I sat in the cold, pitch-black dungeon wondering what to do next. I yelled for them to let me out but heard nothing. I tried to kick the door open but to no avail. My eyes were not used to such total darkness. I started to see strange faint images swirling around. After what seemed like an eternity, probably five minutes, they let me out. I wasn't used to being the target of practical jokes and didn't like it. But this was part of the initiation into the ranks. They also booby trapped a door going into the shop where we stored our tools. As I pushed the door open, I got a full plastic bucket of water dumped on me. I started to be more cautious and paid close attention to anything that seemed odd.

Although I didn't like to have pranks pulled on me, I enjoyed doing them to someone else. In the years ahead, Ricky and I added a better climax to the freezer prank. We told the new kid that the foreman wanted him to check and see if the fan in the freezer was running. As soon as he walked in, we slammed the door and dropped a bolt in the latch so it couldn't be opened. We let him sit in the cold, pitch-black freezer for a few minutes to ponder the situation. When we thought he had settled down and was just biding his time waiting to get out, we lit an M-80, threw it in the door and slammed it shut again. An M-80 is like a firecracker on steroids. After the explosion, we opened the door and the victim came staggering out. He was now a member of the team.

Sometimes the pranks had an unexpected ending. One such prank occurred in July when we were vaccinating the kits for virus enteritis, distemper, and botulism. Vaccinating the mink was hot, tiring work that went on for several weeks. The procedure started with us boys catching a kit in each hand using the heavy leather gloves. We then carried them down the aisle of the shed to Blake and Bob to be vaccinated. When it was our turn, we held the kits out in front of us so Blake and Bob could easily grab a hind leg with one hand and give them a shot with the other. They used an automatic syringe with a flexible tube connected to a bottle of vaccine. They didn't change needles after each vaccination. Instead, they used the same needle until it became dull. After the kits were vaccinated, we carried them back to their cage and caught the next pair. Although the kits were young, we still had to be careful. They now had grown needle-sharp teeth and would bite us if given the chance.

Since we could catch the kits faster than they could be vaccinated, a line formed as we waited for our turn. It was a tiring and boring job. As we stood in line, we had to be careful not to get too close to the person in front of us. If we did, the kit would likely bite the person in front of us on the butt or the back of an arm.

Unfortunately, whenever I got bored, I would think up some type of diversion, usually at someone's expense. One day, I was standing in line behind Ricky who was waiting behind Brian as his kits were vaccinated. On a whim, I twisted around and gently nudged Ricky on the butt with my elbow. He thought one of my kits was too close and twisted around to his left to see what was going on. As he did so, the kit in his right hand got too close to Brian and bit him on the butt. Brian, who had warned Ricky several times to quit crowding him, let out a curse and dropped both his kits. As Ricky turn back around to see what Brian was yelling about, Brian punched Ricky in the head. Ricky promptly dropped his kits and the fight was on.

Blake was taken back by the sudden outburst. He wasn't sure what had happened. All he knew was that he had two kids throwing punches and wrestling while their kits were running in every direction. After the initial flurry of punches, Brian and Ricky stepped back to size up the situation.

During the lull, Blake said, "Boys, boys, knock off the bullshit. This isn't a damn boxing tournament."

Ricky said, "Don't tell me. I was standing there minding my own business when Brian punched me in the head."

Brian glared back at Ricky. "Like hell you were minding your own business. One of your damn kits bit me on the butt. Why don't we have one bite you on the butt and see how you like it?"

Blake looked a little annoyed. "I told you two to knock it off. I'm sure it was an accident. Let's get back to work."

Ricky and Brian stood glaring at each other for a few more seconds and then Brian reluctantly left to clean and bandage his wound. Ricky and I captured the stray kits and went back to work. Fortunately for me, neither Brian nor Ricky figured out what or who had precipitated the fight.

Of course, I didn't feel compelled to tell them.

Several days later it was my turn to be surprised. We were still vaccinating kits and it was getting late in the day. I became tired of holding the kits out and started to let my arms rest closer to my body. The kits' heads were just far enough from my stomach that they couldn't bite me. As Blake went to give one of the kits a botulism shot, the needle skidded off the inside of the kit's leg and stuck me the stomach. Blake reflexively pushed the plunger before he realized what had happened. I had just been vaccinated for botulism.

Uncle Blake and I both looked down at my stomach. There was a pinhole in my shirt surrounded by a small red spot. I couldn't believe what had happened. I looked back up at Blake then back down at my stomach. When I unbuttoned my shirt there was a small puncture wound.

I asked Blake, "What made you think I needed to be vaccinated?"

Blake said, "Shit, this hasn't happened before. I'm not sure what to do."

"Well, it's a new experience for me too."

Blake thought for a few seconds and then said, "We should probably wipe it off with alcohol. If you start feeling bad, you'd better head to the house."

Initially, my stomach hurt a little, but not too much. I swabbed the puncture wound with alcohol and went back to work catching kits. That night, my stomach developed a large, red splotch and began to really hurt. By the next morning, I was running a fever and felt terrible. Blake took me to the doctor but he just shook his head. This was a new experience for him also. He didn't know of any treatment for a botulism injection intended for a mink, particularly 16 hours after the accident.

I continued to feel worse during the day and ended up in bed, deathly ill. It was ten days before I was back to work. By then, fortunately, all the kits had been vaccinated. I decided it was a good idea to think about what could go wrong with a situation. I clearly needed to watch after myself and not trust others to do it for me, particularly when I was far away from home.

All of these pranks and escapades helped relieve some of the boredom and tension on the mink ranch. More importantly, it bonded us together, like an extended family. Although we would sometimes argue or have disagreements, overall, we watched out and took care of each other. It was a way to survive in an otherwise boring work environment. Learning this proved to be invaluable in my professional career that was still years into the future. People did a much better job when they felt like they were part of a "family."

Notwithstanding the depressing summer, there was one perk. I returned home and started the school year relatively rich compared to my friends. Although I was only making 25 cents per hour, I didn't have much opportunity to spend it during the summer. Thus, I had over $100 when I returned to school. This was at a time when a hamburger cost 25 cents and a Coke was a dime. Now I could spend the money how I wanted. My friends were jealous. I started to appreciate the benefit of having money at a very early age. I also started to think about what I could do as an adult that would provide a decent living, preferably without working in the hot sun with smelly mink.

CHAPTER 5

The Age of Science

Experiments sometimes provide unexpected lessons

As a young boy, I was always curious about how things worked. I still am. This curiosity was nurtured by my dad as I helped him fix things. It seemed like he was always tinkering with something. If he was changing the spark plugs in the old black and white Oldsmobile, I would stand on the bumper next to him and peer under the hood to watch him work and hand him the socket wrench and spark plugs. His big hands, much bigger than mine, wielded the tools with purpose and ease. He knew what he was doing and I was in awe of him as he explained how spark plugs functioned and why they mattered. If he was changing the brakes, I would crouch down next to him and hand him the brake shoes. Although I didn't always understand him, I listened as if he preached gospel.

By letting me watch, listen, and participate, Dad taught me the value of knowing how things worked. Dad's job as teacher continued when I started helping him do electrical work. In addition to his job as a motor inspector at U.S. Steel's Geneva plant, he ran his own electrical contracting business. When I was only eight, Dad had me install outlets and switches in a bowling alley he was wiring. Although I wasn't much help, it got me out of the house and gave my mother some time to unwind.

Dad helped me understand the workings of electricity and these lessons served me well in my career. And while I was too young to know it, it was the beginning of the rest of my life of figuring out how things worked. Dad taught me that if I approached a problem logically and thought things through, I could figure out almost anything. By feeling this way, my curiosity blossomed and I started to explore things on my own, particularly if I could use my knowledge to torment my siblings. My curiosity was further spurred along by world events.

The nightly news in the late 1950s and early 1960s made it seem like I was living in a science-fiction novel. It had only been a few years since the first atomic bombs were detonated in 1945. They not only ushered in the atomic age but also the beginning of the Cold War with the Soviet Union. As I sat on the floor in front of our small black and white TV watching the news, the narrator, Walter Cronkite, frequently announced that there had been another open-air nuclear test. This was often at Yucca Flat, Nevada, which was only 300 miles away. Since we were downwind, I became worried as I listened to my parents discuss the possible effects of nuclear fallout. I might get sick and die or mutate into a zombie. In retrospect, that might explain a lot about me.

The nightly news also provided updates on the Space Race. This race officially began on October 4, 1957, when the Soviets launched the first satellite, Sputnik, into orbit. This was followed up by their November launch of the first animal, the dog Laika, into orbit. Watching the news, I learned that winning the Space Race was important. The rockets being developed could also carry nuclear weapons to destroy other countries.

I was very anxious to get updates on whether the U.S. was catching up with the Soviet space program. America finally launched their first satellite into orbit at the end of January 1958. I sat in rapt attention when Walter Cronkite interrupted a program to show the launch of a U.S. rocket. I couldn't believe it when a rocket exploded on the launch pad. Sometimes, just when I thought we'd finally had a successful launch, the rocket would veer off course and explode in the air. Cronkite had the embarrassing task of trying to put a positive spin on America's rocket failures.

In addition to updates on the Cold War, the news also carried stories about advances in science and technology. Electronics, including radios and TVs, still used tubes. The widespread use of transistors and integrated circuit boards that power today's electronics were still way in the future. And even though we only had small black and white TVs with fuzzy pictures, families would huddle around them each night as if participating in some pagan ritual. During this time, the old prop-driven airplanes were being replaced with jets. It was astounding to think that it was now possible to cross the entire country in six hours. Instead of cell phones, we used operator-assisted phones connected to party lines. After making some nasty remarks about a neighbor while talking on the phone, I learned first-hand that you never knew who might be listening in. This was a time of rapid change not seen before in human history.

My curiosity about technology often manifested itself in interesting ways. One of my first projects was to take apart Dad's mechanical alarm clock. I was seven years old and wanted to understand how it worked. Although it gained 15 minutes a day after I put it back together, I was proud of my accomplishment. This success led me to other endeavors: rockets, high voltage electricity, electronics, chemistry and explosives. I was that kid. My poor parents. Scratch that. My poor siblings.

Despite how it looks on TV, it's not easy to blow things up

My first, but not last, experience with explosives was an attempt to build a small bomb. At first I tried to produce black powder but found that a lot of effort was necessary to grind the components fine enough to generate a decent explosion. I quickly decided the easiest course of action was to use some of Dad's gunpowder. He kept gallon jugs of it in the garage for use in reloading rifle shells. Dad certainly wouldn't miss a little. In my first attempt to build a bomb, I filled a rifle casing with gunpowder. Next, I needed some way to light off my bomb from a safe distance. Fortunately, a friend, Kevin, had told me I could buy a fuse at the local hobby store. I stuck the fuse in the rifle casing, lit it, and ran behind a tree. As I peered around the tree trunk, I was disappointed. There was no explosion. But in the process I'd accidentally designed my first rocket engine.

Experimentation continued until I was eventually able to get a decent explosion. I had to use pistol powder instead of gunpowder in the rifle shell. I hadn't realized pistol powder burned quicker than rifle powder. I also found that model rocket engines I could buy through the mail provided much better performance than my homemade engines. When I mated my bomb to a rocket engine, I had my first bazooka. I launched it from a piece of pipe resting on my shoulder. Aiming my homemade bazooka at a cinder block wall in my friend's backyard, I called out to Kevin: "Light it!" He touched a match to the fuse and the rocket shot out of the pipe with a whooshing sound. The rocket spit sparks as it flew through the air. My invention hit the wall with a loud explosion. Holy cow. What had I done? It was *incredible*. I had done it! I had really created a bazooka! No matter that it only made a small hole in one side of the cinder block, I was sure I could improve it. Unfortunately, or maybe fortunately, before I could test my improved design, Dad noticed the decline in his pistol powder.

"Clark, do you know anything about my missing pistol powder?" Dad asked.

"Well," I stammered. "I used a little to make a rocket." I didn't think it was a good idea to tell him I'd made a bazooka.

"A LITTLE!? There's almost a quart missing. How the hell many rockets did you make?"

"I had to experiment quite a bit before I could get it to fly," I exaggerated.

"Well, I'd better not catch you using it again. And just to be sure you don't, I'm going to lock it in a chest and keep the key in my wallet."

Not only was I grounded for a month, I was out of the bazooka business.

Electricity could provide unexpected entertainment

Knowing my interest in technology, Dad sometimes brought things home he thought would interest me. One of my favorites was a 6,000-volt transformer normally used to generate a spark to ignite a gas-fired steam boiler. It was a black, 6-inch cube with an electrical cord on one side that could be plugged into an outlet. When plugged in, a spark would jump over an inch from the wire on the other side of the transformer to anything grounded, including people. Although the wire had to be within an inch to start an arc, the spark could be drawn out several inches before it quit. It was fun to play with and I used it for all kinds of experiments. It could ignite steel wool, char small pieces of coal, and make an eerie glow if I held the middle of a fluorescent light tube and touched the wire to one end. It also provided a good security system when I was in my bedroom and didn't want to be disturbed.

Unfortunately, the transformer eventually shocked the wrong person. I came home from school one day to a ransacked bedroom. All my science equipment was gone.

"Where's all my science stuff?" I asked Mom.

"At the garbage dump," she said. "I was vacuuming your bedroom and your damn transformer shocked me on the leg."

"So you took EVERYTHING to the dump?"

"Yep. I wasn't sure what else in your room was dangerous and decided you couldn't be trusted. You're just lucky you weren't here when it happened or you'd be at the dump too."

It looked like I would have to find some other electrical device to explore. Maybe the TV. As it turned out, the consumer market for televisions was going through a revolution at this time. In the 1950s, black and white TVs were the norm because few television shows were in color. In the early 1960s, all of this changed. More and more programs were broadcast in color. Although color TVs were expensive, people began to purchase them and they soon became status symbols.

Mom had wanted to replace our old black and white TV for years. It had been purchased in 1955 and had a small, roundish picture tube. Over the years the picture became dim and fuzzy. In

1962, her brother, Uncle Dick, bought a brand-new RCA color TV. He was the first in the family to own one. We all went to his house and gathered around to see it. We were startled to see the color of Lucille Ball's red hair and the green forests and blue skies in the many western shows. Mom redoubled her efforts to get a new TV.

Finally, after two years, Mom wore Dad down and he purchased a new, Zenith 22-inch color television housed in a big wooden cabinet that stood on four legs. Inside the cabinet was a large picture tube surrounded by many smaller tubes used to amplify the signal from the antenna. There was a large knob on the front of the set for tuning in stations. There were other knobs for controlling the volume and adjusting the picture's color and brightness. Mom proudly showed it off to her friends and neighbors, many of whom didn't yet have a color set.

During this time, I had been reading about color TVs and the technology making them possible. One of my favorite sources of information was the magazine *Popular Science,* which explained how the color television worked and the purpose of each component. After reading the article, I was sure I was now an expert. About a month after Dad brought the color TV home, I had my chance to test my knowledge.

My parents decided to take a trip to West Jordan to visit Grandma and Uncle Dick. They would be gone for the day so I'd have plenty of time to explore the TV's inner workings. As soon as they were out of sight, I unplugged the TV, moved it away from the wall and removed the back cover. Peering inside, I could see a maze of tubes, wires, and a couple of transformers, including a high voltage one. Based on my earlier experience, I knew to be careful with it.

First, I removed and inspected the smaller tubes, trying to determine which were rectifiers and which amplified signals. Next, I removed the wire harnesses going to the tubes and carefully unfastened the transformers. Although the picture tube was 22 inches across at the front, it necked down toward the back of the TV. Here I found the magnetic yokes I'd expected. The yokes controlled the electron beams that made the picture on the screen. I noted the yokes' orientation and carefully removed them from the back of the picture tube and then lifted the picture tube out of the cabinet. The cabinet was now essentially empty with a pile of electronic parts scattered around the carpet in the front room.

Me at age twelve with my siblings (guinea pigs). Front row (left to right): Brad, Machell. Back row (left to right): Stan, Clark

I was diligently inspecting the parts when I heard the front door open. When I looked up, I was alarmed to see Mom standing in the door. Their trip had been aborted due to thick fog that had rolled in from Utah Lake and covered the highway making driving slow and dangerous. Initially, Mom stopped moving and just stood there looking like a deer in headlights. I did the same. Mom apparently couldn't believe what she was seeing. Then, she grabbed the hair on each side of her head and screamed. Dad peered around her to see what was going on. His eyes got big.

"Oh, shit," he said.

He carefully grabbed Mom by the elbow and led her out to the car. After she was seated and the car door closed, he came back in the house.

"I'm taking your mother out for a long lunch," Dad said. "When we return, that television had better be back together and working like new or there is going to be hell to pay."

After they left, I diligently reassembled the TV taking special care to align the picture tube using the magnetic yokes. The information provided by *Popular Science* had proven invaluable. When my parents returned, the TV was back in working order. Mom flipped through the channels and scrutinized the picture closely but could find nothing amiss. However, I was still under strict instructions to never, ever, mess with the TV again.

It's a good idea to lock your door while taking a nap

After the color TV fiasco, I was ready to go back to experimenting with chemistry. I was always looking for an opportunity to learn something new, particularly if it gave me a chance to test it on my siblings. One day, I was helping Mom clean the basement bathroom. As I was cleaning under the sink, I came across a can of Drano. We would normally put Drano crystals down the sink drain when it was clogged. The Drano crystals would react and dissolve the hair, soap, and other gunk to open the drain back up. Not surprisingly, the skull and cross bones on the back of the can caught my attention. It contained a long warning about things not to do with Drano. Towards the end of the warning, it said, "Toxic, chlorine gas will form if Drano comes into contact with a liquid chlorine bleach such as Clorox." Although I didn't know much about chlorine gas, this seemed worth investigating.

Next to the bathroom was the laundry room with the detergent and, more importantly, the Clorox bleach. It also contained shelves of quart-size glass Mason jars Mom used when canning fruit. I rounded up a couple of quart jars and the jug of Clorox bleach and headed back to the bathroom where I closed and locked the door. I poured an inch of bleach into one of the jars and then dumped in some Drano crystals. I was amazed when the mixture immediately started bubbling and heating up. Stranger still, the bubbles contained a greenish yellow gas that accumulated in the jar as the bubbles burst. I was totally baffled that the gas stayed in the bottom of the jar instead of rising up like steam and escaping. It was like something from a science-fiction movie. The gas was like a weird liquid that moved around slow and could be poured from one jar to another. What in the world had I made?

I carefully took a whiff of the gas. It stung my nose and eyes almost like they had been exposed to fire. This definitely had potential. My laboratory was across the hall from the bedroom I shared with Stan. He happened to be napping so I carefully took a jar of the gas, snuck in and poured a little over his head. As soon as he inhaled the fumes, he jerked awake and started to gasp and cough.

Then he yelled, "What are you trying to do, kill me? What was that?"

"I found a way to make chlorine gas using Clorox and Drano," I said.

"Well, don't ever do that to me again. I thought I was going to die."

"Yeah, I sniffed it and it seemed pretty bad."

Stan thought about it for a few seconds and then said, "Let's make another batch and try it on Brad."

I was surprised. This was totally unlike Stan. Maybe my mischievousness had worn off on him.

We generated another bottle of chlorine gas, decanted it into a clean jar, and put a lid on it. We snuck upstairs and headed to my youngest brother's bedroom. Brad was lying on his side in bed, happily asleep. I carefully opened the jar and poured a little of the gas out. The greenish-yellow vapor oozed out of the jar and slowly drifted down over his head. As soon as he inhaled a little, he bolted upright and started to gasp. Then Brad started to scream that he couldn't breathe. Mom came running in from her bedroom.

"What the hell is going on here?" she asked.

I wanted to hand the bottle to Stan, but he was trying to sidle away from me.

Brad gasped again. "I can't breathe! I can't breathe!"

Mom looked at me. "What did you do to him?"

"I made a little chlorine gas and wanted to surprise him."

Mom was not amused. Fortunately, Brad started to breathe easier and settle down. I tried to explain that this was just a harmless science experiment, but Mom wasn't buying it. Grounded again. The bleach and Drano were put back in their proper places and I was told to never so much as touch them again. And, even today, if I mention this to Brad he gets mad, and for a good reason. Years later, while studying chemistry in college, I learned chlorine was one of the poisonous gases used against enemy troops in World War I. Many soldiers exposed to it died from asphyxiation or had permanent lung damage. After WWI, international law banned its use as a weapon. Fortunately, there was no permanent damage to my siblings other than a little emotional trauma. Brad still says he hopes to get even with me some day.

When something doesn't seem right, don't trust it

Despite Mom's previous admonition, I still continued to experiment with electricity and chemistry. In one experiment, I was able to combine both. During the late 1950s and early 1960s, I watched the TV show, *Mr. Wizard*, which covered such things as how to build an electromagnet and how to generate electricity. Volcanoes were made that spewed foam when vinegar was added to baking soda. The host, Don Herbert, explained the science behind the experiments. The show was immensely popular. I watched the show regularly and occasionally duplicated the experiments, sometimes with unexpected results.

During one show in the early 1960s, Mr. Wizard demonstrated how to decompose water into its constituent gases, hydrogen and oxygen. He collected the gases in two clear glass jars. At the end of the show, he careful lifted the inverted bottle of pure hydrogen. Lighting a match, he moved the flame to the bottom of the hydrogen bottle. I was surprised when it didn't explode. Instead, a faint blue flame moved up the bottle as it consumed the hydrogen and then went out with a pop. Mr. Wizard explained that since the hydrogen was pure and needed oxygen to burn, it could only do so at the interface between it and the air. I was hooked.

The chance to have a flame in a bottle was exciting. The first step was to find a non-conducting container for the water. I found a plastic washtub and moved it to my laboratory, the basement. I filled it with about 4 inches of water. Next, I rounded up a couple of Mom's Mason jars. I was finding they were excellent lab equipment and would be perfect for collecting the hydrogen and oxygen. I filled the jars to the brim with water and covered them with a piece of her wax paper. Taking care not to let any air in the bottles, I slowly flipped them over and submerged the open end in the plastic tub of water. With the mouth of the bottle underwater, I removed the waxed paper. The water in the tub kept air from getting in the bottles.

Next I needed two electrodes. I searched around in the garage but didn't find anything that would work. After considering the problem for a while, I cut open a couple of flashlight batteries and removed the carbon electrodes in the center of each battery. The acid was washed off and the electrodes left to dry while I searched for some copper wire. Fortunately, Dad had a ready supply in the garage. The two bottles were propped up on short blocks of plastic and an electrode placed under each.

The final component needed for the experiment was a source of DC (direct current) electricity. Mr. Wizard stressed that this was essential. From working with Dad, I had learned that batteries produced DC while the house outlets supplied AC or alternating current. Mr. Wizard used a large battery in his demonstration. I searched the garage and Dad's van but couldn't find any large batteries I could use. I did, however, locate the transformer for my model train set. Dad had taught me that AC current could be converted to DC current using rectifiers. Reasoning that my train used DC current, I was sure that the model train transformer also had rectifiers inside the black box. I hooked up the train transformer to the wires running to the electrodes and turned it on. Small bubbles started to form on the electrodes but they weren't filling up the bottles very fast. I left it running overnight.

Awaking the next morning, I raced out of my room and over to the corner of the basement to check on the experiment. One bottle was almost completely full of gas but the other one was about three-fourths full. This puzzled me. Mr. Wizard had explained that since water is H2O, it contains twice as much hydrogen as oxygen. One bottle should be twice as full as the other. Although this seemed strange and bothered me, I rationalized that Mason jars were not laboratory glassware and probably didn't contain exactly the same volume. It didn't dawn on me that the train transformer primarily put out AC rather than DC current. Both bottles contained a mixture of hydrogen and oxygen.

Following Mr. Wizard's dumbass example, I decided to light the fuller hydrogen bottle so I could see the pale blue flame move up inside the bottle. I lit a wooden match with my right hand and lifted the fullest bottle of hydrogen with my left—

Opening my eyes, I couldn't figure out where I was. It took a few seconds for the room to quit spinning. I didn't feel so good. I felt nauseated and dizzy. The back of my head hurt. Slowly, I realized I was lying on my back in the basement looking straight up at Mom standing over me. Had she done something to me?

As I blinked my eyes, Mom said, "I think you've gone and killed yourself this time, Clark."

Mom helped me sit up and wiped away the blood drizzling from my nose. I had no memory of the explosion and no idea how long I was unconscious. I couldn't move or feel my left arm. My right arm wasn't quite as damaged. Although my hand and lower arm were numb, everything above the elbow worked. The skin on my arms and face was bright red and felt like it had been scraped with sandpaper. It turned out that the sharp explosion had pulverized the bottle containing the hydrogen. All that was left of the bottle was fine silica sand all over the basement floor. This explained why the glass fragments from the bottle hadn't shredded me. The explosion was so sharp that it had disintegrated the bottle and nearly shattered my hand. But I had finally managed to create a good explosion.

Mom shook her head and said, "I had better get you to the doctor."

She had to help me to my feet and into the car. As we drove to the local hospital, feeling began to return in my arms and hands. It was not pleasant. They felt like they were immersed in fire. Apparently, the nerves were pissed off at the treatment they had received. At the hospital the doctor was not overly sympathetic. He had occasionally dealt with the damage I'd done to my siblings and as he was bandaging me up he mostly commiserated with my mother for having to put up with me. He said that it appeared that I hadn't done any permanent physical damage. However, he couldn't do anything about my mental problems.

Although my hydrogen and many other experiments were dangerous, they had taught me a lot. I gradually realized I could figure out how almost anything worked if you gave me enough time. I decided that I wanted to become a scientist or an engineer but didn't really think I was smart enough. People were always telling me I was a dumbass and my teachers said I wasn't very smart. I only tolerated school because my parents made me go. And my grades reflected this. But now I realized grades would be very important if I wanted to be accepted by a university. I started to worry about whether there was any chance I could find a way to get a college to let me in.

CHAPTER 6

Junior High School Revelations

Sometimes you learn something unexpected in school

My newfound knowledge of technology was often useful in school. I was usually ahead of the class in discussions of science and how things worked. Plus, my production and testing of chlorine gas on my siblings taught me to be cautious with my shenanigans. Another problem I needed to learn to deal with was bullies. My initial lesson with a bully occurred when I was in first grade.

I started first grade in the fall of 1957 at the ripe old age of six; I didn't want to go because I didn't have any friends at school. My creative excuses such as a stomach ache or a sore foot made it hard for Mom to get me out of the house. When she finally did, I slowly trudged down the street with occasional stops to look at the clouds or the birds in the trees. At first Mom couldn't figure out why she was getting calls from the school about me being tardy. After all, the Park Elementary School was just a little over a block away. Eventually, she figured out what was going on and told me there would be serious problems if I was late again. The tone in her voice convinced me she meant it.

Initially, I was very shy and just played by myself during recess. Finally, some of the boys took pity on me and asked me to play marbles. I suspected they were just after my marbles but I was glad to be included. They of course did win a lot of my marbles since they had to teach me how to play. First rule they explained was that we drew a three-foot diameter circle in the dirt. This was our arena where we each placed one or two of our marbles near the center. Next, we took turns shooting and trying to knock a marble out of the circle. We did this by kneeling down just outside the circle and placing our "shooter" marble on our forefinger. We then used our thumb to flip it into the circle. If we were able to knock a marble out of the circle, we got to keep it. If the shooter stayed in the circle, it was fair game for anyone lucky enough to knock it out later.

The kids were right to think I was an easy mark, and I was in the beginning. But I had a very competitive spirit and quickly figured the game out. I started to win more than my fair share of marbles. Unfortunately, one of the regular players, Lynn Renaulson, didn't like me winning.

Playing marbles was not my first encounter with Lynn. We had been in the same kindergarten class the previous year, but he had started school a year later than was normal. He had black hair, stood a couple of inches taller than me, and weighed quite a bit more. He was a big boy whose size intimidated me. He would often knock me down and make fun of me while I laid helpless on the floor. Lynn had an older brother who liked to torment him and beat him up, and so when Lynn was around kids his own age he wanted to treat them the same way. And for some reason he particularly enjoyed bullying me. Early on, I determined he was definitely stronger than I was, since he continually pushed me around and took my toys. It was embarrassing. If I saw him coming, I would try to hide or at least get out of his way.

Not surprisingly, I soon found out that Lynn didn't appreciate me winning his marbles. If I happened to win, he would push me down or hit me and take my marbles. I thought I could avoid the problem by not playing marbles with him, but it didn't help. He just started taking my marbles anytime he caught me on the playground. I finally told my teacher, Mrs. Wheelwright, about what was going on. No good. If she forced him to give my marbles back, he would just catch me the next time we were at recess, beat me up, and take my marbles again. And since anytime I tattled on him I got beat up, I gave up on that approach. I tried to fight back when he would bully me, but he was bigger and stronger and it just made the beating worse. I hadn't thought it was possible, but school was becoming even more miserable and I didn't know what to do about it.

Finally, it dawned on me that maybe I didn't need to win a fair fight. Instead, I would make sure he realized there would be serious consequences if he messed with me. That way he'd decide to leave me alone. I just had to wait for my chance. It happened the next morning at recess while Lynn was playing marbles.

Lynn was bent over preparing to take his turn concentrating on trying to figure out his best shot. While he was distracted, I snuck up behind him, reared back, and hit him as hard as I could over his right ear. The blow knocked him onto his side. I then jumped on him and beat the crap out of him. I was out of control as I released my months of frustration and humiliation on him. Fortunately, the bell rang so I hurried to class. He returned a little late from recess holding a paper towel to his nose.

As might be expected, he caught up with me after school and beat me up. When he was done, he stood there glaring at me.

"Okay," I said, "we're even."

"What do you mean we're even?" asked Lynn.

"You just got even with me for what I did this morning," I said. "But if you ever mess with me again, you'd better watch your back every second because sometime when you're not looking, I'll beat the crap out of you again."

Surprisingly, that ended Lynn's reign-of-Clark bullying. Based on that experience, I resolved to never let anyone ever bully me again. If they did, they would have to suffer my reprisal. Sometimes it would be a fair fight. Sometimes I would have to take a different approach. And I could be creative, but I'd make sure they didn't want to mess with me in the future. It didn't take long for word to get around that I wasn't someone to mess with. Unfortunately, my need to keep from being bullied extended to adults, even teachers.

There was one teacher in particular in junior high school that I had problems with: Mr. Partington, my shop teacher.

You don't always need to get even

Mr. Partington was a lot like the deputy sheriff, Barney Fife, on the old *Andy Griffith Show*. He was an aggravating know-it-all who liked to flaunt his superior knowledge and power over the class. Since I couldn't bring myself to be awed by his knowledge of such things as using a table saw to cut a board, Mr. Partington and I had a long-running feud with neither one of us wanting the other to get the upper hand. When he did something to embarrass me in front of the class, I did something to get even with him. I wouldn't let anyone, including a teacher, bully or make fun of me in front of my friends and classmates.

The shop area was divided into three rooms. The large main room contained work benches, drill presses, table saws and other such things. Behind the main work area was a regular classroom where we received lessons and worked on small projects. Thus, the shop provided plenty of area for me to carry out shenanigans.

One day Mr. Partington laughed as he pointed out to the class the poor paint job I'd done on a model house. I retaliated by taking the cover off of an electrical junction box and disconnecting the power going to the drill press. I then replaced the cover. It took him several days to figure out what was wrong. He initially thought the motor was burnt out. My electrical experience gained from working with Dad came in handy. On another occasion, he laughed as he pointed out to the class the ugly hat rack I had built. In reprisal, I enlisted the help of a couple of friends to act as lookouts while I wired an Auto Fooler to the on/off switch of the table saw. When attached to the spark plug of a car, an Auto Fooler would scream and emit smoke when the driver tried to start the car. It then exploded with a loud bang as the finale. In this case, I taped one to the underside of the table saw and connected the wires to the on/off switch. When Mr. Partington turned on the saw, the Auto Fooler ignited and began screaming while blowing out smoke. He took off screaming as he ran to get out of the shop.

It exploded just before he got to the door. He was suspicious I had perpetrated the prank, but fortunately, my lookouts didn't rat me out.

The feud continued for several months and finally reached its apex a month after Christmas. My anger was brought to the boiling point as Mr. Partington demonstrated his homemade, electrical continuity tester in the classroom. We'd been making crude electrical motors using thin electrical wire wound around our own rough iron frames. To test whether we had any open circuits, we used Partington's homemade tester. He had mounted a white porcelain light socket on a small wooden plank and attached an electrical cord that was plugged into an outlet. Another cord ran from the light socket to two electrodes that when touched together turned on the light.

Mr. Partington explained, "You can check whether your wiring makes a proper circuit by touching an electrode to each end of the circuit. If the bulb lights up, you know you have a complete circuit."

I raised my hand. When he pointed to me I said, "Shouldn't we be careful not to touch the bare electrodes with our bare hands? It would seem like you'd get shocked."

"No, you won't get shocked," he sneered. "You will just feel a little tingle. The resistance of the light bulb protects you from the 120-volt electricity."

He demonstrated this by grabbing an electrode in each hand. He smiled when several classmates gasped at this brazen act.

"I would have thought a so-called electrical expert like you would know this," Partington said.

The class pointed at me and giggled a little bit.

"Your lack of understanding makes me wonder whether you even know how to turn on a light."

Now the class broke out in full-on laughter.

I slumped down in my seat in embarrassment. I could barely wait for class to be over so I could get away from the snickering. But while I waited, I developed a plan to get even. It was based on my experience in dealing with the old electrical system in our family's house. Instead of breakers to protect the circuits, it used fuses that were screwed into sockets. Unlike breakers that could be reset if they tripped, the metal filament in a fuse would burn in two and the blown fuse would need to be replaced with a new one. Sometimes, I would blow a fuse at the house during an experiment and not have a replacement. Dad showed me that I could unscrew the fuse and place a penny in the bottom of the socket and then screw the fuse back in. This shorted out the fuse so the circuit would work. I just had to be careful not to overload it since there was now no overload protection. I reasoned that the same strategy would work on a light socket. I also, unfortunately, had plenty of experience with being shocked by 120-volt electricity while helping Dad. I found that without the resistance of a light bulb, it wasn't pleasant. But it wouldn't kill you as long as you could jerk free of the wires.

Since our class was held late in the morning, Mr. Partington often went to the bathroom when class was over. And on the fateful day he didn't let me down. As soon as the bell rang, he headed out the door. I then cautiously snuck back into the classroom and removed the light bulb from the socket of his homemade tester. Then I dropped a penny into the socket and replaced the bulb. Although the whole thing had only taken 20 seconds, I heaved a sigh of relief when I exited the classroom without being caught.

Fortunately, me and my friends had lunch right after shop, although Partington had to teach another class before he got a break. I told my friends that there might be a show in Partington's next class while we had lunch. We quietly snuck back and peered through the windows into the classroom to watch the demonstration.

Mr. Partington proceeded to provide his explanation of the continuity tester. I had expected he would first show them how the tester worked. We would get to see him burn up someone's motor in a blinding flash while it tripped the breaker. I started to panic when I realized that instead, he launched into a discussion of my "stupid" question about the tester shocking someone. He once again grabbed an electrode in each hand. This was immediately followed by his eyes bulging out as he started to scream. He then commenced to shake and dance for a few seconds as 120 volts of electricity surged through his body. Finally, he was able to pull himself free. My friends and I, along with the class, initially gasped in surprise and then laughed our asses off. I decided it was time to make a quick getaway to the school cafeteria.

As the day rolled on, all of the students were talking about Mr. Partington's fiasco during our class breaks. They laughed about his "dance routine" and wondered how he could have been so careless. It was proving to be one of the most notable events of the whole school year. I didn't know whether to be proud or scared. Not surprisingly, the school launched an inquisition to determine who had pulled the heinous prank. They were taking it seriously and interviewing students. This didn't look good.

That night, when Dad got home from work, he asked me to step into his bedroom.

"I was talking to Ted Leifson today," he said. Ted was a family friend who worked as a general contractor but also served as the justice of the peace for Spanish Fork.

"Ted told me there was a problem at the junior high today."

Shit. I tried to play it cool.

"Apparently, someone played a prank with a homemade conductivity tester and the teacher got shocked," Dad said. "Do you know anything about that?"

"I heard that it happened," I said with an innocent face. "But I don't know anything about it."

Dad stared at me for a few seconds while he considered the situation.

"I don't know," he said, skeptically. "Putting a penny in a light socket sounds exactly like something you would do."

I was starting to sweat now.

"It wasn't me. Honest."

"If you're lying, you're just digging a deeper hole for yourself."

It was certainly starting to feel that way.

"You would be better off confessing your sins now," he added.

Confessing didn't seem like a good option as long as there was a chance Dad wouldn't find out. I went with a move more daring than the conductivity tester: I lied straight to my father's face.

"It wasn't me," I said. "Someone must have been out to get

Mr. Partington." That was only a partial lie, and it did not feel as bad as the outright lie I had told earlier.

Dad put his hand on his chin while he thought about it and stared at me for a few seconds.

This is it. I'm done for.

Finally, Dad said, "I'll drop it for now. But you'd better be telling the truth."

My stomach was in knots.

"Now get out of here and get ready for dinner." And with that I thought the matter was settled.

However, within 48 hours, the day of reckoning came. I found out my friends couldn't be trusted when under pressure. During the inquisition someone squealed on me. I was chewed out by the principal and suspended from school for two weeks and warned that I'd be expelled if anything else happened. I was also banned from taking shop for eternity. Surprisingly, neither of my parents were there for the discussion. Maybe they'd called Mom but she wouldn't come in.

In any case, I felt sick that night as I sat in the front room waiting for Dad to come home from work. When he arrived, I told him we needed to talk.

"I thought we might," he said.

Back to the bedroom for another closed-door session with Dad. After the rock throwing fiasco that led to my exile at the mink ranch, Dad was always the one who dealt with and disciplined me.

"I've got something to tell you," I said.

He waited for me to continue. It took more courage than lying to him a few days earlier had. I felt horrible. Dad had always told me that he trusted me to be honest with him. Now he would know I'd lied to his face.

"I was responsible for the fiasco with Mr. Partington," I said. "Because of this, I've been suspended for two weeks. If anything else happens, I'll be expelled and have to find somewhere else to go to school."

"I wish I could say that I'm surprised," Dad said, shaking his head. "I ought to kick your butt."

I was expecting that.

"But experience has shown that it won't do any good," he said.

I wasn't expecting *that*. I expected that he would yell at me and vent his frustration with trying to raise me. Instead, he just looked sad. And I felt terrible. I'd really let him down. His disappointment was so much worse than his rage.

"I'm really sorry about this," I said. "I just thought it would be a funny prank."

"Clark, that's the problem," he said. "You need to start thinking. You are too old for this dumb shit."

He was quieter now, speaking in a voice I had not heard often. It wasn't a good voice to hear. If you've disappointed someone you hated to disappoint, you know what I'm talking about. I knew he was serious and that I needed to take him seriously.

"You have a lot of potential, but if you don't straighten out, it'll be wasted. You need to think about this. Figure out what you want to do with your life and quit doing dumb shit that will land you in jail."

We sat there in silence for a few seconds. I wasn't sure if he was done, but I didn't dare ask.

Finally, he said, "Go on, get out of here."

I had finally begun to learn a lesson at fourteen that I should have learned at six. At this stage of life, I learned by experience if I learned at all. I had almost a decade worth of experience and had only learned a few of the things I should have.

Of course I was grounded during the two weeks of my suspension. Sitting around home for two weeks was not much fun. Unlike today where you can play video games and get on the internet, there was nothing to do. Since my friends and siblings were in school, I just did chores all day. It was like solitary confinement. But it gave me plenty of time to follow Dad's advice and think about the stupid things I'd done and what I wanted to do with my life. It was one of those times that I hated it while it was happening, but in hindsight it was one of the best things that could have happened to me. In my younger years I had a lot of miserable moments that later shaped who I became as an adult. Apparently, I needed to be miserable to learn anything. It's kind of a tough way to learn.

You may be smarter than you think

When the suspension finally ended, I was glad to get back to school despite being teased by my friends. A couple of months later, however, I had another surprise. I was on my way to English class when the guidance counselor, Mr. Jones, caught me in the hallway. He told me he wanted to talk to me in his office. As I followed him down the hall, I wondered what I was in trouble for now. I had been trying to be on my best behavior and couldn't think of anything I'd done. Whatever it was, I hoped it wasn't too serious. I didn't want to have to find another school.

Or explain it to Dad.

As we walked into his office, Mr. Jones waved me into a chair on the other side of his desk. I sat down cautiously, preparing for the worst.

"Let's get right to the point," he said. "Did you cheat on the aptitude test?"

What? It was like a shot out of the blue. Of all the things I had actually done, cheating on the test never crossed my mind. The entire ninth grade had taken the state-wide test several months earlier. I had not given it a second thought. Until now.

"No way," I said. I knew I hadn't cheated. "Why?"

"Did you look at your neighbors' answers or something?"

"Did you see my neighbors? I'd be an idiot if I used their answers."

I was starting to get upset. Of all the things I'd done, I didn't want to be punished for something I hadn't done. This was starting to feel like the rock throwing incident with Stan that got me exiled to the mink ranch. I needed to be careful.

"There's no reason to cheat," I reasoned. "It wouldn't impact my grade or anything."

"Well," he said, "this doesn't make any sense. Salt Lake just called to congratulate us on the job we're doing. They let me know that one of our students, you, scored in the top 10 individuals in the state."

I didn't believe it.

"Knowing you...that doesn't seem likely," he added.

It didn't seem likely to me either. I was taken aback. It didn't make sense. It seemed to me that others remembered things much quicker and were smarter than me. I was a slow learner and had trouble memorizing facts. Some of my peers could easily remember things and always did well in class. Instead, I had to study things until I understood how they worked. Then I could remember them. You can see how that worked well for science and math, but for English...not so much. There, the rules were not built on logic. Unlike the smart kids, my learning style was very tactical and hands-on. Once I figured it out, I had it. But that took time.

"I swear I didn't cheat," I said. "I don't know what to tell you."

The counselor thought about it for a few minutes while I squirmed in my seat. It felt like torture. Silence could sometimes get me talking, but I had nothing more to say.

"I can't see how you'd cheat. But if you're really that smart," Mr. Jones finally said, "why do you do such stupid things?"

I shrugged.

"Clark," he said, sounding like my father, "you need to knock off the nonsense. You should be getting straight A's in school. Based on the test, you can be anything you want. But, based on your experience in shop, you're on a path that will take you to jail."

Hearing this from yet another person was starting to make me nervous. Mr. Jones talked to me for a few more minutes, telling me that I was just starting out and needed to think about the consequences of my actions and what I wanted to do with my life. He then sent me on to English, my least favorite subject. As I walked down the empty halls to class, it seemed crazy that he and Dad were saying the same thing. Were they right? I thought about it periodically during the day—and the remaining school year.

What they said stuck with me after school ended and I started my sixth summer in exile on the mink ranch. I had a lot of thinking to do. While working on the mink ranch, I considered what it would be like if I had to do this type of manual labor for the rest of my life. But based on what Mr. Jones had said, maybe I really could make it through college and get a degree. I thought I'd really enjoy becoming an electrical engineer. I had previously thought about becoming an electrician. I already had a lot of experience. But electricians didn't get to design anything. They followed someone else's plans. But an electrical engineer got to design and look after the construction of things. Plus, they made lots of money.

The more I thought about it, the more convinced I became that I wanted to become an electrical engineer. I decided that there would be no more shenanigans, or at least very few for the near future. Instead, I would buckle down and work hard to get good grades. It would also help if I stayed out of jail. I kept this in mind during the summer as I dealt with the mink.

CHAPTER 7

The Mink Ranch Revisited

It's easy to be stupid, but it takes imagination to have fun doing it

Despite my protests, I was exiled to the mink ranch every summer from 1961 until after I started college in 1969. For the first few summers, Dad tricked me into believing my uncle absolutely needed my help. He came up with a lot of excuses. Sometimes one of the workers quit without notice. Or maybe they needed extra help because they were building a new mink shed. It had to be me because I was such a valuable worker. Dad was smart not to tell me what was really going on. I would have been mad and sad if I'd known it was because my mother didn't want me around. But after the first few years I accepted that I was going to spend the summer at the mink ranch.

Initially, I bunked with my grandmother. But after a couple of summers she'd had enough and had better things to do with her time. Then I was handed off to my uncle Blake. I also spent a couple of summers working at my cousin Rick's mink ranch and bunked with him. I even got to live by myself in Uncle Dick's shop for the last two summers. The shop was a separate building where I had a makeshift bed and only went to Grandma's house for meals. I had a lot of freedom and could run my own life. How could anything go astray having a teenage boy, me, look after himself?

During my early years in exile, I was terribly homesick. I didn't have anyone to play with. Grandma's TV had limited reception so it was no help. Sometimes, I would go hiking with Grandma's dog, but mostly I just sat outside watching the birds and clouds until it was time for dinner. Fortunately, I eventually became good friends with the people I worked with and they invited me to do things with them even though they were much older. We would go fishing or rabbit hunting at night. Sometimes my friend Bob picked up a couple of six packs of beer and took me rodding on State Street in Salt Lake City. Although he was twenty-two years old and I was only fifteen, we tried to pick up girls. It didn't turn out well. Even though I had a beer in my hand, I just couldn't convince a twenty-one-year-old girl that I was in her league. It probably didn't help when she slid over next to me in the back seat I cowered against the door. The most I'd ever done before was kiss a girl.

I also learned that alcohol didn't improve a person's judgment. On one occasion, Bob pulled into a parking lot on the west side of State Street.

"Clark," he said, "it's your turn to drive."

I was stunned.

"You've got to be kidding." I said. "I'm only fifteen and don't have a license. Besides, I've been drinking too."

"Maybe, but you're still in better shape than me. I can't afford to get a drunk driving ticket."

With that he opened his door and climbed out. I reluctantly climbed into the driver's seat. Fortunately, it had an automatic transmission. Unfortunately, although I'd driven Dad's pickup on dirt roads in the mountains, I didn't know what I was doing in downtown Salt Lake.

"Which way do you want to go?" I asked.

"North," Bob said.

"Which way is north?"

"To the left."

I put the car in drive, pulled up to the parking lot exit, and watched until there was a break in traffic. Then I hurriedly made a left turn. But there was an island dividing the lanes going north and south. So up over the island we went, scraping the bottom of Bob's Pontiac GTO as we headed down the road.

"That could have gone better," Bob said. "If you'd turned right and made a U-turn at the next intersection the car would have been a little happier."

"I told you I didn't know how to drive."

"I'm starting to think that you may be right. Still, it's better for you to get a ticket than me."

Easy for him to say.

When I was sober the next day, I realized how lucky we'd been. I wasn't sure how he'd have explained to the police that he'd let a drunk 15-year-old drive his car. Luckily, we didn't find out, but this wasn't the only stupid thing that happened on the mink ranch.

The cat fiasco

Besides the fun I was having with my older friends at night, there were the ongoing shenanigans during the day at the mink ranch. Sometimes these involved stray cats. People often hauled their unwanted cats out to the country and dropped them off by the side of the road. The cats were not accustomed to being in the wild and were ill-prepared to take care of themselves. They had to scrounge food and defend themselves from predators. They quickly became feral and were not to be messed with.

The cats were always hungry and the smell of the mink feed attracted them to the mink ranch where they hoped to grab an easy meal. However, to get at the mink feed they had to find a way into the 200-foot-long mink sheds.

Unfortunately for the cats, the shed made it difficult for them to get at the mink feed. But occasionally a cat would find a way in for a snack but then be unable to find a way out. When we'd come in the shed the next morning we'd discover the cat and the fun would begin.

Since the cats were feral, they didn't want to be caught and would tear into us if cornered. Catching them required the heavy leather gloves normally used when handling the mink. But even then we had to be careful. Unlike the mink, the cats could sometimes bite through the leather gloves or twist their bodies around so they could tear into our arms with their rear claws.

Normally we released the cats and seldom saw them again. If one did make a habit of getting in the sheds, we could usually discourage it by tying one end of a string to the cat's tail and the other end to an empty pop can. Upon release, the cat would take a few steps, hear the can clanking along behind it and take off running. The cat apparently thought something was chasing it. We'd laugh as it raced through the fields jumping over fences.

The most infamous adventure with the cats took place when I was 16. My cohort, Ricky, and I were making our morning rounds and discovered a cat. Although Ricky was a year younger than me, we had worked together for several years and were good friends. Walking in the shed, we were startled to see a large cat on top of a mink pen eating the food. The cat stared at us for a few seconds then jumped and ran down the aisle of the shed. We put on the heavy leather gloves and took off after him. Ricky managed to corner it at one end of the shed. Unfortunately, Ricky didn't know any better and lunged directly at the cat. The cat thought there was no way to escape and attacked Ricky. It leaped onto his right thigh, dug in with the claws of all four feet, and starting biting his leg, tearing out pieces of his jeans and leg.

Ricky was so surprised, all he could do was stare wide-eyed at the cat and scream. I ran over and slapped the cat with my gloved hand knocking it loose. The surprised cat looked at me for a second and then ran to the opposite end of the shed. Ricky was shaking so bad that I had to help him sit down in the aisle. It took a few minutes for him to calm down. Then I cautiously walked to the end of the shed to deal with the felon.

Warily, I approached the cat while standing on the right side of the aisle. This provided a potential escape route for the cat on the left side. We stood there in a kind of stalemate for a few seconds. Finally, the cat couldn't stand the tension any longer and tried to dash by. I waited until it was almost even with me and then lunged at it, grabbed it around its neck holding its tail. Although it struggled, it couldn't get loose and I was careful to make sure that it couldn't bite me or tear into me with its hind claws.

Ricky was adamant that this cat deserved special treatment. After some thought, we came up with a "brilliant" idea. First, we tied a can to its tail and then loaded it into a portable cage used to transport mink which we placed in the trunk of my car. At our morning break, we told the foreman we were going out for snacks and headed to the local grocery store.

When we arrived, we were fortunate to find a parking spot near the entrance. I put on the leather gloves and wrestled the cat out of the carrier but kept it in the trunk so it wasn't visible to people passing by. Ricky then wandered over to the store entrance and acted as lookout. When no one was walking toward us in the parking lot or near the doors on the inside of the store, he signaled. I quickly carried the cat over, Ricky opened the door, and I tossed the cat in. When the cat landed on the floor, it heard the can clang behind it and took off down the aisle. Of course this took the shoppers for a loop.

We stood mesmerized as we watched the circus. The cat shot down an aisle between shelves of food causing some women to scream and throw things in the air. When it reached the end of the aisle, it tried to turn the corner at full speed but its claws couldn't get traction on the tile floor. It slammed into a cooler, finally made the corner, and then took off up the next aisle with more women screaming and food being thrown in the air. At this point, Ricky and I came to our senses and decided it was time to make a hasty retreat.

I waited a few days before heading back to the store for snacks. I was surprised to find wanted posters taped to the light poles in the parking lot offering a $200 reward for information leading to the identity of the person or persons that turned a cat loose in the store. I decided to not press my luck and climbed back in my car and drove to a mini-mart for snacks.

Several days later, one of Uncle Blake's friends stopped by the mink ranch to visit and asked if we had heard about the cat fiasco at the grocery store. Ricky and I looked at each briefly then shook our heads no. He said a cat turned loose in the store ran up and down aisles terrorizing shoppers while making a big mess. It finally became exhausted and stopped to catch its breath near the meat counter.

A stock boy, thinking it was someone's house cat, attempted to pick it up. Bad decision. The cat was really pissed off and tore into him. The cat would threaten to attack anyone that got near it. It took almost 20 minutes to herd the cat out of the store. He concluded with the news that the store manager was offering a reward for information about who'd done it. We decided it was best to avoid the store for a few months. Maybe I needed to consider what could go drastically wrong with a shenanigan. It made me nervous to be a wanted man.

The war with Howard

Based on my experience with Lynn Renaulson in first grade, I wouldn't tolerate being bullied. I felt that if you let someone push you around too much without retaliating, the abuse only got worse. Unfortunately, I still hadn't figured out a constructive way to deal with this type of problem.

One of Uncle Dick's former employees, Howard Quid, lived in an old log house next to the mink ranch. When he had worked on the mink ranch, we kids hadn't gotten along with Howard. He always thought we should do the work that he didn't want to do. He continually came up with schemes to shift work on to us. The feud continued even after he quit and found another job. Although he had a new employer, he still lived next to the mink ranch in the log house. Unfortunately, we boys had to walk down an alley that ran alongside his back yard in order to get to the lower half of the mink ranch. If Howard happened to be outside, he would unchain his German Shepherd and turn him loose on us. The dog would jump over Howard's fence and chase us. Howard laughed as he watched us scramble to get away from his dog and into a mink shed. We were able to get some revenge by throwing firecrackers at the dog when he was chained up and Howard wasn't around. In fact, after a few firecrackers all we had to do was hiss as we walked by and the dog would think we'd lit another firecracker and dive into his dog house. However, this wasn't adequate retribution since it didn't impact Howard. After considerable thought, we finally came up with a proper scheme to enact our revenge.

Although I generally slept outside alone at night, sometimes one or two of my coworkers spent the night with me. On the night of this infamous adventure, I invited Ricky and Brian to a sleepover. Since Grandma was watering her lawn, we bedded down in my uncle Dick's back yard. It was a relatively warm, moonless night so we lay on top of our sleeping bags while we discussed our plans and waited for the neighbors to go to sleep. When the houses around us had turned dark, we decided it was time for our sneak attack.

We put on our shoes and headed down the alley leading past Howard's back yard. We snuck along without talking, careful not to make any sound. As we closed in on Howard's house, we could dimly make out his bedroom window. We knew from previous experience his windows were different. They were designed with the glass window on the outside and hinged at the top. The screen was on the inside of the window and had a hole in the bottom of the frame. Since Howard didn't have air conditioning, he could push a wood dowel through the hole in the screen frame to raise up the bottom of the window and let cool air in. The bottom end of the dowel rested on a wooden stop on the window frame inside the house. On this hot night, it almost looked like the house had sets of small wings sticking out all over the house.

The three of us carefully climbed over his three-foot fence and then tiptoed up to his bedroom window. It was very dark inside the house, but we could hear Howard snoring softly. While Brian lifted up the bottom of the window, Ricky pulled the dowel out of the hole. This provided a direct opening into the house. I then cautiously put a red phantom in the hole, lit the fuse and waited.

A red phantom was one of the fireworks bought in Evanston, Wyoming. When the red phantom ignited, it started to scream loudly and shot out fire. We were surprised when the fire propelled it into Howard's bedroom. We were even more surprised to see that Howard's bed was directly below the window. The red phantom landed in the middle of his bed as it continued to scream and shoot out sparks. It sounded like a falling bomb in an old war movie.

Howard jumped from the bed and joined his wife in the screaming. He then yelled, "The Russians are coming!!" and started to run from the bedroom. Unfortunately, the bedroom door was closed and he hit it at full speed and bounced back. About this time, the red phantom exploded and Howard took off running again, and again bounced off of the bedroom door. We decided it was time to cut out of there. We were laughing so hard we could hardly get back over his fence.

We quickly crawled into our sleeping bags. We kept laughing as we retold the story. We had gotten our revenge. After a while, I finally drifted off to sleep.

Sometime later, a bright light in my eyes interrupted my dreams. I thought one of my companions was playing a joke on me.

"Get the damn light out of my eyes," I said.

A strange voice said, "Watch your mouth."

I was still struggling to shift from my dream to reality and couldn't figure out what was going on.

"Get that light out of my eyes or I'm going to kick your ass."

"I said, 'Watch your mouth.' This is the police. We're here to investigate a complaint."

I bolted upright. Two police officers were standing alongside my uncle Dick. Howard Quid was standing behind them. The police officers didn't ask whether we had done it, but just started to chew us out. They said we had trespassed and would be liable for any damage. They also said that all kinds of bad things could have happened to Howard due to our prank. I wasn't so sure they were all bad but thought it best to keep my mouth shut. At the end of the lecture, my uncle confiscated our fireworks. He told us that he wasn't happy about getting up in the middle of the night to hear about our damn stupidity.

As the police were preparing to leave, their final words were, "You boys need to leave Mr. Quid and his wife alone."

At this point, Howard leaned around from behind the officers and said, "And that goes for my dog too."

We were lucky that we didn't get into more trouble over the incident. However, our objective was achieved. We had our revenge on Howard and he no longer turned his dog loose on us. We'd reached a truce.

The freedom I had on the mink ranch turned out to be very educational. When I thought about it later, I realized that driving a car while underage and drunk was stupid. And, although the pranks relieved some of the boredom of the mink ranch, I began to appreciate they could go too far. The prank with the cat in the grocery store had resulted in a wanted poster. If the store had found out who released the cat, I not only would have been liable for the damages but could have been arrested by the police. The incident with Howard had actually resulted in a visit by the police. That was bad enough, but it would have been much worse if we'd started a fire or Howard had been seriously hurt. I was beginning to see that I needed to exercise some judgment. The shenanigans were fun and relieved tension, but I had to avoid those that might get me in serious trouble. I resolved to try to think things through better in the future. I still made some bad decisions but at least my thinking had started to move in the right direction.

Living in the shop during my last few summers on the ranch taught me a lot. No one paid any attention to what I was doing or where I was. Having this freedom at such a young age taught me lessons others didn't learn until much later in life. I knew from experience that doing heavy manual labor in the hot sun for minimum wage wasn't much fun. I was getting an appreciation for how much it cost for an adult to live. This provided a lot of incentive to go to college, and if I was smart enough, I could make a decent living while working in a comfortable environment.

CHAPTER 8

How to Screw Up Without Really Trying

Some lessons aren't taught in school

As the fall of 1966 approached I was excited. I would get to abandon the mink ranch two weeks early to start training for the high school football team. Previously, I'd played football regularly with the neighborhood boys on my friend Jerry's large lawn. I really enjoyed it and had been able to hold my own, even with the older boys. Now, I was finally old enough to have a shot at playing on the high school football team. Football was important to me for two reasons. First, I really liked playing the game and, second, football players were the big men on campus. They attracted the hot girls. I was definitely interested in girls. At the mink ranch, there weren't any girls, hot or otherwise, except the much older ones I met rodding State Street with Bob.

With all this in mind I was also worried that it would be difficult for me to play football and do well academically. I still wasn't convinced I was very smart, and I really wanted to go to college to become an engineer. I knew I wouldn't have a chance unless I quit my shenanigans and got A's in school, particularly in math and science. But I figured if I was careful, I could get my studies done and still have time for football practice.

During the two weeks before school started, the Junior Varsity team practiced football twice a day for two hours. Since high school in Spanish Fork was only a three-year program, only sophomores were on the Junior Varsity team. But even without older players, four hours of football in Utah's August heat exhausted me. First, there was warm-up which consisted of jumping jacks and sprints. Next, we practiced specific plays over and over again until we got it right. After practice, I showered, changed clothes, and then hiked a mile uphill to my house. By the time I got home, I didn't have enough energy to do much except whine. I quickly found Mom wasn't sympathetic enough to drive me to practice. She didn't have much to do with me if she could help it. I decided to take the matter up with Dad. Even though he couldn't drive me because of work, he might be able to plead my case with Mom.

Dad listened to my complaint and said he'd see what he could do. A few days later he said, "I've come up with a solution to your problem of getting home after football practice. Get in the car."

Huh? Get in the car? How was getting in the car going to convince Mom to drive me to practice?

I climbed in the car with Dad and we headed down the street. Although I was confused and started asking him questions, all he'd say was "Wait and see." My confusion deepened when he stopped at Mose's garage.

Mose was one of Dad's drinking buddies who happened to own a garage. When we got there, we spotted Mose's brown hair lurking over a car. The garage was in an old service station he had converted into an auto repair shop. The large white building had six stalls where cars could be repaired. Next to the garage he had a weed-strewn lot filled with all kinds of old cars in various states of disrepair. Some were available for sale and some were being stripped for parts. Dad took me over to a 1959 Pontiac Bonneville. I was not impressed. It was a light green monster with four doors, twin tail fins, and four headlights. It's only saving grace was that it had a V-8 engine.

"What do you think?" Dad said. "Mose wants $300 for it."

"I was kind of hoping my first car would look a little hotter," I said.

Hot girls and hot cars went together.

"Dad, I don't see how it resolves my problem of walking home from school. I'm only fifteen and don't have a driver's license."

"If you buy it I will work things out so you can drive it to school. But only to and from school, nowhere else."

I was stunned. I never imagined my dad would let me drive before I had a license. This would definitely resolve the problem of getting home after practice. I was also thinking about the girls.

"On second thought, this works for me," I said. I figured I could always trade it out later.

"Then go ahead and drive it home. I'll let Mose know you'll pay him in the next few days after you run by the bank."

The money I'd made at the mink ranch was proving beneficial.

"Also, make sure you park it on the far side of the driveway in front of the boat."

Maybe that was to protect the boat from errant rocks during rock throwing contests.

My 1959 Pontiac Bonneville

Besides getting to and from school, the car definitely helped me pick up girls. Although my Pontiac wasn't much to look at, no one else my age owned one. Giving a girl a ride to school wouldn't technically violate Dad's instructions. So my mother's refusal to drive me to practice ended up helping me know new girls, and I took the opportunity when I got it. It was good to have something to perk up my spirits. The football season had turned into a complete disaster—the JV team had lost every game so far.

I was pondering the football fiasco one night when an unexpected headache arose. I was watching TV when Mom told me that a couple of boys were asking for me at the front door. It seemed strange that Mom didn't know who the boys were since she knew all my friends. I pondered this as I walked to the door and out onto the steps. I was surprised to see two boys, a year ahead of me in high school, wearing their blue WojWoda sweaters. The WojWodas were a high school gang unique to Spanish Fork initially founded to do service projects, but there was always an occasional wild party. Over the years, the service projects dwindled and the wild partying increased. I would often see them drinking beer while rodding Main Street in their cars. They got into all kinds of mischief and an occasional fight. The school had banned the gang due to the partying and fighting. Still the WojWodas continued to operate, but they didn't wear their sweaters to school. They would have been my kind of guys before I decided I wanted to go to college.

"I'm surprised to see you guys," I said, "is there a problem?"

I was hoping I hadn't inadvertently offended a WojWoda. I hadn't fought one of them and based on their reputation, I didn't want to.

The larger of the two, Tiny Larsen, spoke up. "We're here to offer you the chance to join the WojWodas. You'll fit right in and have a lot of fun. What do you think?"

Oh, shit. What do I do? If I don't join, these guys will make my life miserable for the next three years. I had seen the abuse they heaped on someone who offended them. And I suspected that either one could beat the crap out of me. But if I joined, the drinking and mischief would likely eliminate any chance of me going to college. I'd shown I could get into plenty of trouble on my own. Having WojWodas around to egg me on would only make matters worse. I decided to try and dodge the problem.

"Can I think about this?" I asked.

"Nope," Tiny said. "The initiation starts right now. You either come with us or you're out of consideration. You won't get a second chance and we will make sure that you'll wish you'd joined if you don't," he said glaring at me.

I was in a bind but decided to wimp out. I would go along for now and find a graceful way to flunk the initiation during the next two weeks.

"Give me a minute to tell my mom and I will be right with you," I said as they walked back to their car.

We drove to the city park where we waited in the dark to see who else was joining the club. Eventually, me and ten other idiots were surrounded by twenty WojWoda members. Then the abuse began. They had us bend over while they whacked us with a paddle. After each whacking we had to say, "Thank you, sir, can I have another?" Over the next two weeks, we helped them with various projects. In one case, I helped Tiny Larsen with his job of milking cows at a dairy. They would also embarrass us at school by having us pounce on random girls walking down the hall and give them a kiss. After the first day, the girls shied away from us when they saw us coming.

Partway through the initiation, the coach of the varsity football team, Coach Andersen, caught up with me after football practice.

"Clark, wait up," he said. "I want to talk to you."

I stood and waited as he walked over.

"I understand you're joining the WojWodas."

Uh oh. This could be trouble.

Coach Andersen continued, "You should rethink that. If you join, you won't be able to play football and I will be very disappointed. You have potential and will likely be on the varsity team next year. But you can't play if you're a WojWoda."

I heaved a sigh of relief. The coach had given me a way out.

"Thanks for letting me know," I said. "I'll let them know that I can't join."

That night I caught up with Tiny and told him I needed to drop out because of football.

Tiny stood there for a few seconds looking at me.

"Coach Anderson told me the same thing," Tiny said. "But I am still playing football. He's just bluffing. You had better stay on board or we'll make sure you regret it."

We discussed it a little longer, but it was evident that Tiny wasn't buying my excuse. The net result was that I ended up becoming a "proud" member of the WojWodas. A week after completing the initiation, I drove to Salt Lake to get my custom-made sweater. My fellow WojWodas and I wore our sweaters after school as we rodded Main Street in our cars. It also turned out Coach Anderson wasn't bluffing. Beginning with my high school class, no WojWoda played football. Stupidity had struck again. Now the question was whether I could minimize the damage to my academic career.

Not surprisingly, joining the WojWodas didn't help my reputation at school. WojWodas got into all sorts of trouble. At football games, we'd sit in the opposing team's bleachers and heckle their fans and cheerleaders. On the weekends, we'd break into the school to play basketball in the gym. One night we thought Igor, the biology lab's skeleton was bored just hanging around in the classroom and that he'd like some excitement like rodding Main Street. We had him sit in the back seat of the car. My friend, Alan, lay on the floor and raised his hand with a beer taped to it to salute passing cars. We almost caused a couple of wrecks.

The front and back of my WojWoda sweater

All of these dumb shenanigans meant that during Monday morning announcements we were often called to the principal's office. Typically, we received an ass-chewing followed by additional hours of detention. I accumulated a lot of hours of detention over my next three years of high school. These were supposed to be worked off by helping the janitors after school. Eventually there were so many hours I just gave up.

There was one shenanigan that still riles up some people. It started one Friday afternoon when we were drinking beer and driving around the rural roads in the farmland as we often did. As we drove along we usually discussed what was going on at school or girls that were reportedly frisky. On this occasion, we were discussing the Junior Prom being held that night.

"I can't believe none of us have dates for the prom," I said.

"Most parents won't let their daughters date us," Gary said. "They seem suspicious of our intentions."

"Still, it would be fun to see the girls all dressed up."

About this time we came upon a turkey farm. Several hundred fully grown turkeys were contained in a large, fenced area.

"I know where we could get a date," Sheldon said. "We could take some of those turkeys to the prom!"

"What?" we said in unison. We knew Sheldon worked at the farm but didn't realize he was that attached to the turkeys.

"Sure. They lead a miserable life being penned up like that. They would really enjoy being our dates and the chance to get out for the Junior Prom."

I pulled over next to the farm and Sheldon climbed over the fence and herded the turkeys to one end of the enclosure. He then caught and handed four turkeys over the fence so that we would each have a date.

Heading back to town, we decided the turkeys felt bad because they'd never flown. We remedied the situation by holding them out the windows by their necks. As we drove along, they spread their wings and maneuvered as if they were really flying. I think they were pretending to be eagles.

The Junior Prom was being held in the high school cafeteria. Although we arrived two hours before the prom, we didn't think the turkeys would mind being early. We were able to find a window that wasn't properly latched, opened it, and pushed the turkeys inside. I'm sure they were excited to have flown and attended a prom on the same day.

However, it turned out the turkeys didn't behave themselves over the next few hours. The prom-goers found the decorations in disarray and turkey shit all over the place. Trying to evict the turkeys added to the mess. Besides more shit, they now had feathers scattered around that added more damage to the decorations. Apparently, we should have given the turkeys a few pointers on how to behave.

There was a lot of talk Monday morning about the turkeys at the prom. Some of my classmates asked whether I was involved. To deflect their suspicions, I suggested it was probably some kids from either Springville or Payson. Both high schools were our mortal enemies. The students in charge of decorations for the prom were particularly pissed off. After spending most of the afternoon decorating, they were distressed when they returned and found such an ungodly mess. Even decades later, when I mentioned my role in the fiasco to one of the decorators, she told me she wasn't surprised but was still totally pissed off. Such was the impact of a few beers on teenagers.

Going into competition with the state

Obtaining the beer that fueled this type of behavior was difficult. First, we had to find someone who would buy it for us, usually at a premium. And we couldn't always find someone. If I tried to buy beer myself the store clerk almost always asked for my ID. It would make life a lot easier if I just had the proper identification. A forged driver's license seemed to be the best solution to the problem.

At the time, paper driver's licenses were still used in Utah and the minimum age for drinking was twenty-one. Thus, licenses issued for those under twenty-one were tinted green while those for adults were yellow. About this time, I happened to discover that the library at nearby Brigham Young University had one of the newly invented black and white copiers. No place else that I knew had one. They were that rare. I experimented with it and found that it provided a good, crisp black and white image, and so I made copies of both the front and back of my driver's license. At home, I covered up critical information such as name, date of birth, and license number using Wite-Out. The edited documents were then taken back to BYU and multiple copies made.

Since the copies were black and white, I needed to add the correct color. Borrowing my mother's license, I shopped around the local hobby store until I found a translucent, yellow spray paint that matched perfectly. On a warm calm day I hung the copies on our clothesline and lightly sprayed them with paint to produce a nearly perfect match to an adult driver's license.

After the paint dried, I carefully cut out the front and back sheets of my new license. Not wanting the license to be brittle, I purchased rubber cement and used a thin layer to glue the front and back together.

The next problem was the license number. The numbers on the official licenses were red and twice as tall as the other print on the license. After some thought, I headed down to the local stationery store. There, I was able to find a rubber stamp that produced the same size and style of numbers as used on a real license. The stamp was made so that rubber rings could be rotated to provide different six-digit numbers. I also bought a red ink pad. At home, I made up a license number similar to my mom's and carefully stamped my forged license using red ink.

I now had a nearly perfect blank Utah driver's license. The next task was to fill it in. The font produced by my parents' mechanical typewriter did not match that used by the state of Utah. Checking around, I found that none of my friends had a suitable typewriter either. After a few weeks, I happened to check the typewriters used in the typing lab at the high school. These were IBM Selectric typewriters that used the elite font—a perfect match! I posted a lookout at the door and snuck into the typing lab during lunch. Using the fake name of Robert Clarke and a made-up birth date, I was able to complete my driver's license.

The next Friday, I traveled to the nearby town of Springville to try out my new license. I didn't want to run into someone that knew me while I was buying beer. I also had one of my friends drive. He was waiting in the car with the engine running in case I needed to make a quick getaway. After loading a case of beer into a shopping cart, I pulled up to the checkout counter. The clerk asked to see my ID. After briefly looking at it, she rang up the beer and sent me on my way. My buddies and I heaved a sigh of relief as we headed for the rural roads west of Spanish Fork to drink beer and swap stories.

Based on the success of my license, I decided to enter the driver's license business. Using BYU's copying machine, I started to manufacture licenses by the dozens. I sold them for $50 apiece, which was a lot of money back in 1967. But even at that price it was hard to keep up with demand. I had developed a lucrative business.

After a couple of months of forging licenses, I was alarmed one afternoon when the chief of police, Ned Grant, pulled up to me in his patrol car as I was walking through the high school parking lot.

"Clark, hop in the car," he said. "We need to go for a ride."

This was a totally unexpected event that scared the hell out of me. Due to some previous encounters, he knew my name. I nervously climbed in the car and we drove off.

"Clark," he said, "the state of Utah would like to believe that they have a monopoly on the driver's license business."

Uh oh. I wondered how much he knew.

"I can see why they'd feel that way," I said.

"It has come to my attention that you're in competition with the state." Chief Grant looked over at me. "It would be a good idea if you exited the business before I'm forced to throw you in jail."

"Thanks for the advice. You can consider me out of the business."

"And if anyone asks," he said, "this conversation never happened."

"My lips are sealed."

He then drove me back to the parking lot and dropped me off. The other students walking to their cars wondered why I was being dropped off by the chief of police, but I didn't say a word.

My brief stint at forgery ended abruptly. I was out of the driver's license business but fortunately not in jail. Also, the school hadn't found out that I was using their typewriters as part of the forgery operation. If they had figured it out, it might have ended my chances for graduation and college. And despite my actions and dumb WojWoda shenanigans I really wanted to go to college. To do this, I knew that I needed to shape up before my luck ran out. In particular, I would need to take and pass advanced math and science with good grades. The WojWodas might be the death of my dream to go to college if I didn't make some changes.

CHAPTER 9

Dr. Jekyll Goes to High School

Sometimes, you're not as dumb as you think—or act

My friends worried about my gang activities. Their concerns were based on the heavy drinking, occasional fistfights, and my clandestine shenanigans often under investigation by the high school. Even the relatively benign shenanigan of turning the turkeys loose at the Junior Prom had elicited an investigation that lasted several weeks. Unfortunately, my reputation preceded me as I started high school which caused my teachers some concerns.

Although I tried to stay out of trouble during class, occasionally someone would try to bully me. I still wouldn't tolerate it. One such incident occurred early in my high school career during chemistry lab. At the time, we were studying how certain chemicals increased the electrical conductivity of water. The teacher, Mr. Nelson, explained that one chemical, sodium chloride or table salt, did this because it ionized when dissolved in water. Our lab class on this particular day was designed to allow us to observe this phenomenon.

At the beginning of the lab class, Mr. Nelson divided us into groups of two. Each pair had their own work area on one of the lab benches. We were given a large glass beaker and told to fill it with 750 milliliters of distilled water. The idea was for us to observe the increase in conductivity as we weighed and dissolved small amounts of salt in the water. I was a surprised by the simplicity of the test equipment. Instead of using a meter to measure the conductivity, we were using a light bulb. The greater the conductivity, the brighter the light. After weighing out and stirring in each addition of salt, we lowered two electrodes into the beaker. Then we flipped on a switch that allowed the current to flow through the solution and then through a light bulb. Since distilled water was a very poor conductor, initially the bulb didn't light up at all. But as more salt was dissolved in the water, it became a better conductor. This allowed the 120-volt electricity to flow through the water so the bulb would begin to glow. The more salt we added, the brighter the light.

Unfortunately, just as the lab got underway, a pair of boys a year ahead of me in school began making snide remarks. They didn't think a WojWoda could possibly do the experiment correctly.

"Hey, Clark," John said. "I thought they'd banned WojWodas from class. The teachers didn't want to waste their time on retards."

Initially, I tried to ignore him and go on with the experiment. However, I could hear some giggling which started to embarrass me.

After a few minutes John fired another shot. "Clark, that light bulb isn't the only thing around here that isn't very bright."

John's partner, Brad, decided to join the fun. "Yeah, your light bulb has been out for quite a few years."

There was more giggling, only louder this time. I wasn't sure how to deal with this. I wasn't used to verbal sparring. My normal way of dealing with this type of situation was to punch the person. But I didn't think it would be a good idea to start a fistfight in the classroom with the teacher nearby. I just tried to ignore them as their snide remarks continued and the snickering and giggling grew louder. But I was not about to tolerate this bullying without some type of repercussion.

As I thought about what possible actions to take, I realized the test equipment was similar to that used in Mr. Partington's class in junior high. Despite the punishment I'd received for using it back then, it seemed like a good way to get even with my harassers.

And they shouldn't get shocked, just surprised. Without the resistance of the light bulb, the surge of electricity should just vaporize some water. I waited until they headed to the scale room to weigh out more salt. In the brief time they were gone, I removed their light bulb, dropped a penny in the socket, and hurriedly screwed the bulb back in. Back at my station, I casually looked around the room. No one was paying any attention to me. Everyone was absorbed in running their own experiments.

After a few minutes, my antagonists returned and added more salt to the water. At this point, the water was a good conductor. I watched from a safe distance as they stuck the electrodes into the beaker of salt water. When they turned on the switch, the surge of electricity vaporized some of the water, which blew the rest of the water out of the beaker. They let out a scream and threw their notepads in the air. When the screaming ended, they were standing there wide-eyed with water dripping off of them. They looked like fools. I had my revenge.

Mr. Nelson rushed over to see what had happened. He was looking around and talking to people, but no one had seen anything. Fortunately for me, only a few minutes after the "explosion" the bell rang and class was dismissed.

The next day, Mr. Nelson caught me in the hall as I was about to enter the classroom.

"Clark, I need to talk to you," he said.

This surprised me and made me very nervous. Maybe someone had ratted me out after all.

Mr. Nelson continued. "I found a penny in the bottom of John and Brad's light socket. It's what caused yesterday's explosion."

I didn't like the direction this conversation was going. It looked like I was screwed.

"I heard about a similar incident that happened at the junior high in Mr. Partington's class not long ago. I'm not looking for a confession, but nothing like this had better happen again or you won't get off the hook so easily. Now get into class."

I couldn't believe I was being let off the hook. I heaved a sigh of relief as I hurried to my seat. I also resolved that I wouldn't do anything like that again, at least not in Mr. Nelson's class. I wasn't about to press my luck. But that wasn't the only problem my reputation caused.

Mr. Backman, my algebra teacher, couldn't believe his eyes when he saw me in his class the first day. As he began his introduction to algebra, he kept looking at me. It made me feel very uneasy. When the bell rang at the end of class, he caught me by the elbow. He waited until the other students were gone then spoke up.

"Mr. Huff, are you sure you belong in this class?" he asked. "This isn't an easy course and I won't tolerate any cheating."

I wasn't sure what to think. It felt like he didn't want to have to deal with me in his class.

"I'll need this class to get into college," I said. "I hope to become an engineer."

Mr. Backman stepped back in surprise and his eyes got large. "An engineer!? You've got to be kidding me! I can't believe you think that's possible."

"You may be right, but I thought I'd give it a shot."

With that he just shook his head and sent me on my way. But he continued to watch me in class. Closely.

Surprisingly, I generally didn't have much trouble understanding algebra. It was logical and made sense to me. I understood why certain methods worked to solve problems so it was easy for me to remember. And, unlike English, there weren't exceptions to the rules. All of this meant that, despite limited studying, I aced the first test. Mr. Backman was suspicious, particularly since he seldom saw me take notes. After handing out our graded tests, he asked me to stay after class.

"I would like to know who you cheated off of," he said.

I couldn't believe he thought I'd cheated. This started to seem like my conversation with the counselor after the junior high school aptitude test.

I stared at Mr. Backman. "I didn't cheat."

"I'm not convinced. There's something fishy going on here and I'm going to keep my eye on you until I figure it out."

After we stood looking at each other in silence for a few seconds he sent me to my next class. But this wasn't the end of it. He kept watching me in class and started to ask me questions even when I didn't raise my hand. Several weeks later, when we had our next test, he stood at the back of the classroom where I couldn't see him. However, after the test, several of my classmates mentioned that he watched me the whole time. They wondered what was going on.

He apparently wasn't happy when he found that I also aced that test. He moved me so I was seated in the first row directly in front of his desk. He also moved some other students so I was no longer surrounded by friends. Despite his precautions, he was flabbergasted when I aced the next test and then the test after that. He asked me to stay after class again. I wondered what he was going to accuse me of this time.

"Clark, you've convinced me," Mr. Backman said. "You really do understand algebra."

I hadn't expected this.

"I want to apologize for being skeptical. I just couldn't imagine how anyone that would get in the mischief you do could be that smart. You need to grow up and knock off the nonsense. You have a lot of potential and probably can be an engineer if you just quit doing stupid things."

I wasn't sure what to think. On the one hand I felt proud that I had impressed him. On the other hand, he would likely get on my case if I didn't quit screwing around.

"I appreciate you taking the time to tell me this. I'll try not to disappoint you."

With that I hurried on to my next class. But this was a turning point in my relationship with him. After that he would sometimes catch me in my hallway to see how I was doing. And surprisingly, he would sometimes hitch a ride from me when he needed to go to a meeting at the junior high school. It was clear our relationship had changed when I was driving him to the junior high one time and had to make an abrupt stop at a red light. A half empty bottle of whiskey rolled out from under his seat. I was startled. I'd forgotten that I'd left it there the night before. He picked up the bottle and looked at it for a few seconds then looked at me.

"I suggest you remind your dad not to leave booze under

the seat when he borrows your car," he said. "You might get in trouble."

He then slid the bottle back under the seat and we continued on our way. He also wasn't the only one who decided I could do algebra. A few of my close friends also caught on.

One day, my friend Sheldon approached me and said he was having a problem with algebra. I thought he meant he was having difficulty solving a problem and so I told him I could help him with it later in the day. He said it was going to take longer than a few minutes. He and four other friends were struggling to pass algebra and were afraid it would jeopardize their chances of going to college. He wanted me to tutor the group on a regular basis.

Me?! I was astonished.

I agreed to help them but explained I wasn't sure how good of a teacher I would be. This was going to be a new experience for all of us. I held class a couple of times a week in Dad's garage. He never parked a car in it and had converted it to a game room which included a pool table. I threw a piece of plywood on the pool table and my "students" used it for their desk. Since I had to figure out how things worked in order to remember them, I explained algebra by taking them down the path I'd followed. I would just recite my thought process when I'd figured out how something worked. From the expressions on their faces, I could see it was making sense to them. They said it was like someone had turn on a light. They were very appreciative, and they all passed the class. It apparently meant a lot to them. Fifty years later, Sheldon surprised me and came by my house to let me how much the experience had helped him.

Although I could excel in math classes, it wasn't particularly fun. Physics, on the other hand, was much more interesting. I started physics my senior year, in the fall of 1968. The Space Race, between the Soviet Union and United States, was entering its final stage. Both countries wanted to control outer space since it could be used to deliver nuclear weapons. They also wanted the prestige of being the first on the moon and might even claim the moon as their own. The news was filled with stories about space walks, rendezvous with space capsules, and space capsules orbiting of the moon. It seemed like something was going on every month.

Physics played into this. As the year went along, I could tie in many of the lessons to what was going on in the news. We'd learned about gravity and how inertia allowed an object orbiting the earth to offset it. The rocket engines I'd tried to make as a young boy followed the rule that for every reaction there was an equal and opposite reaction. Thus, it was no surprise at the end of the year I chose to build a rocket as my senior project.

My teacher, Mr. Small, divided the class into groups of two. I was paired up with Doug. After some discussion, we decided to design and build a solid fuel rocket from scratch. We designed the rocket engine including the nozzle which was formed from a cut-off rifle shell. The fuel was a mixture of sugar and saltpeter that I had learned about from my friend Kevin's older brother. We worked on the rocket diligently for several weeks. It took longer than I expected to design and assemble, and I was surprised when Mr. Small allowed us to launch it from the high school's lawn. Apparently, the principal was surprised too. The rocket didn't fly very high and crash-landed on the school's roof. There was a concern the roof might catch fire so the janitor had to quickly climb up to retrieve it. I found out later that afternoon that the principal had a tense discussion with our teacher. I hoped that this wasn't going to cause a problem with my graduation.

Graduation, or is it?

At the start of my senior year I began making plans for college. Dad let me know he wouldn't be able to provide any financial assistance so money was going to be tight. I decided to go to an in-state college, the University of Utah, to keep costs down. In order to apply, I would first need to take the ACT test. At the time, the U of U used it rather than the SAT to evaluate college applicants. Neither my friends nor I studied for the test. We just went over to the neighboring town of Provo and took it in a large room at Brigham Young University.

As I walked into the room I was very nervous and a little shaky.

There were literally hundreds of kids there. Maybe I should have studied after all. However, when it was over I was surprised that it hadn't seemed too difficult. A day or two later, as I listened to my friends complain about the test, I started to worry that it hadn't seemed hard because I hadn't understood the questions. The math problems they'd had trouble with had just seemed logical to me. As it turned out, I did well on the test. Although my scores were not as good as on the aptitude test in junior high, they were above the 90th percentile in math and science. My lowest score was in English where I was only in the 80th percentile.

My next problem was to find teachers crazy enough to provide letters of reference. Several teachers were somewhat hostile toward me, particularly my English teacher. Fortunately, I had a pretty good relationship with Mr. Small, my physics teacher; Mr. Backman, my calculus teacher; and, Mr. Bartholomew, my engineering drawing teacher. All three agreed to provide references. In December of 1968, I filled out my college application and sent it off. Then I waited and worried whether the U of U would be crazy enough to accept me.

As I waited to find out if I was accepted, one evening in March of 1969, Mom told me that someone named Dr. Olsen from the University of Utah wanted to talk to me on the phone. This was an unexpected development that made me nervous.

"Hello," I said. "This is Clark Huff."

"Hello. This is Dr. Olsen, the head of the Department of Metallurgy at the University of Utah."

Department of *what*? Metallurgy? I'd never heard of it. This was really confusing.

Dr. Olsen continued. "Unfortunately, your application to enroll at the university in electrical engineering arrived late. By the time they received your application, they were already full. However, they were impressed with your qualifications and knew there were a few openings left in metallurgy so they forwarded your application to me. In fact, based on your grades, ACT score, and letters of recommendation, we would provide a scholarship to cover tuition and books plus a living allowance if you would switch to metallurgy."

I was stunned and excited. This would resolve the problem of paying for school. But what in the world was metallurgy? I had no idea. I'd have to go to the library and find out.

"Thank you for your consideration, Dr. Olsen," I said. "I'd like to take you up on the offer. What do I need to do?"

"We will send you the paperwork to apply for the scholarship and to change your major."

I thanked him again and we said our goodbyes. I wasn't sure that I wanted to be a metallurgist but figured I could stick it out for a couple of years while I took the basic classes all engineers took. Then if I didn't like metallurgy, I could always change majors at the start of my junior year.

When the paperwork arrived, I learned that I would be applying for the D.C. Jackling Scholarship. I was excited that I'd not only been accepted by the university but had a scholarship to cover most of my costs. With it and the money I'd make working in the summer, I would be in good shape financially. The whole thing seemed too good to be true. And it almost was. The whole thing depended on me graduating from high school.

A few weeks before the graduation ceremony the principal called me into his office. As I hurried down the hall I wondered what I was in trouble for this time. When I arrived, the secretary waved me into his office.

"Clark, we have a problem," the principal said. "During your three years in high school you managed to accumulate a record 184 hours of detention. Unfortunately, you've only worked off 15 hours. The rule is, you can't graduate unless the detention is worked off. There's no way you can do it before school lets out. You aren't going to be able to graduate. You will have to come back next year."

I couldn't believe it! I'd never taken the detentions seriously. After I reached about 30 hours of detention, I just ignored it. It was a boring to do janitorial work after school and it cut into my fun. Now the detention problem had reared its ugly head. This could be serious.

"Isn't there some way to get around this?" I pleaded.

"I don't think so. If we made an exception for you, no one would take us seriously."

I considered my situation. The thought of telling my parents, particularly Mom, that I would spend another year at home going to high school made me nauseated. And it would really piss me off to miss a year of college after I'd received a scholarship at the University of Utah. I might not get a scholarship the next time around.

"Are you sure you want me back for another year?" I said. "I'd think it would be better for the school if you didn't have my poor example to lead students astray. Besides, it will look bad if a person that has received one of the best scholarships isn't graduated by his high school."

"I don't know," he said. "It still sets a bad precedence."

I stood there nervously as he thought it over for a few minutes. It seemed like an eternity.

Finally, he said, "I think you may be right. It would be better if you became someone else's headache next year. Congratulations, Mr. Huff, you're on your way to college."

With that he shook my hand and sent me out the door. Later in the week, I started to wonder if the principal had been playing with me all along. Maybe it was his chance to play a joke on me or to get even for all the headaches I'd given him. I thought about asking him, but decided I'd better let sleeping dogs lie.

On the night of graduation, I put on my cap and gown and headed down to the high school auditorium. Since I was graduating with honors, special gold cords were draped across my shoulders and hung down each side of my chest. I was standing around visiting with friends before the ceremony when a girl, Betty, from the junior class came up to me.

"You disgust me," she said.

I was startled. I couldn't think of anything I'd done to her.

Betty continued. "I can't believe you would beat someone up and steal their honor cords."

"What are you talking about?" I asked. Her outraged comments made no sense to me.

"There is no way you are an honor student. You're called to

the principal's office at least once a month to be disciplined. You should be ashamed of stealing someone else's cords."

No matter how much I explained the situation, Betty wouldn't believe me. Nor was she alone. As part of the graduation ceremony, we each got to walk across the stage to receive our diploma as they announced our name and any awards or scholarships we'd received. When it was my turn, they first announced I had graduated with honors. The audience looked at each other in stunned silence. They couldn't believe what they had heard. Then it was announced I'd received a full scholarship to attend the University of Utah in engineering. After a few seconds, the shocked audience burst out in laughter. They thought it was a joke. They had only seen the wild side of my personality—the WojWoda side. Few of them had ever taken a technical class with me and so they didn't know I could think and do the work. They were surprised I had graduated at all and knew my "supposed" recognition and awards must be a joke. The disbelief carried on after the ceremony when people would come up to me and ask if I'd really received a scholarship.

A few days after graduation I started my last summer at the mink ranch. As the mink and I tormented each other, I thought about the lessons I'd learn during high school. Despite joining the WojWodas, I made it through to graduation. But just barely. I'd come close to being expelled or going to jail. If I hadn't lived in a small town, I wouldn't have made it. I resolved to never again let peer pressure force me into doing something stupid. For this reason, I absolutely would not join a fraternity while in college. And I would think more about the consequences of my actions when considering doing something stupid.

On the other hand, the educational side of high school helped to convince me I might be capable of going to college and becoming an engineer. I had done well in my technical classes and obtained A's. I'd even tutored some of my close friends. But in college I would really need to buckle down and study. I knew that I wouldn't have time for the heavy drinking and partying I'd gotten away with in high school. I would leave that by the side of the road, at least most of the time.

CHAPTER 10

Not All Lessons are Taught in Class

Stress can be a bitch

I returned to the mink ranch one last time. It still wasn't much fun, but knowing it would be my last time there I looked back on all I'd learned. There I was treated like an adult. No one paid any attention when I came home at night or asked me what I'd been up to. So by now I'd already sown my wild oats and learned the consequences of doing dumb things. Most teenagers were on their own for the first time when they graduated high school. As a result, they often did crazy, stupid things when they started college. Not me. I was already through that phase, although I'd barely survived it. Now I was ready to move on and start a new, responsible, and mostly sober phase of my life. And based on my experience at the mink ranch, I would focus on my education to acquire a degree that would translate into gainful employment and help me launch a career and not just a job. It was now time to take the first step and go to college.

College was a big mystery to me, kind of like a black hole. Although we know about black holes, we haven't really seen what happens inside their event horizon. No information leaks out. This was similar to my situation; I had no idea what went on inside a college campus. Neither my parents nor anyone else I knew had graduated from college. I hadn't even visited the University of Utah campus so I didn't know what it looked like. This lack of information started to stress me out. And since I would be staying with my grandmother to reduce costs, I would need to commute to school daily. Unlike today, there was no GPS system for navigation. I had to buy a road map of Salt Lake City and work out my best route based on limited information.

At the end of June, I received an "invitation" to attend a mandatory, two-day orientation at the university in early July. I would have to drive up one morning, spend the day, sleep in a dorm room, and drive home the next afternoon. I drove up the first morning and was surprised at how long the trip took. I hadn't accounted for the rush-hour traffic in Salt Lake City. The drive took almost 40 minutes and included lots of cursing at drivers that darted in and out of traffic and cut me off. The net result was that I showed up late for the orientation. Not a good start. Fortunately, the guide was still discussing the university and hadn't begun the walking tour.

After I introduced myself, the guide finished his presentation and we headed out to see the campus. The university is located on the east edge of Salt Lake City in the foothills of the Wasatch Mountains, 400 feet above the city. The view was spectacular. Downtown Salt Lake sprawls across the valley floor to the west and the Wasatch Mountains rise immediately to the east. Walking along, our guide explained the general layout of the campus and the type of classes taught in each building. I was amazed that the campus covered over 400 acres. There were about thirty large buildings separated by lawns and sidewalks. It looked like some sort of maze. What the hell had I gotten myself into?

At the bookstore, I was disconcerted to find out they didn't just hand out textbooks at the beginning of class. I would have to buy mine before classes started. And they were expensive! I started to stress out even more. I hadn't realized there would be costs other than tuition. I soon learned there were even more expenses, like lab fees and parking passes. On top of this, student parking was located on the perimeter of the campus—not very convenient. No matter where I parked there would be a lot of walking during the day. And I'd better walk fast. Some of my classes were over a half mile from each other and I only had ten minutes in between to get to them on time.

In late July a registration packet arrived from the university including a list of the classes I needed to take. Although some classes were mandatory, I was surprised to learn that others were just broad categories. I could choose what I wanted to take for general education, English, and physical education. At the time, the university still divided the school year into quarters. For my first quarter, I planned to enroll in freshman chemistry including a chemistry lab, calculus, English, and economics. I was also required to take a metallurgical engineering seminar each quarter. Surprisingly, most classes were only taught two or three times a week. I had expected each class would be taught five days a week. The packet also explained that I had to go back to the university on registration day to enroll in classes. This required walking around the campus to find the sign-up sheet for each class. Then, if the class had free seats and it was the right time, I had to manually sign my name and Social Security number. Since freshman got to register last I found there were few options to choose from.

My first class typically started at 7:45 a.m. and I was usually done for the day by about 2:30 p.m. The exception was the four-hour chemistry lab on Friday that started at 5 p.m. It pissed me off that I had to hang around the chemistry building until 9 p.m. on Friday night. By Friday afternoon I was worn out and just wanted to unwind and have some fun. Apparently, the university wasn't too concerned about infringing on a freshman's free time.

I didn't have the best start on my first day of college. I still wasn't used to rush-hour traffic at 7:30 in the morning and ended up late for my metallurgy seminar. Then a little later in the day I got lost and managed to arrive late for freshman chemistry. As I walked through the door, I found myself in a large auditorium filled with over 600 students. Being late, I had to sit near the back. Although the stage with the professor was lit up, the rest of the auditorium was dark, kind of like coming late to a movie theater. This was a far cry from high school chemistry which was taught in a regular classroom with about twenty students. When I sat down I saw that the professor was already at the podium.

"Good morning. I'm glad you're all here," Professor Ragsdale said. "Unfortunately, I have some bad news."

I sat up and paid attention. What in the world had happened?

"Most of you won't make it," Professor Ragsdale continued. "Few students are up to the intellectual challenge of chemistry. Look at the person to your right and left."

I felt a little awkward as I sized up my neighbors.

"If you do make it to the end of the school year, you aren't likely to see either of your neighbors. They won't make it. By the end of the year, we will be meeting in a much, much smaller classroom."

After his pep talk, several students stood up and left. More followed during the coming weeks. And I could understand why. We were learning difficult concepts at a much faster pace than high school. I was determined to succeed and was worried about what he'd said. Plus, I also felt lonely. In Spanish Fork, I went to school with the same kids year after year. However, at the U of U, I didn't know anyone to talk with or to help me with my studies. My concerns increased even further as the midterm exams approached. Unlike high school, I now had to stay up until midnight most evenings just to get my assignments completed. Chemistry was a particular problem. To understand and remember something, I had to have a picture in my mind of how things worked. It was difficult to imagine the various electron shells of atoms and how they affected the way they grabbed onto each other to form bonds and compounds.

I continually worried about my scholarship and had to maintain a B average in all my classes to keep it. I wouldn't be able to afford college without it and knew that if I didn't pass chemistry and calculus I would be screwed. They would boot me out of the engineering program. Just to make matters worse, it was apparent that the kids from the large, big city high schools were way ahead of me in class. They had already gone through most of this stuff in their high schools' advanced science and math classes. This was more like a review for them. They were just coasting along. Yet, these were the students I had to compete against since we were graded on a curve. Thus, the week before mid-terms, I was a nervous wreck as I left a confusing chemistry lecture.

That's when my vision failed.

I started to have problems as I hurried down the sidewalk on my way from chemistry to calculus. As I walked along, my vision became fragmented. I was puzzled. What was happening? It kind of looked like I was next to a large bed sheet on a clothesline that had jagged pieces cut out of it. These "holes" were where I could still see my surroundings. But the angular pieces of my surroundings were hard for my brain to process. I couldn't identify what I was looking at or what was going on around me. It was very confusing. The pieces were surrounded by blank areas. However, after a few seconds, the blank areas gradually expanded and soon there were no colored fragments left. I was blind. I felt my way to the edge of the sidewalk with my left foot and sat down on the grass.

My mind was jumping around trying to figure out what had happened. I didn't have a headache. Maybe I'd had a stroke or developed a brain tumor. What the hell should I do? How would I get home? Did I need to get someone's attention and have them call an ambulance? What about calculus? I was going to be late and I absolutely needed to pass the class. My mind jumped around and my thinking became illogical. This was scaring the hell out of me. I damn sure didn't need this complication in my life with all the stress I was already under.

To my relief, after about ten minutes, my vision began to clear. I was able to get up and walk. However, everything looked strange. Colors seemed to be somehow brighter and there was kind of an aura around things. I made it to calculus, arriving only a little late. But it was hard for me to pay attention to the teacher.

As the day went on, I felt fine and wondered if the loss of vision had really happened. I decided not to worry about it. It must have just been a fluke. However, a few days later it happened again while driving to school. Fortunately, it was only in one eye. This made driving difficult since I didn't have any depth perception, but at least I could still drive. Naturally, my vision waited until I was safely in the school parking lot before it returned. A couple of days later, it happened again during class. I couldn't deny there was a problem any longer and finally headed to the school's infirmary to see a doctor.

After describing the situation to a nurse, I was asked to take off my clothes and put on a robe. I was surprised and uncomfortable when a 30-year-old female doctor walked in. I wasn't used to being naked around strange women. She listened to my concerns and asked me to remove the robe while she checked me out. I was extremely embarrassed to have her checking me out, particularly when she inspected me for a hernia. They drew blood and then she sent me to the main hospital to have X-rays taken of my head. I had an appointment to return in three days for the results. I decided to wear my best underwear just in case.

Three days later I was back at the infirmary nervously waiting to hear the diagnosis. I was somewhat disappointed when the female doctor didn't want me to see me naked again. Apparently, I hadn't impressed her much.

"Clark," she said, "I have some good news and some that isn't quite as good."

I braced myself.

"The good news is that it doesn't appear that you've had a stroke or a brain tumor. In fact, we have pretty much ruled out any physical cause for your problem."

I felt somewhat reassured but waited for the rest of the story.

"The bad news is that you are probably having optical migraines. Unfortunately, there isn't a treatment. You're just going to have to learn to live with them. They shouldn't be a serious problem. They are often brought on by stress so you need to try to ease up."

Easy for her to say. But I heaved a sigh of relief and decided to put the whole fiasco behind me.

By coincidence, I visited my parents a couple of weeks later and decided to let them know about the migraine fiasco.

"I've started having a strange problem," I said. "A couple of weeks ago, I lost my vision for several minutes. Since then it's happened a few more times. I visited a doctor and found I'm having optical migraines."

My dad looked startled. "I'll be darned," he said. "I had the same problem."

What?! I couldn't believe what I'd just heard.

"During a championship baseball game in high school I was playing second base and my vision failed as a runner was headed from first to second. I didn't see the ball coming and it hit me in the chest and dropped to the ground. The runner made it all the way to third before the shortstop got the ball. The coach had to pull me out of the game. After the game, I told my dad, your granddad, what had happened. He said he'd had the same problem when he was younger. It pissed me off he hadn't told me sooner. If I'd known, I wouldn't have panicked."

I glared at him a few seconds.

"Well, I sure as hell understand that," I said. "The last few weeks would have been a lot easier if I'd heard your story sooner. Apparently, more than just migraines run in the family."

As the school year continued, an occasional optical migraine would torment me. However, they were just a minor nuisance now that I knew what they were. Despite the distraction, I endured my freshman year. On top of that, by the end of the first quarter I had caught up with the big city boys. They could no longer just coast along in class. Now we all had to study hard to learn new things. The playing field had been leveled. And as time went on, I gradually felt more comfortable with college. I knew where all the buildings were and how things worked on campus. I eventually found a route to school that avoided the worst of the rush-hour traffic. I also developed some engineering friends which gave me someone to talk to about problems. And although it was a lot of work, I did survive chemistry and got two B's and an A for my effort. But, Professor Ragsdale had been right. By the third quarter, chemistry was taught in a much, much smaller classroom.

Toward the end of the school year, I was starting to enjoy college. It was exciting to learn how the universe worked. Unfortunately, I had to spend a lot more time studying than my peers. I still couldn't remember something unless I visualized how it worked. For me, that meant I had to imagine how electrons acted in their shells to understand chemical bonds or think through the tug-of-war with gravity and fusion in a star to understand why big stars burnt their fuel faster. But at least all the studying kept me out of trouble. There was little time for drinking, partying, or shenanigans. Furthermore, I maintained better than a B average. I was going to keep my scholarship for another year. Now I just needed a summer job to gain experience and provide some extra money. Even with a good scholarship, college was expensive. I had no intention of working on the mink ranch.

CHAPTER 11

The Burgin Mine

Finding creative ways to die, and getting paid for it

As the end of my freshman year in college approached, I hoped to spend the summer in Spanish Fork for the first time in ten years; if Mom would let me. I was excited at the prospect of being with my friends rather than babysitting mink. I heaved a sigh of relief when Dad called a week before school let out and told me Mom would let me stay in my old bedroom. To add to the good news, one of Dad's friends, Stan Richardson, found me an opportunity for a summer job. Stan was a paving contractor with connections to businesses near Spanish Fork. He arranged an interview for me at the nearby Burgin mine. The mine produced ores containing precious metals from deep underground. Metallurgy was then used on the surface to separate and upgrade the ore before shipment to smelters. I hoped to get a job in the refinery since it would give me experience in my major.

On the appointed day, I headed to the Burgin mine located near the town of Eureka, Utah, for my interview. This made me nervous. Although Eureka was only 25 miles away, it was an alternate universe compared to Spanish Fork. My hometown was a small Mormon community of about six thousand people. The streets were laid out in a grid. Although it was a small town, there were nine Mormon churches, several nice restaurants, and only one bar and one liquor store. People and children casually walked the streets.

Eureka, on the other hand, sprang into existence in 1869 when gold was discovered in the area. Miners from all over the country flocked to Eureka to get in on the action. The streets wandered all over the place as if they were laid out by following a rambling cow. The town contained a wide assortment of salons and brothels. The miners worked hard but drank harder. Fistfights were an accepted form of recreation. Unlike other Utah towns, stabbings and shootings were a regular occurrence. In Eureka, you could find anything you were looking for, if you had enough money. This was the exact opposite of what I was used to.

I started the trip for my interview by driving through the green farmland south of Spanish Fork. After about 10 miles, I turned west and began to meander through hills pockmarked by red and black mounds of rock from old mine excavations. I was surprised to see steam rising from ponds and streams near the highway. Apparently, there was geothermal activity in the area. Finally, I turned left onto the Burgin access road and spied the mine buildings and other large structures as I came around a curve in the road. The sight caused my heart to race.

I was a little lightheaded as I walked into the administration building. This would be my first job interview. After filling out a job application, the receptionist took me back to see the head of Human Resources. I sat there nervously while he scanned the application. After a few routine questions he hired me on the spot. Stan Richardson carried some weight around here. However, I was distressed to learn that a job in the refinery wasn't available. Instead, I would be working in the underground mine. My first shift would begin that night. I would work the graveyard shift from 11:00 p.m. until 7:00 a.m. the next morning for the entire summer. I headed home, made a futile attempt to take a nap, and then prepared for my first night at the Burgin.

Leaving for work at 9:30 p.m. was strange. It seemed like I should be heading home to go to bed. When I reached the mine and parked my car, I found the change house and walked in. It was a large, steamy room with long rows of benches, wire baskets hanging from the ceiling, and a crowd of men in various stages of undress. There was a large communal shower on one end of the

Burgin mine headframe: the office and change room are on the right

room and vending machines on the other. I felt very nervous. It was like being a foreigner in a strange land. By watching the others, I learned that the basket was for my street clothes. I began to undress and place my clothes in an unused wire basket. The basket hung from a thin chain that ran up to a pulley on the ceiling. This was so I could hoist the basket and my belongings to the ceiling and attach a padlock for safekeeping. Unfortunately, no one told me to bring a lock. As the men stood around in various stages of undress, they kidded with each other and discussed local happenings in Eureka. I quickly realized I was not only a naïve new employee, but the youngest person in the room. This made me even more nervous as I undressed. I tried not to look at anyone and just concentrated on getting into my work clothes as quick as possible.

My anxiety increased further as I overheard discussions about their recent adventures in the mine. I couldn't figure out what they were talking about. I had no idea what terms like station, raise, skip, and stope meant at the Burgin. Plus, the conversation was intermingled with foul language. They never spoke a sentence without using an assortment of vulgar words. Swearing seemed to be an elevated art form with them. There were also detailed discussions of their sexual exploits and who could be exploited. I was hoping not to be on that list.

What the hell had I gotten myself into?

After dressing in my work clothes, an older man walked up to me and asked if I was the new employee, Clark. Apparently, I was easy to spot. John introduced himself as the foreman for the 1,200-foot level where I would be working. John was a husky fellow at 6 feet, 2 inches tall with black hair. He explained that the levels were named based on their depth below the surface. Thus, I would be about the same distance underground as the Empire State Building is tall. There were also 1,000-foot and 1,300-foot levels. As we headed toward the mine shaft, John stopped in front of a large, square wooden board with rows of metal hooks. There he explained how to "tag in."

"Everyone," John said, "has two brass tags assigned to them."

He handed me two tags with the number 6116 on them.

"When going underground, place one tag on a peg on the board. That way we know you're underground."

"What about the other tag?" I asked.

"You keep that with you so we can identify your body in case you're smashed or charred in a fire."

This didn't make me feel any better.

The foreman then took me down a flight of stairs through a short tunnel to the mine shaft where a large group of men were waiting in the boarding area.

"Stay here," John said. "When they announce they are loading people for the 1,200-foot level, climb on board the man cage. When you get there, wait for me at the station."

I didn't dare ask him where the station was. I'd ask one of the workers after the boss left.

After 10 minutes, they announced they were loading men for the 1,200-foot level. With considerable trepidation, I climbed aboard for my first ride down the shaft. They crammed twelve of us into a six-by-six-foot area and closed the access gate. We started to drop slowly down the shaft but the speed kept increasing. Looking through the wire mesh surrounding the cage, the I-beams in the shaft became a blur as they whizzed by. I heard a noise from deep in the shaft that was getting closer as we descended. I was startled when another man cage shot up past us. I soon learned that a cable ran from the cage on our side of the shaft up and over a pulley in the head frame and then down the other side of the shaft to a second man cage. This helped to provide some counter balance for the hoist.

As we traveled down the shaft, the surface lights quickly faded and the noise from the surface ventilation fans faded away. In the darkness, we turned on our head lamps. I was immediately told to watch where I aimed the light when it got in another miner's eyes. When we approached the 1,200-foot level, the hoist slowed and gradually came to a stop. After we got off, they closed the doors and the man cage shot up the shaft to get the next load of miners.

There was a large group of men loitering near the shaft when I got off the cage. I walked over and stood near the edge of the group and found out this was the station. I looked around and saw I was in a 60-foot-long chamber about 20 feet wide. The far end of the chamber was connected to a large tunnel with railroad tracks that passed by.

"Where does that tunnel go?" I asked the man standing next to me.

"That's the main entry. Go to the right and you'll reach the area being mined. The escape shaft is to the left, in case you ever need it."

As I waited, the men around me talked about recent events and continued to kid each other. Finally, the boss, John, showed up. First, he barked orders to the other miners and sent them on their way, then he turned to me.

"Everyone works in pairs," he said. "That way if something happens to one of you, the other one can go get help."

Maybe the mink ranch wasn't such a bad place after all.

"I am pairing you up with Paul Jolley. He's another college student who's only been here a couple of days."

It turned out Paul and I worked together the entire summer. And despite the fact he attended Brigham Young University, one of University of Utah's chief rivals, we became good friends. On the first night, the boss assigned us to dig the "piss ditch" which was a trench alongside the railroad tracks. It carried any water that escaped the active mine area downhill to the shaft so it could be pumped to the surface. The miners also urinated in it, hence its name. Unfortunately, the ditch was in solid rock so we had to use jack hammers to dig it. This turned out to be a hot, miserable job. Since we weren't provided hearing protection, it was tough to endure the ear-splitting noise. We found out later that the foreman was just trying to get us to quit because he didn't want to have to babysit two college kids. However, after a couple of nights he finally gave up and assigned us to haul timber.

The mine used 10-inch square wooden beams that were 12 feet long to shore up unstable mine entries. Our job was to transport loads of the wooden beams from the shaft to a storage area. We quickly learned that the beams were heavy—particularly if they hadn't been cured properly. At the station, we loaded them on a flatbed rail car to transport them to the storage area. To help with this task and to transport ore, the mine was equipped with a narrow gage railroad. The electric engine that pulled the cars was about as long as an automobile, but the cab wasn't enclosed. My dream as an eight-year-old of becoming a railroad engineer had finally come true.

Initially, the mine was very confusing. It was a three-dimensional maze which made it easy to get lost. I wasn't used to thinking in three dimensions. Things became even more perplexing at the mine face. The entries followed the ore veins all over the place. Because Paul and I received no safety training, we didn't know which areas of the mine were unstable or how to use the equipment safely. We had to rely on the other miners to tell us what to watch out for or, more often, figure it out from our own painful experience.

A prelude to hell!

Over time, we gradually learned more about the mine and occasionally helped out when an unusual problem developed. One evening, the foreman told Paul and I to help replace a water pump that had failed. Twelve of us "lucky" individuals trudged up the main entry until we reached a side entry leading to the pump. We were divided into three-man teams. A guy named Mike joined Paul and I to make up our team. The teams took turns and while one team worked in the side entry to remove the pump, the others rested in the main entry.

When our fifth turn came with the pump still not removed, we were worn out before we'd even started. It was miserable to wade up the side entry in 6-inch-deep, 152-degree water. Although the pump was only 400 feet away, it seemed much further. The air was 120 degrees and foggy with hot water dripping from the ceiling. Reaching the pump, we worked to hook a chain to the pump to hoist it out of the water. As we worked, Mike told us he was sick of this nonsense and was going to get the damn pump out this time or else. When Paul and I were ready to head back for a rest, Mike refused to leave the pump. A few minutes later, Paul and I saw Mike staggering like he was dizzy. We looked at each other for a second, then rushed forward and caught Mike just as he collapsed.

"What do we do now?" Paul asked. "I don't think we'll be able to drag him out and neither of us have first aid training."

I looked at Mike. His face was becoming darker.

"Ah, shit," I said. "He's not breathing. We've got to get him out of the heat. And we'd better hurry or he won't make it."

An adrenaline rush kicked in giving us the strength to lift Mike's arms over our shoulders. We raced down the entry as fast as we could regardless of the splashing. Unfortunately, in the heat and humidity, the hard work was starting to make us dizzy.

Getting near the base camp, we started to yell for help. Fortunately, they heard us over the noise and four men raced up and took Mike from us. At the main entry, they lay Mike on his back to look at him. By now, his face had turned very dark. Fortunately, one of the men knew first aid and took over. He pried Mike's mouth open and found that he'd swallowed his tongue. Using his grimy finger, he dug Mike's tongue out of the back of his throat and pulled it forward. Mike immediately began to breathe on his own.

Damn. I wished I'd thought of that.

After a couple of minutes, he regained consciousness and was soon sitting up drinking water.

A few minutes after that, John the boss showed up. Someone had let him know what was going on.

"How are you doing?" he asked Mike.

"I'm not feeling too good. I have a throbbing headache and feel sick to my stomach."

"Well, just sit here and cool down for a while. When you feel up to it, get someone to walk with you back to the station where you can rest for the remainder of the shift. The rest of you dumb son-of-a-bitches can get back to work before I fire your asses."

With that he walked off. I was appalled by his lack of concern. I couldn't believe someone had almost died and that's all the foreman said. John didn't seem to care at all about us, just whether the work was getting done. I was also starting to get more of an appreciation of how dangerous the mine was. I was looking forward to getting back to hauling timber. At least we knew what we were doing and understood the risks.

If something doesn't feel right, it probably isn't

On another occasion, Paul and I were asked to investigate why water quit draining from one of the stopes, or excavation sites. As Paul and I walked into the maze of entries, we speculated why the flow of water had dried up. This normally didn't happen. We walked to the stope, climbed the ladders and, after catching our breath, headed along the horizontal entry. Due to the poor ventilation, it was hot and humid. I was surprised when we came to a crude rock dam that stretched across the entry.

"Why in the hell," I asked, "did someone dam up the water?"

Paul stood there shaking his head. "This doesn't make any sense. The water will eventually wash it out."

"Maybe it's a practical joke or something."

The dam was about 3 feet high and made of large rocks stacked haphazardly. This puzzled me. I climbed up on the dam and found a small lake of steaming hot water. I stood there perplexed trying to figure it out.

What in the hell was going on?

Suddenly, I felt my hair stand on end and reflexively jumped back off the dam. A few seconds later, a large two-foot-thick, six-foot diameter slab broke loose from the ceiling and crashed down where I had just been standing. If I hadn't moved, it would have smashed me flat.

Paul gasped. "Oh my gosh. Are you all right?"

"I'm okay. But I may need to change my shorts."

As the realization of what had almost happened sunk in, I had to sit down. It was now clear that a partial collapse of the roof had created the dam. The slabs had been breaking loose from the roof and stacking up on the floor. Apparently, my subconscious realized I was in danger before I did. If I hadn't jumped right then, I'd be dead. When we told the foreman he just shrugged his shoulders. Apparently, it was just another Tuesday in the mine. He told us he'd assign a team to drain the lake and remove the dam.

Going on a trip without leaving the mine

As the summer drew to a close, I was anxious to be done with the Burgin mine. Compared to the mine, school now seemed like a breeze. And with all my adventures, I felt like it had been a year since school let out. But as luck would have it, the foreman, John, assigned me one final odd job. I was to check whether any rubble needed to be removed from a stope before mining resumed. After the previous episode, I was leery of stopes and even more nervous when I learned I'd have to do it alone. The foreman sent Paul on a different errand while I handled this trivial assignment.

I made my way along the main entry to a vertical shaft that went straight up to a mine tunnel or stope. The shaft was kind of like the stairwell in a tall building except there were ladders instead of stairs on one side and a "laundry chute" on the other side for ore. The shaft was eight feet square and went straight up 85 feet.

At the top was a horizontal entry going to the area being mined. I started climbing the first ladder and after 20 feet got off on a small landing. There, I could move sideways a couple of feet so I could climb the next ladder. But since there were no guard rails at the landing, I had to be careful not to slip and fall down the ore chute. After climbing straight up 80 feet, I stopped to catch my breath before climbing into the mine tunnel.

After resting a few minutes, I climbed the last five feet and crawled out onto the rock floor of the mine entry. As I stood up, my headlamp briefly illuminated the bottom of a layer of gas three feet above the entry's floor. It shimmered like an upside-down mirage. I briefly wondered if it was the bottom of a layer of the "bad air" seasoned miners had warned me about. If it was, I thought I would feel like I was suffocating and could just hold my breath and climb back down to the fresh air. Standing up in the entry I took a breath. There was a momentary sense that I was in serious trouble. Then my vision went blank. The whole thing happened in less than a second.

As I looked at the ants crawling around I tried to understand what they were doing. They seemed strange but I was very tired and went back to sleep.

There were the ants again. There were only a few of them and I wondered why I was looking down an ant hole at them. But again, I was overcome by sleep.

Now, there was a single ant looking up at me and waving as he called out my name. *What was going on?* I began looking around but nothing made sense.

Slowly, I realized I was looking straight down a large hole. The men walking past the hole were so far away, my brain interpreted them as ants. My mind was reeling as I sorted things out. The ant/person calling my name looked familiar. With a jolt, I realized it was the John the foreman and that I was underground in the Burgin mine. My thoughts swirled around for a few more seconds before I fully realized the situation. I yelled to the foreman and let him know that I would be down in a minute. It actually took several minutes for me to get my strength back so I could climb down the ladder. Descending, I quickly realized my coordination was gone and I had a severe headache and nausea. Upon reaching the bottom I explained what had happened to John. He told me I could rest for fifteen minutes to clear the gas out of my system. Then I was to get my ass back to work.

As I rested, I thought about how lucky I had been. After passing out, I had fallen from the stope to the landing five feet below. The good news was I was out of the poisonous gas. The bad news was I'd almost slid into the ore chute. My head was over the edge so that I was looking down the chute to the mine entry 80 feet below. If I had slid any further, I would have plunged to my death. But if I hadn't fallen down to the platform, the gas might have killed me. I was anxious to be done with the mine.

Fortunately, a few weeks later, I was headed back to college. Despite my hopes that I could use my college education at the Burgin mine, it hadn't work out. However, it did provide plenty of money for the upcoming school year. They paid me $12 per hour plus time and a half for overtime and two and a half times my regular pay if I worked weekends. This was when many of my friends were making $3.25 per hour at their summer job. And, fortunately, or maybe unfortunately, I had learned some valuable lessons that wouldn't be taught in school. I'd learned that just because you were the boss, you didn't have to pretend to know everything. You could learn a lot by listening to those working for you.

On one occasion a miner told the foreman, John, that a section of the roof in an entry needed to be shored up. John told him he had his orders and to get his ass back to work. A few nights later, that section of the mine collapsed which needlessly put people in danger and disrupted mine production. On another occasion, he told several of us to pack a large fan out of an area of the mine. One of the miners assigned to the task told John it wouldn't fit through a narrow spot in the entry. John told him to quit whining and get to work. The net result was that me and four other miners were trapped behind the fan for four hours while they used jack hammers to enlarge the entry. If they had enlarged the entry first, we wouldn't have gotten to take a four-hour nap on company time.

Unfortunately, I also learned that the workplace could be very dangerous. The roughly 300 miners working at the Burgin suffered a severe accident about every nine months and a fatality every one to two years. And, despite the hazards, we received no safety training. If I ever became a boss, I'd make sure my employees received training to understand and avoid the dangers they would be faced with. They wouldn't be left out on their own like the foreman had left us. They would also be trained in first aid so they could help an injured coworker. This would be good for employees but also the company. I was convinced that a safe work environment would ultimately reduce costs and attract better workers.

CHAPTER 12

A Fourth of July Celebration Gone Astray

Stupidity strikes again

My time at the Burgin mine helped feed my fascination with explosives. I had always been fascinated with them, but my homemade bombs weren't very spectacular. Unfortunately, at least from my point of view, my most spectacular explosion was when I blew myself up while making hydrogen in my parents' basement. Even though it almost killed me, it didn't dampen my enthusiasm. At the Burgin, explosives were used daily to blow rock loose from the mine faces. Thus, working there created a dilemma. On the one hand, I had decided to quit doing anything that would get me thrown in jail. On the other hand, it presented the opportunity to easily get some quality explosives. You can guess which argument won out. I would celebrate the Fourth of July in style.

It is strange to think about it today, but back in 1970, the Burgin mine didn't keep track of its explosives. Old cases of dynamite as well as bags of ANFO, an explosive made from ammonium nitrate and fuel oil, were routinely stored in the open. Fortuitously for me, it was often near the employee parking lot. So it was relatively easy one night, when I showed up for work early and no one was around, to load a half case of dynamite and several bags of ANFO into the trunk of my car. I carried the blasting caps out of the mine in my empty water jug.

Since I was staying with my parents for the summer, I stashed the dynamite and blasting caps in my basement bedroom but left the bags of ANFO in the trunk of my car. However, I was careful to store the blasting caps away from the dynamite. Without the caps, the dynamite wouldn't explode, or so I was told. I thought everything was set for a memorable Fourth of July celebration. However, as usual, there were complications. When my friend, Terry, drove me home after an evening of partying, I discovered a pile of clothes on the front lawn. Upon closer inspection, I realized they were mine.

This doesn't look good.

I took a deep breath and tried to look nonchalant as I walked into the house. Dad was sitting in a lounge chair in the family room waiting for me.

Another bad sign.

"How are things going?" I asked.

"I'm doing okay," Dad said. "But you're not. You're out of the house."

Uh oh.

"Any particular reason?"

Dad glared at me. He was clearly pissed off.

"During dinner, your mother mentioned she'd had found a box of flares in your bedroom. She didn't think you would mind if she borrowed a couple and put them in the trunk of her car in case of an emergency. This puzzled me since I couldn't figure out what you'd be doing with a box of flares."

I started to sweat. I suspected I was in serious trouble.

Dad continued. "I walked out and looked in the trunk of her car and discovered the flares read 'Caution, Dynamite, Class A Explosive.' When I checked your bedroom, I found a half a case of dynamite in your closet and a box of blasting caps in your sock drawer. I decided it was time you moved out before you killed us all."

I tried to explain that the blasting caps were not near enough to the dynamite to detonate it. Dad wasn't convinced. He heatedly explained that I should find other lodging in order to increase my life expectancy as well as his.

I spent the next few days living out of my car with the explosives keeping me company in the trunk, except for the blasting caps which were in the glove box. However, I was allowed to return home to do laundry and shower. Each day, I spent a little more time at the house. Dad gradually got over being mad and let me move back in on the condition I wouldn't bring any more dynamite home.

Fortunately, the Fourth of July was rapidly approaching. This year it was on a Saturday which meant my friends and I would have the day off. My buddy Alan volunteered to pick me up along with my friends, Kevin, Blaine, and Sheldon. When Alan arrived, I was surprised to see him driving his dad's new Oldsmobile Cutlass. He made sure we understood not to get anything on the seats or floor mats. His dad was very protective of his new car.

As we transferred the explosives to the trunk of Alan's car, we discussed possible locations for our "celebration." Obviously, we needed to find an isolated spot. After considering several options, we decided someplace in the mountains. It would provide the solitude we needed if we didn't want to get arrested. We headed east of town, passing orchards and farmland along the way. After a few miles, we entered the mouth of Spanish Fork Canyon. Here the view abruptly changed. The flat lands of the valley gave way to the steep walls of the canyon and the vegetation changed to trees and scrub brush. About six miles up, we turned left onto the Diamond Fork road. It was a side canyon that offered, we hoped, the remoteness we needed. As we drove along the winding road, we passed random groups of cattle wandering along grazing on the open range. Occasionally, a jack rabbit took off through the brush. We eventually turned right onto a dirt road, crossed a small bridge over a stream, and climbed up from the valley floor to a relatively level bench on the side of the mountain. Here we found a small, grassy clearing surrounded by trees. On the far side of the clearing we spied a badger hole.

"This looks like the perfect spot," I said. "We shouldn't have any visitors and a badger was good enough to dig us a hole."

The badger hole appeared abandoned. It was about nine inches in diameter and sloped slightly downward. Looking in, I could see the hole made an abrupt turn to the left after about five feet. We immediately started preparing for our Fourth of July celebration.

First, I took seven sticks of dynamite and bundled them together using black, electrical tape borrowed from Dad. Then, I inserted an electric blasting cap into the center stick.

"Sheldon," I said, "see if you can find something we can use to push the dynamite into the hole."

Sheldon looked around and found a large, dead tree branch lying on the ground. I used it to push the dynamite into the hole but was careful that the blasting cap's wires didn't get tangled up. After the dynamite was in place, we got two sacks of ANFO out of the trunk of the car. The ANFO was granular, kind of like fine water softener salt contaminated with oil. We poured as much as we could into the hole and then used the tree branch to push it back with the dynamite. Then we'd pour some more in the hole and repeat the process. It took us a little while to get all of the ANFO in. From my experience at the Burgin mine I knew that we needed to find some way to plug the hole. Otherwise, the explosion would just "bootleg out," blowing fire out the hole while doing little damage. This would make a lot of noise but not do much else. The only thing we could find to plug the hole was an assortment of 6-and 8-inch rocks. They would have to do.

"Sheldon, can you get the spool of wire for me?" I asked.

Sheldon fished it out of the car and brought it over.

"What's this for?" he asked.

"Since we're using an electric blasting cap, we have to use electricity to detonate it. It wouldn't be very smart to stand near the dynamite when we connected the battery. The spool of wire will let us get a couple of hundred feet away so that when the explosion goes off we won't get hurt."

Or so I hoped.

Fortunately, I had also been able to appropriate a roll of "lead" wire from the Burgin. They used the small diameter, 2 conductor wire to connect explosives to the electrical source used for detonation. Normally, a spool contained close to 400 feet, but some of the wire had been used. This unfortunately left only 200 feet but it would have to do. I connected the wires from the spool to those of the blasting cap and unrolled the spool as I crossed to the other side of the clearing. At this point, I discovered that I hadn't brought along a portable battery. Apparently, planning was not one of my strong points.

After a little thought, we decided we could use the car battery. Since we didn't have any way to remove it, Alan pulled the car over to the end of the lead wire. He thought it would be a good idea to park it sideways so we could hide behind it just in case we misjudged our danger.

Since I was never underground when they detonated explosives at the Burgin mine, I was not aware of how big of an explosion seven sticks of dynamite and 80 pounds of ANFO would make. Based on the explosives I'd made, it seemed like 200 feet would surely be far enough away that we would be safe.

I took a deep breath and touched the wires to the battery.

There was a stupendous boom as the rocks shot out of the badger hole like howitzer shells and the ground shook. The rocks were a blur as they whizzed past us and slammed into trees. The aspen trees were shattered by the impact. At the same time, a small pine tree and a piece of earth roughly 30 feet in diameter over the badger hole was torn loose and launched into the air...the tree looked like a rocket as it raced skyward. We stood mesmerized as we watched it go.

"Ah, watch out!" I said. "All that shit is going to rain back down."

We looked at each other and then tried to dive under the car. Unfortunately, the low clearance of the Oldsmobile made that nearly impossible. But with considerable effort our heads and shoulders were mostly protected. Lying face down in the dirt under the car, we heard loud bangs as rocks bounced off the hood and roof and debris landed around us.

The very loud "boom" that accompanied the explosion echoed back and forth between the surrounding hills for almost ten seconds. The nearby cattle grazing on the open range were startled. When the rock barrage ended and we crawled out from under the car, we could see the ass end of cattle going over the hills in every direction.

We all agreed that it was time to make our getaway. We suspected anyone within five miles would come to investigate after hearing that wild explosion and we didn't want to be caught with the remaining explosives still in the trunk. Jumping into the now-dented car with the cracked windshield, we took off. About ten minutes later as we were heading down the canyon, a string of eight deputy sheriff cars passed us going up the canyon. We were surprised and then scared. It was surprising that they had gotten here so quick to investigate the explosion. I was afraid one of them might get curious about the dents in the car and the cracked windshield and pull us over. Fortunately, they drove on by and headed up the canyon. I found out later that the deputies weren't after us. About an hour before the explosion, a fisherman had fallen in the river and drowned ten miles further up the canyon. The deputies were going to investigate the incident when they passed us.

Needless to say, Alan's dad was not happy about the condition of his new car. It took several weeks to get all the repairs completed, primarily due to waiting for parts. And it still wasn't quite like new. Things were a little testy between Alan and his dad for several months.

Overall, it had been an interesting day. I had finally witnessed a noteworthy explosion of my own making. In fact, almost fifty years later, I met up with the participants of the adventure at our fiftieth high school reunion. We compared notes and laughed about the fiasco. But driving down the canyon the day of the explosion it wasn't a laughing matter. It was clear that I was treading on thin ice. After all of the years doing illegal activities, I finally realized that my stupidity could put me in prison and ruin my life. I resolved to never do anything that stupid again. And I never did.

CHAPTER 13

College Didn't Teach Me Everything

You may be worth more than you think

Iwas preparing to start my sophomore year in college and reflected on how lucky I was to have survived the summer. I could have easily been killed by an accident in the Burgin mine or when I dynamited the badger hole. Based on my near-death experiences, I resolved to never work underground at the Burgin again. Unfortunately, this was reinforced later in the school year.

A workmate from the Burgin called to tell me my good friend and work companion, Paul Jolley from Brigham Young University, had been killed in a mine accident. After I left for school, he decided to continue working at the Burgin mine to build up his college funds. He was killed when a large slab of rock broke loose from the ceiling, fell, and crushed him. When I learned about Paul, I was devastated. It was a struggle for me to get past it and get on with my studies. I kept thinking of how we helped each other and all the fun we'd had.

Just to further aggravate the situation, my optical migraines decided to return. They hadn't plagued me during the summer but made a guest appearance whenever I was under stress, like cramming for an exam. Although I was learning to deal with them, they were still a nuisance. However, as the year went on, the stress eased up some as I finished my basic classes in preparation for starting the engineering program in earnest.

At the start of my junior year, I finally gave my grandma a break by moving out. Together with a couple of friends we rented a house within walking distance of the college campus. But despite the increased freedom, there was very little partying. Like me, my roommates were serious about graduating from college and knew they'd better study if they were going to make it.

Continuing into my junior year, school became much more difficult. The class size in the metallurgical engineering program was much smaller since few students were enrolled in this field. I found that the metallurgical processes we were studying were completely foreign to me. I'd never even heard of them before. Since I couldn't remember things unless I understood how they worked, I had to spend a lot of time studying. I still felt like an idiot compared to my classmates who seemed to be able to remember things with hardly any studying.

Surprisingly, during that same year, I also started dating an old high school classmate, Betty Pinegar. We hadn't dated in high school because her mother absolutely forbade it. Being a school librarian, she had heard all about my mischief. Besides, Betty was the girl who chewed me out for stealing someone's honor cords at my high school graduation. Based on that incident, I suspected she didn't have a very high opinion of me. But now that she'd graduated from high school and was no longer under her mother's supervision, she thought it would be fun to date one of Spanish Fork's "bad boys."

At the start of my senior year in college, I proposed to Betty and she accepted. Her mother wasn't enthusiastic. She thought I would be a poor addition to the family. Despite this, we were married in December and moved into an apartment. It was a good arrangement for me. Betty worked as a secretary to pay the bills and I screwed off at school.

As college graduation approached, I had a sense of accomplishment. I had managed to disengage from my destructive high school behavior and had earned a B.S. degree in metallurgical engineering. And much to Betty's amazement, I even graduated with high honors. My old high school friends were astounded. Although I hadn't received any financial assistance from Dad, the scholarship and my job at the Burgin allowed me to graduate with no debt. Now if I could only land a well-paying engineering job.

In the early spring of 1973, I started looking for work in earnest. Unfortunately, the country was sliding into a recession. Companies weren't hiring unless absolutely necessary. Normally, recruiters swarmed the university campus in the early spring. Not this year. After six weeks, I had only met two recruiters looking for metallurgical engineers. I was starting to panic. It appeared my efforts to avoid hard manual labor would be in vain. I hated to think of the embarrassment of spending four years getting an engineering degree so I could flip burgers at McDonald's. Although Betty was still working, she might get testy if I just laid around the apartment. Particularly since she was now pregnant.

Of the two recruiters, the first was from a company named Texasgulf. They were looking for a metallurgical engineer for their Moab, Utah facility. This was an unusual operation since it used solution mining to produce potash, whatever that was. The second potential job was at U.S. Steel's Gary, Indiana, facility. Since the Texasgulf job was in a part of the country I knew and enjoyed, I favored it. I had never spent much time outside Utah and was nervous about moving away. The nightly news didn't help my uneasiness since it continually talked about the crime, murders, and drug trafficking that went on in the rest of the country.

I was excited when a few weeks after the campus interviews, I received a phone call from Bob MacAdams, a member of Texasgulf's Human Resources department.

"Clark," he said, "the management team at Moab would like to get to know you better before we make you an offer." Oh, boy.

"What do you have in mind?" I asked.

"We would like you to visit Moab so that we can look you over and so you can see our facility. If it works for you, we will have the company plane pick you up Thursday morning at the Salt Lake Airport. We can have you back in Salt Lake by Friday afternoon."

I was dumbfounded. I was so naïve that I had no idea companies had their own planes. To think that Texasgulf would send one for me was mindboggling.

"That works for me," I said. "I'm looking forward to meeting the people and seeing the plant."

As the day of the trip approached, I was nervous. Although I'd had brief interviews with the two recruiters, I had never been interviewed in depth for a professional job. I had no idea what I should wear, what kind of questions they would ask, or what I should take on the trip. On top of that, I'd never flown anywhere before. Everything would be a new experience.

To alleviate my fear of traveling, I decided to visit the Salt Lake Airport the day before my trip. After wandering around the commercial terminal for a half hour, I finally went to the information desk. I was surprised to learn that Texasgulf's plane wouldn't be allowed at the commercial terminal. Instead, they would have to use the private terminal on the far side of the airport. I hadn't realized there were commercial and private terminals at major airports. It was good I'd checked things out in advance. But it didn't help my nerves. What else didn't I know?

On the day of the trip, I was uneasy as I walked into the private terminal. How would I find my pilot? I needn't have worried. Just inside the door, a gentleman walked up to me.

"Are you Mr. Huff?" he asked.

I drew in a breath. No one ever called me "mister" except when I was in trouble with a teacher.

"Ah, yes, sir," I said.

"I'm Johnny Sparks. Let me take your bags and I will escort you to the plane."

Another surprise. I'd never had anyone carry my luggage before. We walked out and boarded an eight-seat, twin-prop plane. Once airborne, I was provided a drink and a snack. I squinted as I peered through the bright sunshine at the terrain below. The plane made a steep climb as it gained altitude to fly over the Wasatch Mountains and their snow-covered peaks. Although I had hiked the area, I quickly became lost. Nothing looked the same from the air. The confusion continued as we flew southeast. The mountains gave way to a reddish-colored desert with deep canyons. In the distance, bluish-gray mountains poked up from the flat desert terrain. Although they appeared to be nearby, we didn't seem to be getting any closer. The flight took a little over an hour which was a lot better than four hours by car. When we landed, I couldn't see any sign of a town. I learned that Moab was eighteen miles away and located in the bottom of a deep canyon. Bob McAdams was waiting for me at the airport. After collecting my bags, we headed for the Texasgulf plant.

At first there was only silence as we drove along. I was very tense and didn't know what to say. I just sat there looking out the window as we drove down the highway. I was pleasantly surprised by the brilliant blue sky. With the low humidity, the air was clear, and our surroundings were vivid. Finally, I gathered up my nerve.

"What are those mountains?" I asked Bob.

"Those are the LaSalle Mountains. They are almost thirty miles away."

I was surprised. This was a welcome change from smoggy Salt Lake City.

At first, we drove along a drab sagebrush flat but soon dropped into a long canyon. As we traveled down the highway, the canyon walls rose to become dazzling red cliffs that towered over us.

Bob explained that Moab was the gateway to both Canyonlands and Arches National Parks. Clearly, there was a lot of spectacular scenery to attract tourists. When we reached the muddy Colorado River, we turned right and headed downstream. Bob explained that if we'd gone straight, we would have ended up in Moab in a few more miles. I was captivated by the river scenery. In some places, there were shallow areas in the river with sand bars and groups of geese paddling around. In other areas, the swift current was visible as it boiled up around obstacles and then tumbled down the canyon. Soon we entered a large basin and I could see the Texasgulf facility a short distance away. At least I'd have a scenic drive to work. If I got the job.

At the plant, we pulled up to the admin building and Bob escorted me to a conference room. A secretary, Marge Phillips, brought me a cup of coffee and after a few minutes, Bob's boss, Dick Reynolds, walked into the room. He provided a little background information about Texasgulf's potash operation. I learned that potash is the primary source of potassium, one of the nutrients required by all life. Bob handed me a small bottle of potash. It consisted of large, white crystals that looked like water softener salt. At their urging, I opened the bottle and tasted it. It was salty but with a much sharper bite than table salt.

They explained that millions of tons of potash are used worldwide to fertilize crops. Unlike the Burgin ore body, the potash ore body was a relatively flat layer about 12 feet thick located 3,200 feet underground that extended for miles in every direction. It turned out that the Moab facility was unique in that it used solution mining and solar evaporation to produce potash. Nowhere else in the world was potash produced this way. Most producers used underground mining equipment combined with a refinery on the surface.

Moab facility with warehouses and loadout in the foreground

After the brief orientation, Bob provided a more detailed explanation as he took me on a tour of the facility. We began our excursion at the intake structure on the bank of the Colorado River where river water was pumped to the treatment facility. There, the muddy water was clarified to remove silt. From the treatment plant, we followed a 10-inch diameter, steel pipeline to one of the injection wells. The wells allowed the water to flow into the mine workings 3,200 feet below us. Since the potash and salt in the ore bed were soluble, the water dissolved them to form a brine solution.

Next, we stopped at a well next to a small, cinder block building. Bob explained that this was where the brine was pumped from the mine and began its journey to the solar ponds. The solar ponds surprised me. I was expecting something like a pond you might see at a city park. Instead, I was driven around 23 large ponds that covered almost a square mile. In the solar ponds, the hot desert sun evaporated the water and deposited a mixture of potash and salt on the pond's bottom. Once a year, the solids were "harvested" from each pond using road construction equipment. The solids were then sent to the plant for processing.

At the plant, the salt and other impurities were separated from the potash and sent to the tailings area. The high-grade potash that remained was then dried to remove the residual water and sized to remove the dust. The finished product was stored in one of the large, 100,000-ton warehouses to await shipment.

After the driving tour, we walked around the plant area, visited the refinery and sizing plants, and talked to the people in the lab and maintenance shop. The people were friendly and asked questions about where I was from and how I liked living in Salt Lake. They joked with each other and seemed to enjoy working together. This seemed like an alternate universe compared to my experience at the Burgin mine.

At the end of the plant tour, we headed back to the conference room. There, Bob explained that my job would be to provide technical support to the refinery to improve the process and make it more efficient. Although I found the potash technology interesting, this was the first time I'd ever heard of it. It scared me to think that I was going to be the person they relied on for technical support. In the era before the internet, it was difficult to find information unless it was available in a library, and I doubted the library carried many books on potash technology. In other words, Texasgulf wouldn't be hiring much of an expert.

That night I had dinner with Bob and Dick at the Sundowner

Restaurant. The next day, Bob drove me around town so that I could get an idea of the living conditions. The highway passing through town also served as the city's Main Street where the grocery stores and shops were located. As we moved away from Main Street, there were numerous houses and a few apartment buildings. There was also a small hospital to take care of health problems and to deliver babies. In many ways, Moab was very similar to the town I grew up in, except there were more motels to accommodate the influx of tourists and more bars to accommodate the miners. That afternoon, Johnny Sparks flew me back to Salt Lake.

Despite my concerns about not knowing the process, I hoped to get the job. I was excited when Bob called me at my apartment a few days later and offered it to me. He said they were willing to pay me $950 per month. Bob explained that this was a salaried position so I wouldn't be paid overtime. I immediately accepted the job which seemed to surprise Bob.

When school finally let out for the summer, Betty and I rented a moving van, loaded up our few belongings and headed to Moab. We rented the basement of a small house. It wasn't too fancy, but it was about all we could afford. Since we only had one car, it was fortunate I was able to carpool with a couple of other workers. As I settled into the job, I was proud to have landed such a well-paying job coming right out of college.

A few months later, I was talking to one of my new friends, Bill, who was a mill operator. In theory, I was supposed to be helping him improve the performance of the plant, but he was explaining to me how the plant worked. After a while, we decided to take a break in the control room.

"Clark," Bill said, "I hope you don't mind me asking, but how much are they paying you?"

My pride at landing such a high-paying job got the better of me. I thought I'd brag a little.

"I am making a whopping $950 per month," I said.

Bill looked startled.

"You've got to be kidding," he said with a look of disbelief on his face.

I felt smug.

"I think you got screwed," Bill said. "I make $1,050 per month, more if I work any overtime."

I was stunned. How could someone with no college education make more than an engineer? After a little, good-natured kidding, Bill went back to work. I was glad to get away and hurried up to Bob MacAdams' office. He confirmed what Bill had said and told me they'd have paid me quite a bit more if I'd negotiated with them. He said he was very surprised when I'd immediately accepted their first offer.

I couldn't believe I'd been so stupid. I'd worked my butt off in college for four years so I could make less than an hourly employee that I was supposed to be training! I just hoped my family and friends didn't find out about this or I'd never hear the end of it.

CHAPTER 14

Learning to be the Boss

Just because you're the boss doesn't mean you know anything!

My career as an engineer began on June 8, 1973. Technically, I was only an associate engineer at Texasgulf's Moab facility, but I was still excited and very nervous. That morning, as I drove along the Colorado River to my new job, I hardly noticed the spectacular cliffs lining my route. When I reached the office building, Bob McAdams of the HR department greeted me at the door. He introduced me to the office staff and then escorted me to the conference room. There, I met another new employee, Paul Stewart. Bob explained that, as new employees, we would have to undergo employee orientation. We spent the morning with Bob learning about the company's work rules. After lunch, Bob sent us to the safety supervisor, Mel Peterson. Mel explained that we would now undergo three days of safety training.

I was stunned!

At the Burgin mine, I hadn't received any safety training, even though I handled explosives. I was surprised that Texasgulf actually looked after its employees. I also learned that handling explosives without the proper training resulted in immediate dismissal. I'd have to watch my step. After we were through with the safety training, we were turned back over to Bob.

"Clark," Bob said, "you'll be reporting to Don Mobley, the operations superintendent. His office is down in the lab building. You can head on down—he's expecting you."

"What about me?" Paul asked.

"You'll be a technician reporting to Clark. You'd better ask him."

I just stood there wide-eyed with a dumb look on my face. I didn't know what to say. Then I saw Bob was smiling. He was joking with me! I couldn't believe it. A member of the management team had just pulled a practical joke! Maybe I would fit in after all.

After a few seconds, Bob said, "For now, Paul, you will report to Don while Clark learns the ropes."

With that, we headed down the hill to Don's office. There I was surprised to learn I had two more people reporting to me, Gene and Jake. Gene, like Paul, was a technician. Fortunately, Gene had worked at Texasgulf for over ten years and knew what he was doing. The superintendent suggested that Paul work with Gene to learn his job. That sounded like a good idea to me. I was to spend the first few months working with Jake in tabulating daily production information. This would help me get an understanding of what was going on in the plant. After spending a month working with Jake to learn where all the process streams went, I would work with Gene to learn how to gather samples and improve the performance of the refinery. To sum it up, my first four months at Texasgulf was a humbling experience. After four years of college, I was being trained by two people who barely had high school diplomas.

I soon learned that Moab's unusual technology had only been in use for a year so I asked Don about it. He looked startled. He had assumed I knew that the technology wasn't proven before I accepted the job. I should've asked more questions during my initial interview. If the technology failed, I was out of a job.

"Texasgulf," Don said, "began to develop the potash mine in the early 1960s. Initially, the plan was to use normal mining technology. A 22-foot diameter shaft was sunk to access the ore body while the refinery and surface buildings were completed. Production began in 1965."

Don continued. "We soon discovered that the potash bed was much more distorted than anticipated. This made mining at Moab very expensive and Texasgulf's potash facility uneconomic. It couldn't compete with the Canadian potash mines where the beds were flat. Thus, Moab had a major problem."

"So," I asked, "what happened next?"

"In 1968 we started looking for alternatives. Finally, we hit on the idea of solution mining. Since potash is highly soluble in water and we're located in the desert, we would let Mother Nature do the work. Water from the Colorado River would dissolve the ore and the hot desert sun would evaporate the water and deposit the potash in ponds. In 1970, we shut down operations to make the conversion. Wells were drilled into the mine and 23 solar ponds covering over 400 acres constructed."

Me, my son, Sam, and daughter, Leslee, viewing Moab's solar ponds from the overlook

Texasgulf resumed operations in 1972 so the technology had only been in use for a year before I hired on. What had I gotten myself into? I probably got the job at such a young age because no one with any knowledge of potash production would want to work here.

Learning to be the straight man

Initially, working with Jake was very confusing. I didn't understand the process so tabulating the information made no sense. One day, I decided to follow the various pipelines around in the plant so I could see where they flowed and how they interconnected. I grabbed a pencil and notepad and headed out into the mill. It was more difficult than I'd expected. The 10-inch steel pipelines formed a complex maze. There were numerous interconnections and an assortment of valves. I had to determine whether the valves were open or closed to know where the flow was actually going. Inside the plant it seemed like every time I squinted up to look at something, a small dust avalanche fell in my face. Apparently, the housekeeping was a little lax.

After a couple of hours, I finally had it figured out. I headed back to the cinder block lab building. Walking through the double doors, I meandered down the hallway into Jake's office. As I walked through his door, a horrible odor almost knocked me down. It smelled like Jake had crapped in his shorts two weeks ago and hadn't changed them. It was unbearable.

"Jake, what the hell have you been eating?" I asked. "Are you sick or something?"

"It's not me," Jake said. "It's that damn Gene. He came in here this morning, snuck up behind me and farted. I've been trying to air the place out ever since."

About this time a lab tech, Reuben, walked in.

"Don't believe him, Clark," Reuben said. "Jake walked into the lab a little while ago and we almost threw up. We are still trying to get rid of the damn smell."

"I swear it isn't me," Jake said looking pretty miffed.

After a few more minutes, I couldn't stand it anymore and told Jake I was heading to the metallurgical lab. There, I found Gene leaning against the wall laughing his ass off.

"What's so funny, Gene?" I asked.

"I decided to get even with Jake for a prank he pulled on me a couple weeks ago," Gene said. "Last year, we ran some metallurgical tests using butyric acid."

Gene nodded toward a brown, glass gallon jug sitting on the lab bench.

"It didn't work in the tests, but we found that it smelled absolutely horrible. This morning I put some on a small piece of cloth, wandered into Jake's office and used a paper clip to attach it to his back pocket when he wasn't paying attention. The odor has been following him around ever since."

When I walked back and told Jake what had happened, he was one pissed off individual. He threatened to do Gene bodily harm if he even stepped in his office again. This situation confused me. Since I was their boss, I was probably supposed to do something. But I wasn't sure how to handle the situation since I was usually the one who pulled the pranks. I had no experience in managing people. However, I soon found that shenanigans were a way of life at Moab.

On another occasion, Reuben was collecting water samples by the river and managed to catch a 30-inch-long rattlesnake. He threw it in a large sample can and hauled it up to the lab. At the lab, he sat the can down in the middle of the floor and called the analysts over to see what he had found. When he took the lid off, the snake scared Dave and he kicked the can over in his haste to get away. The snake raced across the floor to a bookcase bolted to the wall. There it surprisingly found a hole and crawled into the wall where it lived for the next six months, only coming out at night to catch mice when no one was around. The analysts would sometimes see it when they opened the door the first thing in the morning. But as soon as it saw them, it raced back to its hole. When they finally caught it, they didn't kill it. Instead, out of appreciation for a good job it did at eliminating the mice, they turned it loose down by the river.

Other shenanigans involved such things as putting live mice or lizards in someone's lunchbox to watch the reaction when they sat down for lunch. On another occasion they dosed a person's coffee with a chemical used in the lab. Based on previous experience, they knew it would turn his urine blood red. When the victim went to the bathroom, he started to scream as he was standing at the urinal, sure he was bleeding to death. His next thought was that he had picked up a disease from one of the college girls he was dating, possibly Maggie. After confessing his sins, he was really steamed when he found out what had actually happened.

Another shenanigan almost turned into a disaster. A large rubber snake was placed on the visor above the driver's seat in one of the company pickups. When Gerald got in and started driving it up the hill, the snake slid off and landed in his lap. Gerald jumped out of the truck and tumbled down the road. Fortunately, the truck wasn't going fast, and he wasn't hurt. The truck continued along until it stalled in a big dip in the road.

I started to realize that I was on the other side of the prank situation. As the supervisor of this motley crew, I was now responsible for making sure that things didn't get out of hand instead of being the one pulling the pranks. A harmless prank once in a while made for a fun, relaxing work environment and helped us to feel like a family. But bringing a poisonous snake into the lab could get ugly. And we were extremely lucky Gerald had not been seriously hurt when he jumped out of the pickup. After all the years of pulling pranks in my youth, I now found the shoe on the other foot. I had to exercise my authority to keep the shenanigans from getting out of control. However, there were more adventures waiting for me.

There is more than one way to skin a cat

Moab exported potash through the port of Long Beach, California. Since the shipping company didn't make any money when the vessel was sitting in port, we only had a limited time to load it. Otherwise we were charged demurrage. This was often $10,000 per day or more. To help facilitate quick loading, we would send multiple groups of 80-car unit trains to a holding area near the port. When the ship came in, the longshoremen quickly moved the cars to position and began loading the ship. However, preloading the cars meant that some of the potash had sat in cars for a month or more. Not a good situation since potash tended to cake up if given the chance.

Unfortunately, Moab's problems with caking had run up

demurrage charges of almost $50,000 on the last export shipment. The corporate office was not happy. In addition to demurrage, we paid an additional penalty if we "light loaded" the ship. This was when the ship wasn't loaded to its full capacity. Neither demurrage nor light loading was a good thing for Moab.

In late October, Don called me to his office and told me I needed to accompany the general superintendent, AK Gentry, to Long Beach. Unfortunately, I didn't have much time to get ready. We needed to fly out first thing in the morning. Based on the stories I'd heard, I was already mad at the longshoreman before we'd even left town. I'd heard from Don and others that when they had gone to Long Beach the longshoreman had a complete lack of interest in helping with our problem. If the potash didn't start flowing immediately when they opened the gates of the railcar, they just closed the car back up and pushed it down the tracks. Reports were coming in that during the loading of the current ship the longshoremen were pushing an inordinate number of cars aside.

Since AK was a couple of levels higher than me in the organization, I hadn't spent much time with him. I'd heard that AK had come up through the ranks and eventually reached the general superintendent position. Thus, he was a lot older than me and had a lot of experience handling people. But since he'd never gone to college, his technical knowledge was lacking and it was my job to somehow help him solve what to me seemed like a technical problem.

We took an early morning flight the next day to Los Angeles. When we arrived, we grabbed our bags, rented a car, and headed down the road. Since the ship was docked and the longshoreman were working to load it, I assumed we would go directly to the port. Instead, AK pulled into an Albertson's Supermarket. He told me to wait in the car. I was dumbfounded when he came back with a large cooler, a couple of cases of beer, and a bag of ice. It seemed like a hell of a time to have a party. But when I questioned AK, all he would say was "wait and see." Maybe I had been sent with him to keep him out of trouble. I couldn't imagine how he thought a couple of cases of beer would solve the caking problem.

They were expecting us at the port, and we were allowed to

drive right down to the ship loading area. Almost immediately, I became even more irate at the longshoremen. When they opened the gates on a car, if the potash didn't immediately start to flow, they just closed it back up and pushed it out of the way. They didn't even put a car shaker on it to try to break the potash loose. The more I watched, the more pissed off I got. I asked one of the workers where the damn union boss was. He pointed to a guy that was standing nearby watching the circus. I was just about to head over and give him a piece of my mind when AK grabbed my elbow.

"Hold on a second, Clark," AK said. "Let me handle this."

AK sauntered over to the boss.

"Hi," AK said. "I am here from Texasgulf to watch the loading of the ship."

"Hi, I'm the union rep. You got a problem with what we're doing?" he challenged.

The union boss scowled at AK. I think he was expecting a fight.

"It looks like the potash is really being a pain in the ass for you guys," AK continued. "I'm a little worried your crew might be getting dehydrated, particularly in this heat. I've got a cooler full of beer in the trunk of the car. Maybe they'd like to take a break and have a few beers to help cool off."

This confused me. Why the hell were we rewarding them for poor performance? The union boss called the crew over and we shot the breeze for about 20 minutes while drinking beer. But underneath my pleasant demeanor I was starting to get anxious about the wasted time.

I shouldn't have worried. After the beer break there wasn't a car too difficult to unload. If necessary, the longshoremen would thump the car with the switch engine to shake the potash loose. When we started to run low on beer, AK sent me to the store to refresh our inventory, which was about the only useful thing I did on the trip. Toward the end of the day, they also unloaded the cars they had previously pushed aside. I just sat there stunned and relieved. What had looked to me like a major headache and possible argument when we drove up had been resolved by AK with a little diplomacy.

The net result was that for fifty dollars' worth of beer, Texasgulf saved tens of thousands of dollars in penalties. I'd learned a lot about dealing with people during the trip. If I'd been left alone to handle it and gotten into an argument with the union boss, things wouldn't have gone well. Clearly, it was a good idea to try to work with people rather than fight them while trying to solve a problem. I also learned that the best solution to a problem isn't always technical. Needless to say, purchasing beer to use as a bribe was not mentioned in the trip report.

My first five months at Texasgulf hadn't been anything like I'd expected. Instead of using all the science and engineering I studied in college, I was learning things that college hadn't taught me. It was fortunate that I had landed a job that would help me absorb these lessons. And there was still a lot to learn.

He let me sit and think about it for a few seconds. Then he said, "However, it would be good if you learned to present your point of view in a less confrontational fashion. It makes it easier to make the correct decision if egos don't get in the way. We need to work as a team, more like a family. Now, go ahead and get back to work."

As I headed back to my office, I thought about how surprising and exciting things had turned out. Earlier in the day, I figured that by now I would be collecting my things and heading home. Instead, I still had a job and a potential promotion on the horizon. It almost gave me whiplash.

The thought of doing research was also exciting. I had always enjoyed figuring out how things work. This seemed right up my alley. It did, however, seem strange to be heading up a research program when I still didn't know much about solution mining technology. It would definitely be a challenge, but who knew what the future would bring?

CHAPTER 15

Be Careful Who You Piss Off

Words of wisdom

As the end of 1973 approached, I continued to learn more about my job at Texasgulf's Moab potash operation and the company's culture. In early December, I was surprised to find out there was a company Christmas party and the Chairman of the Board, Dr. Charles Fogarty, would be there. He attended the company Christmas parties every year, even visiting the small facilities like Moab. Prior to the official party, he held a meeting with Moab's senior management team in a conference room at his hotel. I was surprised to learn that I, at the ripe old age of 23, was part of senior management.

I was very nervous when I pulled in the hotel parking lot. I'd never attended any meeting with so many senior officials. Dr. Fogarty had brought along his team from the corporate office including the company president. After taking a couple of deep breaths to steady my nerves, I headed for the conference room. Much to my surprise, Dr. Fogarty was standing at the door greeting the guests. He appeared to be in his early fifties and stood about 6 feet tall. His dark hair was thinning on the top of his head and he wore glasses. As I walked in the room, he shook my hand.

"You must be new here," he said. "I don't believe we've met before."

"You're right," I said. "I'm Clark Huff. I started work in June."

"Well, it is good to meet you, Clark. Go ahead and have a seat. I have a message for you, and I think it would be good for the rest of the team to hear it again."

Dr. Charles Fogarty

I found a seat at the large conference table near the people I knew. I wondered what Dr. Fogarty's message would be as I chatted with my neighbors. After the whole group was finally seated, Dr. Fogarty took the floor.

"I know that most of you have heard this before," he said, "but with the addition of Clark to the group, I think it's worth repeating."

The corporate team looked over at me. I felt like sliding under the table to hide.

"Texasgulf's most valuable asset is its people," he paused for a beat. "As long as we have good, dedicated people, we can solve any problem. And because of this, we will always take care of our people so they're there when we need them. We will not lay you off if there's a downturn in the economy. If we have to close a plant, we will find a new position for everyone that is willing to relocate. However, this is not to say that we will tolerate incompetence, lying, or cheating. People that do these things damage the corporation and must be let go. And I had better not find out someone has been promoted just because he's good friends with or sucks up to the boss. That kind of behavior will ultimately destroy the company. We have to have good, competent people in every position in order for the company to survive. Do you understand this, Clark?"

"Yes, sir," I said. "I believe I do."

As the meeting moved on to other topics, I considered what

Dr. Fogarty had said. It was startling. I'd often heard during my summer job that the best way to get ahead was to suck up to the boss. Certainly that was the way it was at the Burgin mine. I'd also heard my fellow workers say they were just cannon fodder. But for the CEO to personally tell me the opposite was astounding. I hoped what he said was true, but based on my experience at the Burgin, I would need hard evidence before I'd be convinced. In the meantime, I had other problems to deal with.

There is more to learn than science

The technology used at Texasgulf's Moab facility was unique. No one else in the world was using solution mining combined with solar evaporation to produce potash. Moab wouldn't have used it either except the facility was desperate to survive. The primary competition, the potash mines near Saskatoon, Canada, used continuous mining machines in the flat potash beds of their underground mines. One man running a continuous miner with its large rotating heads could mine hundreds of tons of rock during a shift. This resulted in very low production costs, making those mines very profitable.

Unfortunately, instead of being flat, Moab's potash bed had large undulations, kind of like broad, 200-foot-tall waves. The continuous mining machines couldn't deal with this. Moab tried to survive by blasting the ore loose using explosives, but this wasn't even close to being competitive with the Canadian mines. For Texasgulf to get any value from their Moab investment, they had to come up with a new mining method. This is where solution mining came into the picture. One of the key people who helped develop the technology was Rudy Higgins.

Rudy was a chemist that worked at Moab in the 1960s. He had been instrumental in developing the idea of using solution mining coupled with solar evaporation and had worked hard to convince senior management to give it a try. When the conversion to solution mining was finally approved, Moab shut down operations and started the two-year conversion project. This consisted of building huge solar ponds, running pipelines, and drilling wells.

Since Rudy was a chemist, he didn't have anything to do while the conversion was underway, so he was transferred to Australia. After a couple of years he was relocated to Texasgulf's Denver office. But despite his other projects, he continued to monitor the situation at Moab. He obviously had a keen interest in whether solution mining was successful.

When I joined the Moab team, the solution mining system had only been in operation a little over a year. Although Moab was currently making money, there was no guarantee it would continue. This meant that the corporate office closely monitored the tonnage of potash brought to the surface as potassium in the brine. Unfortunately, by December 1973 this was declining. Since the volume of brine that could be evaporated in the ponds was fixed, a lower potassium content in the brine meant reduced potash production. Since our profitability was very sensitive to our production rate, senior management was clearly interested in understanding why the brine grade was declining.

The only way to gain physical access to the mine to see what was going on was through one of the 10-inch diameter wells. And any equipment sent down a well had to withstand 1,500 psi of fluid pressure. The net result was that about all we could monitor was the chemical analysis and temperature of the brine being produced from the mine.

Not surprisingly, as Rudy reviewed the monthly data, he would come up with ideas about what was happening. Usually, it involved some mistake in operations that he believed Moab was making. Unfortunately, he often shared these ideas with corporate management. I'd receive memos from him, and sometimes from senior management, as to why we weren't fixing the problems.

Initially, he thought we were doing poor analytical work. Rudy and I argued about thermal energy transfer, problems posed by insoluble materials in the ore, and various other issues. As often happens when there is very limited data, neither of us could prove our theories. Thus, the arguments continued and tempers flared. Rudy was constantly thinking up experiments and tests. It irritated me that my time was being used to conduct useless experiments. During the first six months of 1974, I became very annoyed with Rudy and felt that he was only trying to put the blame for the declining mine production on the incompetence of Moab's personnel. I wasn't convinced he knew what he was talking about and I damn sure didn't need some snooty chemist dreaming up experiments to add to my workload.

That July, I took a week off during the Fourth of July celebration so I could unwind and try get away from Rudy's annoying memos. I headed north to Spanish Fork, my hometown, to see my friends and family. When I got back to Moab after the holiday, I was shocked to learn that while I was gone, the plant manager, Bob Curfman, had died from a heart attack while on the golf course.

This was sad and upsetting. Bob had been doing a good job looking after Moab and I had enjoyed being part of his team. After the funeral, the speculation began as to who would be the new plant manager. We all thought it would either be the general superintendent, AK Gentry, or possibly the operations superintendent, Don Mobley. However, we didn't hear anything from corporate management for six weeks. The suspense was killing me.

Finally, in late August it was announced that Rudy Higgins would be the new plant manager. I was in shock and figured that I was screwed. As plant manager, Rudy had the authority to fire me with no questions asked. It took Rudy a month to get disengaged from his Denver job and make his first appearance at Moab. During this time, I stressed out worrying about the situation and the inevitable confrontation.

By the time Rudy arrived for his first day as plant manager, I was a basket case. I'd given up hope and decided that I might as well quit and get it over with. I figured that if I stayed around, Rudy would just torture me for a month or two and then fire me anyway. And so a preemptive strike was in order. As soon as Rudy settled into his new office, I strode to the admin building to turn in my resignation.

Walking into the office building, I headed down to the executive wing and asked Marge Phillips if I could speak with Mr. Higgins. She walked into his office and came back a few minutes later and told me that Mr. Higgins could see me now. As I walked into his office, he motioned for me to sit down.

"I've been meaning to talk to you," Rudy said. "But why don't you go first?"

Oh, shit. He's going to fire me now!

"Based on our previous history," I said, "I think it might be better if I resigned."

Rudy looked startled. He just sat and stared at me for several seconds. Finally, he said, "I'm sorry to hear that, Clark. Is there any particular reason you're quitting?"

"With all of the arguments we've had over the last few months, I can't imagine you'd want me to stay. I thought it would be easier if I just went ahead and quit."

Rudy sat and thought about it for several seconds. I was on pins and needles.

Finally, he said, "I'm glad you brought this up. It leads into what I wanted to talk to you about."

I could feel my chest tighten up in preparation for the ass chewing.

"I would really like you to stay," Rudy said. "You've demonstrated that you are smart and creative."

I sat there in shock with my month hanging open.

Rudy continued. "You are just the type of person I need to help figure out the solution mining problem. I don't yet have approval, but I plan to set up a new department to do research on solution mining as well as optimizing production. I want to promote you and make you the head of the new department. I would appreciate it if you would reconsider and stay on."

I was absolutely stunned. In my wildest dreams I couldn't imagine Rudy asking me to stay, much less giving me a promotion.

After a few seconds I said, "But what about all our disagreements?"

"Everyone doesn't have to agree with me. Listening to other peoples' views helps me make better decisions. I want you to always feel like you can speak up. However, when I do make a decision, I expect your support and for you to follow my orders."

I couldn't believe Rudy wanted me to stay. After thinking about what he'd said I decided to reconsider. I would give it a try and if it worked out, I wouldn't have to find a new job. If it didn't work out, I wouldn't be any worse off.

"Thanks, Mr. Higgins. On second thought, I'd like to stay."

"I'm glad to hear it, Clark. Welcome to the team. And you can call me Rudy. But I'm surprised you thought I'd fire you. I would have thought by now Dr. Fogarty would have explained that good employees are our most valuable asset. It is more important that you think things through and give me the benefit of your insights than to feel obligated to agree with every idea I have. If you let me do something stupid, nobody wins and we may all be out of a job."

CHAPTER 16

Learning Things When You Least Expect It

It is hard to lead when you don't know where you're going

In early 1975, Rudy Higgins finally received approval to form the Development and Planning Department. I was stunned to learn I would head it up. Even though Rudy had said he would put me in charge, I didn't think it would happen. How could a 24-year-old kid with just two years of experience manage a new department? I felt totally overwhelmed. I had absolutely no idea how to lead a group of engineers or run a research program.

We were doomed.

The department's goal was to keep Moab economic. It was expected that this would require stabilizing or increasing potash production. My new department included a geologist, a chemical engineer, a metallurgical engineer, and two technicians. Bob MacAdams, in HR, did a good job of finding the right people and, a few months later, the department was fully staffed.

Knowing how naïve I was about potash technology, Rudy started sending me to visit other facilities. A few months after my promotion, Rudy surprised me one morning when he walked into my office.

"I've got an adventure lined up for you," Rudy said.

"What's that?" I asked.

"I'd like you to visit the Dead Sea Works in Israel. They produce potash by pumping brine from the Dead Sea into solar ponds and then processing the solids deposited by evaporation."

Damn. I didn't want to visit Israel. The Yom Kippur War between Israel and several Arab states had ended only two years earlier. I was leery of traveling anywhere near that part of the world, particularly for my first trip outside North America. However, I didn't want to look like a coward. Since our solution mining system was our biggest problem and the Dead Sea Works wasn't using this technology, it seemed I could talk my way out of this trip.

"That looks like a waste of time and money to me," I said. "I can't imagine learning anything useful."

"But they do have solar ponds and produce potash, so you should learn something."

"I doubt it. It doesn't seem too tricky to pump brine into a pond and let it evaporate."

"You'd better get used to the idea. Our CEO, Dr. Fogarty, used his contacts at the Dead Sea Works to arrange a visit for you at the end of August, so you're going."

I was screwed.

The trip to Israel was my first excursion overseas. Fortunately, Rudy realized I didn't know much about international travel so he sent along Howard Eastland, the head of engineering at Moab, to try and keep me out of trouble. Howard and I left on our adventure in late August 1975.

First, we made a two-hour drive to Grand Junction, Colorado. From there we flew to Denver and then on to JFK Airport in New York. At this point, I was tired and hoped to sleep on the eight-hour, overnight flight to Paris. I didn't. The jostling, the glare when my neighbor turned on a light, and the noise all kept me awake. After a six-hour layover in Paris, we boarded the seven-hour flight to Tel Aviv.

We were met at the Tel Aviv airport by Jay, a representative of the engineering company, Stearns Rogers. Stearns did business with both Texasgulf and the Dead Sea Works so they volunteered to help us out. I dozed off on the way to the Desert Inn in Beersheba. We had left Moab at 7:00 a.m. and arrived at the hotel at 8:00 p.m. the next evening. After 27 hours of traveling, combined with a time zone change of 10 hours, I was tired, grumpy, and ready to go to bed.

Upon checking into the hotel, I plodded up the stairs to my room. Opening the door, I was hit by a gust of hot air rushing out. Switching on the air conditioner helped. Unfortunately, it sounded like an out-of-balance washing machine on the spin cycle. After 10 minutes, it conked out. Plodding back down the stairs to the front desk, I was informed that no other rooms were available and it would be tomorrow before a repairman could fix it.

Damn.

Now I was mad and tired. I opened the door to my balcony. Although it was hot outside, it was even hotter in my room. I left the door open hoping it would help my room cool down, at least a little. Although it still felt like a sauna, it was the best I could do. I stripped off my clothes, plopped down on the bed, and promptly dozed off.

As the sun streamed into my room, I gradually started to wake up. Laying on top of the covers, I noticed the room was still hot and I was sweaty. Then I noticed the walls seemed to shimmer. Alarmed, I sat up in bed. The shimmering was hundreds of mosquitoes moving around on the walls. Then I noticed I was covered in mosquito bites. Maybe opening the door to the balcony hadn't been such a bright idea.

After a quick shower, I dressed and headed down to breakfast. Jay and Howard were already at a table. As I sat down, I noticed they were staring at me.

"Clark," Jay said, "you need to be more careful about mosquito bites."

"Now you tell me. My air conditioner quit so I opened the door to the balcony to cool off. Being in the desert, I hadn't expected mosquitoes."

"Yeah, mosquitoes can be a problem here. They often carry encephalitis. Most people from North America are not resistant to it. And if you come down with it in Israel, you're in big trouble."

"Why is that?"

"If you go to the hospital, you'll likely catch something there worse than what you already have."

Jay explained that encephalitis would start with a headache and fever and things would go downhill from there. The incubation period was about ten days. Damn, we planned to be in Israel for two weeks.

I was doomed.

After breakfast, we jumped in Jay's car for the hour-long journey to the Dead Sea Works. It was located 1,360 feet below sea level, the lowest place on earth. Being August it was hot. As we reached the rim of the valley and looked down in the deep canyon containing the Dead Sea, I was stunned to see heat waves rising up from the valley like hot air from an oven. It was still morning. What would it be like in the afternoon?

Arriving at the plant, we were escorted to an air-conditioned conference room. There, a couple of DSW employees explained their production process. I was surprised to learn that they didn't just produce potash. The brine from the Dead Sea contained magnesium, bromine, and common salt along with the potash. To increase their income they produced and sold these products too. Maybe we could do something like this at Moab.

Next, we visited their solar ponds. I was impressed. Our pond area covered a little less than a square mile. Their pond area was almost 18 miles long and three miles wide covering about 50 square miles. I took out my camera to take some pictures.

"You can't do that here," our guide said.

"Why not?" I asked.

"We never know when terrorists will use the pictures to plan a missile attack. Our facility is right on the border with Jordan."

I definitely wasn't in Utah anymore.

As we continued our tour, I learned how the brine flowed through their solar ponds. They operated their ponds differently than we did at Moab to optimize the production of byproducts. They also used dredges to harvest the potash while Moab used road construction equipment. At the ponds, they explained that they'd tested the idea of putting dye in the brine going to the ponds to increase evaporation rates. Due to the nature of their brine, dye didn't work for them but they thought it might for us. Although Moab had tested using dye previously, it sounded like it might merit further investigation.

Over the coming days, we investigated not only their solar ponds but also their manufacturing plants used to produce potash and various byproducts. With their large technical staff we also discussed ideas for improving Moab. I was definitely learning a lot about their technology.

At the end of each day, we had dinner with Jay and some of the employees from the Dead Sea Works. They insisted that we sample the local cuisine. I wasn't impressed. After a couple of nights of this, I was hoping we could find a McDonald's. On top of that, driving around town made me nervous. There were a lot of men on the street packing fully automatic rifles. I found out that in Israel when a man or unwed woman turns eighteen they are drafted into the army for three years of active duty. After their mandatory service, they could resume their normal life but still had to serve three months of active duty each year. Because of this they took their weapons home with them.

This was certainly a different world than Moab.

After lunch on Friday, Jay suggested we call it quits for the day and head back to the hotel. As we drove to town, he told us that there was world class snorkeling in the Red Sea. We agreed to meet him Saturday morning in Eilat, a town near where we would be snorkeling. There, we could rent equipment and then make the short drive to Castle Island for our adventure.

First thing Saturday morning, Howard and I jumped in the car and headed out. Our route took us back down into the Dead Sea Valley and then south through a rugged desert region with little vegetation. Every few miles we passed road signs displaying the skull and crossbones symbol with a bunch of Hebrew lettering on the bottom. Above that was the English translation, "Danger. Do not leave the roadway. This area may be mined." These relics of the Yom Kippur War made me uneasy.

When we reached Eilat, we hooked up with Jay, rented snorkeling equipment, bought swimsuits, and headed southwest of town to Castle Island. As we approached our final destination, I suspected there wouldn't be anything interesting to see underwater. With the barren desert surrounding us, it seemed like it wouldn't provide much support for sea life.

At Castle Island, we changed into our swimsuits, grabbed our snorkeling equipment, and headed to the beach. Although the island wasn't too far from shore, we decided to take the ferry. Once on the island, we put on our equipment and waded out to snorkel.

Castle Island located just offshore of Israel

As I laid out on the surface and started to swim toward deeper water, I was astounded. The crystal-clear water made it seem like I was floating in air. Below me were sea anemones with long yellow tentacles waving in the current. Some of these provided hiding places for white-and-orange-striped clown fish. Purplish-gray sting rays with fluorescent green gill slits lay on the bottom. Although the rays made me a little nervous, they paid no attention to me. Further out from shore were large heads of coral rising up from the bottom. Diving down, I looked under the base of the coral heads. A 12-inch-long lionfish surprised me with its dozens of striped, spiked fins poking out in all directions.

We spent the day working our way around the island, exploring the various nooks and crannies and enjoying the diverse marine life. Finally, in the late afternoon we were tired and decided it was time to head back. We climbed out of the water and waited for the ferry ride to the mainland.

While standing there, Howard said, "Clark, you've got a problem."

"What's that?" I asked as I checked myself to see what was exposed.

"Your back has the worst sunburn I've ever seen."

"I can believe it. Since climbing out of the water, it's really starting to hurt." While swimming, the water must have kept my back cool. I should have brought a T-shirt or bought sunscreen at the dive shop.

At the car, I checked myself out. My back had large "water" blisters all over it. They hurt so bad that I couldn't tolerate laying against the car seat. The trip to the hotel seemed like it'd never end. Hurrying up to my room, I jerked off my clothes and climbed in the shower. The cold water felt good as long as I didn't let it beat on the blisters. After showering, I swallowed a couple of aspirins and went to bed. Unfortunately, even laying on my stomach made it difficult to sleep.

The next day, I was tired, had a headache, and had started to run a low-grade fever. Although I suspected this was the result of the sunburn, I worried it might be encephalitis. As the headache grew worse over the next few days, I became more convinced I had encephalitis. This was something of a distraction as we resumed our tour of the Dead Sea Works.

Finally, the day for our trip back to Moab arrived. After Jay dropped us off, we headed toward the terminal building. I found that Israel's airport security was much stricter than that in the U.S. After the inspector meticulously went through everything in my suitcase, I had to pass a cross-examination when I presented my passport. After several attempts to fluster me with trick questions, they finally approved my departure. Next, I climbed on a bus, rode out to the plane, and found my seat. As the plane lifted off the runway and I watched the ground retreat from my window, I heaved a sigh of relief. I was finally on my way back home. Although the return trip included a layover in London, I would be back in a part of the world I was more comfortable with. Arriving in Moab on Friday, I had the weekend to adjust before resuming work on Monday.

I was just starting to settle into my office on my first day back when Rudy walked in.

"I already spoke with Howard briefly this morning," Rudy said. "It sounds like you had an interesting trip."

"It was interesting in more ways than I anticipated," I said.

"Yeah, Howard told me about the mosquitoes and the sunburn. It sounds like it was good I sent him along. Otherwise, you might have gotten in even more trouble."

"It would have been good if someone had given me an idea of how to prepare for the trip before I left."

"You'll know better next time. But the big question is whether you learned anything useful."

I squirmed a little in my seat. I was afraid he might ask this.

"They did have some good ideas about diversifying into byproducts," I said. "They also thought we should do more work in finding a dye to use in our ponds. Although their plant is different than ours, there was still enough similarity to provide ideas on equipment."

"I'm glad you learned something from the trip, despite your reservations. For now, I will let you deal with the work that piled up while you were gone and you need to discuss the trip with your troops. After you've had time to think about it, we can go over things in more detail."

I was glad that Rudy let me off the hook that easy. But in the end, he'd been right. The trip to Israel had taught me a lot and the knowledge would be very profitable for the company. And over the coming years I would visit many more plants around the world. All of these trips helped expand my knowledge about mining and processing. But this first trip to Israel was the most difficult of my career. It is hard to believe I'd been so naïve. I didn't pack a lot of items that I should have like sunscreen and insect repellant, and could have done a better job of looking out for myself. The trip taught me how miserable things could become if I wasn't prepared or did something stupid. In the future, I'd do a little more planning before taking off on an adventure.

CHAPTER 17

Learning to Never Give Up

Learning from failure

After the long, tiring trip to Israel, it was good to be back at my desk to concentrate on solving the mine problem. If I didn't solve the problem, potash production would continue to decline, the Moab facility would become uneconomic, and I would be out of a job. I still couldn't figure out why they appointed me, an inexperienced 24-year-old kid, to tackle such a critical problem. The stress was almost more than I could bear.

Since I didn't know anything about managing a new department, I thought it would be a good idea to hold weekly staff meetings. That way we could keep track of each other's projects and I could get input from everyone on running the department. Our main project was to somehow restore the brine grade from the mine to the level it was at the start of solution mining. However, since we didn't understand why the brine grade was declining, we were driving at night without our headlights on. After a couple of months of discussions and lab tests, I felt it was time to make the decision as to what our first test would be. I called a staff meeting to discuss our options.

After the six of us got our coffee and sat down at the conference table, I kicked things off. "Based on our numerous discussions, it's time to decide what our first test to expand solution mining will be. Does anyone have a suggestion?"

Initially, everyone just sat and looked at each other. Finally, Jim, the metallurgical engineer, spoke up. "I think our best chance is to drill a well outside the old mine workings. We can use fracking to connect it to the mine. This will bring additional potash reserves into production which should increase the brine grade." Fracking was a technology developed by the petroleum industry that used high pressure fluids to fracture rock and open up a path through a formation.

"I've been thinking the same thing," I said. "Does anyone have any other ideas that we might want to try first?"

Everyone just shrugged their shoulders. We discussed a few options but since none of us knew what we were doing, fracking seemed like as good an idea as any.

"Well then," I said, "fracking it is. I'll see if I can get Bill Buchanan to round up the equipment we will need." Bill was in the maintenance department but had a lot of experience with drill rigs.

I discussed my plans with Rudy, the plant manager, who agreed it was a good idea and said to go ahead with the test. Rudy pointed out that it shouldn't be too expensive because I had a couple of free wells at my disposal. During the initial conversion to solution mining a few years earlier, the surveyor screwed up and located two wells outside of the old mine workings. Since accounting had already written them off, this made it cheap and easy to conduct the first test.

Bill immediately got to work on the project. The well was located just south of the plant in some brush near the Colorado River. With the tall, red sandstone cliffs in the background and the river running nearby it was a very scenic location for a test. We cleared the brush away from the well to give us a work area. Bill rounded up the necessary equipment and installed the piping. After only two months, we were ready to begin our first solution mining test. I had the staff gather around the well to witness this momentous occasion.

"Go ahead and start the pump," I told Bill.

Bill opened the valves and the three-piston pump, about the

size of a small Volkswagen, began to chug away. We carefully monitored the pressure as it built up in the well. After about 15 minutes, the pressure reached 5,500 psi. Then the pressure suddenly dropped back down to 3,500 psi.

"What just happened?" I asked.

"I believe we initiated a fracture," Bill said.

"What happens next?"

"The fluid should inflate the fracture and cause it to spread out along the potash bed."

We continued to watch the pressure but had no indication the fracture had found the mine. Over the next couple of hours, the group gradually dispersed. That evening I checked the progress of the experiment on my way home. Unfortunately, the fracture still hadn't found the mine even though it only needed to travel a few hundred feet. I checked the test again the next morning but there was still no success. I was starting to get anxious. The next day was the same, as was the next. After two agonizing weeks I finally gave up. What had gone wrong?

The staff and I discussed the failed test for several months trying to figure out what had happened. Finally, one night while I was lying in bed, I had a burst of inspiration and realized what the problem was. Like most things, the fracture took the path of least resistance. Unfortunately, that path was not toward the mine. This was because the large entries in the mine workings 3,200 feet underground created a stress envelope around the opening. The higher stress in the rock near the mine entries made traveling toward the mine an uphill battle for the fracture.

Damn, it would have been good to have figured this out a few months earlier. Although I had learned something, it was not what I'd hoped for. And as it turned out, I also learned a second lesson.

A little over a month after the failed test a gentleman walked into my office. "Are you Clark?"

"Yes, who are you?"

"I'm Paul, an accountant from the corporate auditing department. Unfortunately, you have a problem."

I sat up as my chest tightened. "What seems to be the problem?"

"You spent almost $20,000 on a solution mining test without

proper authorization. You can't spend more than $1,000 without an approved AFE."

"What's an AFE?" I asked.

"AFE stands for Authorization For Expenditures. You need to write up the project and get proper approval of the AFE before spending the money."

"But Rudy gave verbal approval."

"That doesn't count. You have to have proper written approval. If Rudy doesn't sign an AFE, you will need to pay for the test out of your own pocket."

Damn, another unwanted lesson learned.

As it turned out, I needed to write two AFEs. One for the test that we had already completed and one for our next test, whatever that would be. Once again I listened to suggestions from my staff. Since the rock between the well and the mine was soluble, this time we decided to use water to dissolve a path for the connection.

Fortunately, I had another free well to experiment with. I discussed my plan with Rudy, and once again received his approval. However, this time I prepared the AFE for $30,000 and got Rudy's written approval before spending any money.

I felt optimistic that we had solved the problem as we gathered up the pipe and equipment for the test. First, we used a crane to install a 4-inch pipe from the surface to the bottom of the test well. This was like inserting a straw in a soda bottle. The pipe was the straw we used to get the brine out of the well. The annular space between the pipe and the well casing was like the space between the straw and the neck of the soda bottle. It let the water into the well the way the space between the straw and soda bottle allowed the air to flow in when the soda was sucked out. And since there was a water supply nearby and we only needed a small pump, it was easy to finish the project. Getting ready for the test was almost too easy.

We started the test by injecting a modest 10 gallons per minute of water down the well. At this rate, the brine produced was relatively rich in potash which was good news. Over the next few weeks, I gradually increased the flow rate as the cavern size expanded and provided more surface area for the water to attack.

As the weeks went by, the cavern continued to grow and I kept increasing the water flow. After six weeks, I started feeling confident that the test was going to be a success. Then disaster struck. The potash content of the brine dramatically began to drop. This didn't make sense. In another month, the test well was essentially just producing a salt brine. Something bad had happened, but what?

Rig drilling a test well at Moab

I shut down the test and tried to figure out the problem. Unfortunately, there was very little data. During discussions of the test with geologists at the corporate office, they told me it was possible to sonar the cavern I'd created. Arrangements were made and we lowered the sonar probe to the bottom. Much to my dismay, I found that the shale layer above the potash zone had collapsed and exposed the salt bed above it.

Now everything made sense. Since the water we injected was lighter than the brine in the cavern, it flowed upward like oil flows to the top of water. When the cavity became too large and the shale layer collapsed, the water rose up and dissolved the overlying salt layer rather than the potash. I should have realized that the cavern couldn't get very large at a depth of 3,200 feet before it collapsed.

Another good idea shot to hell.

So far, as the head of a new department for 12 months, all I had accomplished was spend $50,000 of the company's money on useless ideas. Now I was really starting to stress out. I doubted the senior management would tolerate this indefinitely.

I discussed the failure of the solution mining test with the troops. We agreed that we needed to keep the dissolution process in the potash bed, but how? After pondering the problem for several weeks, we decided to try to use a blanket of air in the top of the cavern to protect the overlying salt bed. Unfortunately, we were out of free wells so this test would cost $800,000.

I submitted a request for funds and waited. It took several months to get approval this time. The AFE had to go to the corporate office and corporate management was getting a little leery of my ideas. But eventually they approved the project. As soon as the funds were available, we arranged for a drill rig. It took a month to drill and case the well. We then connected the water piping and the high-pressure air compressor. The third test was ready to begin.

The initial results were encouraging. The brine analysis was as I had forecast and when the cavity was sonared; we found that it was indeed staying in the potash zone. The team and I were excited. But I should have known better. A few weeks later the roof of the cavity collapsed. The cavern had become so wide that it couldn't support the pressure of the overlying rock. The collapse left so many boulders of shale in the potash zone that I once again had a well that just wanted to produce a salt brine.

Now I was really starting to worry about keeping my job. The $50,000 I'd wasted in my first two tests was nothing compared to $800,000.

Developing a fallback position

When I was a kid in Spanish Fork, I had a reputation for never giving up. To my friends' dismay, whenever I played games I would nearly always figure out a way to win, even if it took all night. I felt the same way about solving the solution mining problem. But it was becoming clear that figuring this out was going to take some time. I decided I'd better step back and look at the big picture. My primary goal was to keep Moab economic. Maybe there were other ways to improve the economics and extend the life of the facility.

It dawned on me that there were several large sump areas in the old mine workings that were inactive. I now understood that drilling wells into these areas would bring them into production and increase potash sales. I submitted an AFE for $750,000 for the project and much to my surprise it was quickly approved. I was back in business.

Learning from others' mistakes, I first had the well location carefully surveyed. Bill then used the D-9 dozer to prepare the drill pad. Next, the drill rig was brought in and erected. The rig was the same as those used by the oil industry. The rotary table for the rig was 10 feet above ground level with the top of the rig almost 120 feet in the air.

The well was drilled and brought into production with no difficulty. I was relieved when the potash content of the brine going to the solar ponds increased. I immediately requested and received funds for the next well. When it was also a success, I proceeded with two more wells. Moab's potash production rebounded and stabilized. Although this wasn't a long-term solution, it would improve profitability for several years and buy me some time. I began to wonder what other opportunities might be waiting and remembered my unwanted trip to Israel. I realized that the trip provided two options that were worth pursuing: selling salt and dyeing the brine intended for the ponds. When I discussed these options with Rudy, it was embarrassing to admit that I had gotten these ideas from the trip to Israel.

Selling salt seemed like a no-brainer. The zone being solution mined contained both sodium chloride (salt) and potassium chloride (potash). Both were dissolved and then later precipitated in the solar ponds during the mining process. However, since road salt sold for about a tenth as much as potash, it had been ignored. But the salt was essentially free. It followed the potash through the system to the solar ponds and on to the mill where it was finally removed as an impurity. There would be very little expense to stockpile the salt and then later process it using the existing equipment.

We conducted a study and determined that the changes required in the plant were relatively minor. It would only take a few months to complete and would cost less than $100,000 if all we made was road salt. And since we could produce hundreds of thousands of tons of it each year, it would provide additional income for Moab.

We made the changes to the plant during the next summer outage. In the fall, we initially produced potash while at the same time separating larger crystals of salt and stockpiling them. After producing potash for a few weeks, we switched over and produced road salt using the same equipment used for potash production. The road salt was then stored at the end of one of the large storage buildings. During the winter, we sold the road salt to nearby states.

After several years of successful road salt production, we felt comfortable enough to invest in a bagging plant and began to produce water softener salt. Water softener salt sold for considerably more than road salt and would significantly increase the profitability and life of the Moab facility. Finally, I had a success. Although the long-term potash production problem was still waiting to be solved, I had bought some more time.

How to make a Smurf

Another idea was to use dye to increase evaporation rates in the solar ponds. Since the solar ponds also limited production, if the ponds were twice as large, twice as much brine could be evaporated and twice as much potash produced. Unfortunately, there was no land available for expanding the solar ponds. However, since the brine was relatively clear and the salt was white, the ponds didn't do a very good job capturing sunlight. By coloring the brine, the ponds would become much more efficient at absorbing sunlight and potash production would increase. A black dye would absorb the most sunlight, but any dye would be an improvement.

The idea of using dye in our ponds required some research. There were lots of water-soluble dyes. The trick was to find one that was stable in potash brine for an extended period of time. Sunlight decomposed most dyes in a few weeks. Others were stripped out of the solution when the salt and potash precipitated in the ponds. The trick of finding a dye that would be stable for months was assigned to the chemical engineer, Pete.

Although relatively new at Moab, Pete understood that the solar ponds were not very efficient and was excited to start researching options. First, he built eight test ponds near the lab building. They were 10 feet square and 24 inches deep with plastic liners to seal up the ponds. He added test dye to six of the ponds but left two ponds undyed to act as a reference. Initially, he tried several black dyes since they absorbed nearly all of the sunlight. Unfortunately, none of these dyes stayed in solution for more than a few days. Finally, Pete found a blue dye that would stay in solution indefinitely. At a dosage rate of only eight parts per million, it turned the brine a dark blue and increased evaporation rates by 20 percent.

The next step was a full-scale test of the dye in the solar ponds. The dye was normally used in such applications as liquid toilet bowl cleaners to color the water blue. Because it was so strong, manufacturers of toilet bowl cleaners only needed to order a few hundred pounds of dye at a time. When we ordered eight tons of it, the supplier thought we meant pounds. When we assured him we meant tons he was flabbergasted. Our order would consume almost two months of dye production. We got a volume discount.

The dye was provided as a powder which meant that the best way to handle it was to first dissolve it in a 5,000-gallon tank of water. This allowed it to be easily metered out and added to the brine going to the solar ponds. We rounded up a tank and filled it with water. Upon arrival of the dye, I had my old lab prankster and rattlesnake handler, Reuben, take care of emptying the drums of dye into the tank. He had helped Pete with some of the dye tests and knew he had to be careful not to get any on him. To be safe, he brought an extra change of clothes to work with him that day. But even with this precaution he had trouble. As he carefully dumped drums of the dye powder into the water tank, traces of the dust got on him and his clothes. Although he didn't think he had much dye on him, the dye was so potent that when he showered in the change room, the water turned dark blue. And so did Reuben. Even after standing in the shower for 40 minutes, his skin was tinted blue. He wasn't happy.

The problems continued when Reuben got home that night. When he washed his coveralls, traces of the dye turned everything in the washing machine blue. In addition, Reuben had forgotten about his boots. They were also contaminated with traces of dye. Blue footprints appeared around his house whenever the dye on the floor got damp.

The next day Reuben caught up with me at work.

"I want hazardous duty pay the next time I have to handle the dye," he said.

"You don't like having blue skin?" I asked.

"It's not only that. The wife says I'd better sleep with one eye open if it ever comes home with me again."

Although the sale of salt products and the increased pond production due to the dye helped the financial situation, it only slapped a Band-Aid on the issue. Over the next few years, I developed two novel ideas to solve the problem. For the first idea, a borehole would be drilled from the surface and then "directionally drilled" so that it traveled horizontally under the potash zone. Using this relatively new drilling technology allowed a single well to recover thousands of tons of potash. This technology could provide enough potash to stabilize potash production. Unfortunately, although Moab would remain economic, the solar ponds would limit production to 150,000 to 200,000 tons per year. I eventually received a U.S. patent for this idea.

In the second idea, a new shaft would be sunk to the potash zone. Conventional mining would be used to open up large portions of the ore body. The conventionally mined areas would then be flooded and the remaining ore removed by solution mining. This hybrid system would have the advantage of increasing Moab's production to over a million tons of potash per year. The disadvantage was that it would cost hundreds of millions of dollars to implement and was unproven technology.

As it turned out, my time doing research was coming to an end. But the experience taught me a great deal. I found that every "good" idea didn't necessarily work. There was a huge difference between what looked good on paper and the real world. It also became clear that the more people involved in developing an idea, the better the chances that problems would be uncovered in the planning stage and solved before large sums of money were spent.

Unfortunately for me, I had to learn to deal with failure. But the failures reinforced my tendency to never give up and to think outside the box. Producing salt and using dye in the ponds significantly helped Moab's economics. These lessons served me well during my career and became my hallmark. I was very fortunate to have Rudy Higgins as a mentor. Despite my failures, he continued to have confidence in me and reassured me that I wasn't about to be fired. He was patient in letting me find solutions and, fortunately, I eventually did. Not every boss would have tolerated my stupidity while I was learning. Unknown to me, my tenacity was also noticed by corporate management. This would have a long-term impact on my career. But for now, Rudy had some new lessons for me to learn.

CHAPTER 18

Going to School with the Big Boys

You're never too old to go to school

Unbeknownst to me Rudy Higgins had a problem. In the fall of 1979, he wanted to promote me to general superintendent. Corporate management thought he was nuts. Being only 28 years old, they weren't convinced I was ready for that much responsibility. Rudy finally got them to agree to my promotion on the condition that I first attend the Senior Seminar in Management. This was an intense, three-week crash course in managing people and businesses. Nearly everyone in Texasgulf's corporate management had taken the course. However, it was usually after they had become a vice president or at least a plant manager. The net result was that in October 1979 I was back in school but didn't know why.

The seminar was held at the Hershey Hotel in Hershey, Pennsylvania. The hotel resembled an old estate. There were large lawns including a bowling green in back of the hotel and riding stables. Inside, the hotel was very ornate. We ate dinner on fine china in the grand ballroom.

The first day of class was intimidating. We started the morning by introducing ourselves. Of the 35 male students, most were in their fifties and vice presidents of large corporations. They were surprised when I got up and announced I was the supervisor of the development and planning department at a small production site owned by Texasgulf. I was not alone in wondering why I was there.

The seminar's intense program left little time to relax. We started the day at 8 a.m. and typically worked through until 10 p.m. at night. We were busy with all types of activities depending on our current lesson. This left me mentally exhausted at the end of the day. It was like my college experience but without the sexy girls.

The day normally started with a hypothetical personnel problem we were to solve. The instructor would stand before us and explain the problem that was presented to a supervisor. He then gave us 15 minutes to jot down how we would handle it. Then he would *randomly* select one of us to stand and explain how we'd deal with it. Regardless of what we said, the instructor pointed out flaws in our solution. Every morning I worried that it would be my turn in the box. My classmates had far more experience in dealing with personnel problems and were comfortable speaking to an audience. Not me. I was very nervous any time I had to stand before a group. However, one day a classmate inadvertently helped me feel more at ease.

Fred Constanza was one of my older classmates and as the VP of Operations for Alcoa, he was very experienced in dealing with people. During discussions, he was highly opinionated, outspoken, and hardheaded. It was clear that he felt he knew more than the instructors. He wasn't buying into much of what the instructors said and became grouchier and more outspoken each day. At the beginning of the second week, the question posed to us during our morning ritual was how we would deal with an employee that missed two days of work without calling in. When the errant employee made it to work on the third day, he was poorly dressed and appeared drunk.

"What would you do in this situation, Mr. Costanza?" the instructor asked.

Costanza stood up and faced the instructor. "I'd fire the dumb son-of-a-bitch." He then sat back down. This was one of the shorter answers anyone had provided.

"What if there were extenuating circumstances?"

Fred slowly stood back up. "I've heard all the dumb excuses employees can come up with. It's just a waste of time. You might as well fire him and be done with it." He sat back down and glared at the instructor as if he was waiting to see if he would try to ridicule his answer.

"Well, Mr. Costanza, it turns out that this situation actually happened. And, unlike you, his boss did a little investigating. He found out that a few days earlier, the employee had been in an automobile accident and suffered a concussion. He was in the hospital under sedation for two days. When he finally woke up in the early morning he was confused and disoriented. He wasn't sure where he was, but knew he didn't want to be late for work. He found his clothes, got dressed, and caught a taxi to his job. So, Mr. Costanza, your answer for dealing with an overly conscientious employee is to fire him?"

Costanza's face became red with embarrassment. He was not used to being challenged and clearly was not happy about being humiliated in front of the class. After a few seconds, he said, "Let me tell you something, you dumb son-of-a-bitch. Those that can *do*. Those that can't teach dumb seminars like this. If you knew as much as you thought you did, you'd be running a company. I've had all the bullshit I'm going to put up with. I'm out of here."

With that, he walked out of the class and slammed the door. There was dead silence in the classroom. We sat and looked at each other for a few seconds while we processed what had just happened.

Finally, the instructor said, "It doesn't look like Mr. Costanza is coming back. We might as well continue our discussion."

During our morning break, we spotted Costanza at the front desk checking out of the hotel. He was really going to head home.

The next day, we were surprised when class was interrupted just before lunch. Costanza threw open the classroom door and came stomping in carrying his suitcase. He dropped it with a loud thud, scanned the room, and then fixed his gaze on the instructor.

"You may wonder what I am doing back here. Well, when I got off the plane in San Francisco last night, I found my boss waiting for me. Some son-of-a-bitch had called him. My boss told me that I really needed the lessons being taught in Hershey. He gave me the option of returning to Hershey or taking an early retirement. I considered calling his bluff but decided I didn't want to risk having to look for a new job. I spent the night on the red-eye special flying back here. Needless to say, I'm not a happy student."

With that, he collapsed in a seat and stared at the instructor. The room was silent for several seconds as we looked at each other. I was amazed when the instructor said, "We are happy to have you back, Mr. Costanza. We've missed your input."

I am not sure the instructor was sincere. He was careful not to call on Costanza the rest of the day. But over time, there didn't appear to be any hard feelings. Maybe this was an inadvertent lesson to teach me not to be overconfident.

School can be a little difficult for old fogies

As the class continued, we sometimes got relief from our normal routine by playing management games. After lunch one day, we were divided into two teams and challenged to build a Trojan Horse using supersized Tinkertoys. A foreman was selected for each team and we were told that we needed to follow his instructions as if he were our boss at work. We were given 90 minutes to build our horse. At the end of that time, the horses would be judged based on how big they were, how much they resembled a horse, and their aesthetic beauty, whatever that was.

Unbeknown to us, the real purpose of the exercise was to give us first-hand experience in two very different management styles. The instructors had already secretly selected the foremen for each team. One foreman was instructed to follow the Theory X management style. In Theory X, the boss acts like a dictator. He doesn't ask for advice from his workers and micromanages their activities. The other foreman was to use the Theory Y approach. He would solicit input from the workers, listen to their ideas, and encourage their active participation in the project. I ended up on the Theory Y team.

When the game started, the Theory X team sprang into action. Their boss, Glen, immediately started issuing orders. But there were also conflicts developing. In one case, Glen told a team member to sketch out a design for the horse.

"I can't draw anything. Ask someone else."

"Don't give me any backtalk. We need you to get the horse designed."

Glen then told another team member, "I want you to start building the back end of the horse while John works on the front end."

"I don't have any ability to build things. I'm in finance. I never played with Tinkertoys."

"What part of my instructions didn't you understand? Get to work."

In the meantime, my group was sitting around the table completely unproductive. Finally, someone said, "We should probably do something."

Our foreman, Wayne, said, "What do you think we should do?"

One team member spoke up, "It looks like the other team is drawing up plans for the horse. I used to be an architect; I could draw something up."

"That sounds like a good idea."

Another team member said, "I'll inventory our supplies so we know what we have at our disposal."

We talked about the general design of the horse and how best to proceed. Eventually, several of us volunteered to build the horse based on our design. However, at this point almost 50 minutes had passed and we hadn't actually built anything yet. We observed the other team and started to panic. Their horse was nearly finished. However, there was dissention in their ranks.

Their foreman said, "The horse isn't big enough. We need to take the body of the horse apart and add some pieces to make it longer."

"That's a bunch of bullshit. We don't have the time or the pieces."

"I didn't ask for your opinion. You just need to do what you're told."

"Yes, sir. Anything you say, sir."

One of their team was sitting off by himself. When queried he said, "I'm not feeling well and will be off sick until this game is over."

Our team raced to get our horse completed in time. We talked and exchanged ideas. Although there was a sense of urgency, we were not overly stressed and were working well together. We managed to finish our horse with five minutes to spare. And we won the contest. The other team's horse was in pieces on the table. They had kept taking their horse apart and re-assembling it to make it bigger. Even though the contest was over, they were still bickering and everyone on the team was pissed off at the foreman.

The instructor then explained that the real purpose of the exercise was to show the benefits and problems with different management styles. Generally, Theory Y is best since everyone works together and has the benefit of everyone else's knowledge and experience. However, in emergency situations Theory X is best since there isn't time to debate every option and immediate action is required.

For me, this was an important lesson. I had experienced Theory X management style firsthand at the Burgin mine. It sucked. The only person involved in decisions was the foreman. And he didn't always know as much as he thought. On the other hand, Rudy definitely followed Theory Y. Despite all the bullshit I gave him early in our relationship, he listened to me and didn't get mad. He was able to gather information from everyone and then decide what to do. And we worked well together as a team. It was clear that this was generally a much better way to run things.

An unintentional lesson from the exercise was how hard it could be to change your opinion about someone. The instructor explained that the "foremen" were only acting out the part they were assigned. He stressed that the foremen were following his instructions and the way they'd acted during the game had nothing to do with the way they really were. Despite this, the Theory X team ostracized their foreman. From that day on, they refused to sit near him at meals or interact with him in any way.

Although the games and lectures were interesting, our long days started to wear on me. And while the hotel food was nice, it wasn't what I was used to. To top it all off, there was little free time to unwind. Talking to my classmates, I found I wasn't alone in my feelings. One evening as we stood in line waiting to go into the dining room, one of my colleagues spoke up.

"I've had about all this food I want," he said. "Although it's first class, it's a lot different than what I eat in Louisiana. I'm about a pint low on grease. Why don't we hijack the hotel's bus and go to town for pizza and burgers?"

We all agreed and headed to the lobby. We were able to use the bus as long as their driver came along. He drove us to his favorite bar and grill. We had burgers, drank beer, and played pool. We decided we would stay at the bar instead of going back for our evening "buzz" session. We finally got back to the hotel at about 2 a.m.

We weren't in good shape the next morning. I expected the instructor to chew us out. Instead, he just laughed at our escapades. He said that every class eventually rebelled and that it's good to unwind and let off steam. Compared to others, our rebellion was relatively tame. One class used the hotel's firehoses to stage a water fight. Another locked the instructors in their rooms by tying a rope to their doorknobs and stringing it across the hall to the doorknobs of the opposite rooms. The instructor also said the rebellion was a learning experience. When a group is under a lot of stress, it's good to find a way for them to let off steam, but in a reasonable fashion.

Playing games with the big boys can be tricky

Toward the end of our three weeks of training, we had one final game. That class was divided into five-man teams and we had a two-day contest to see which team could better manage a division of a company. Since Costanza was something of a loose cannon, he was not assigned to any team but acted as the company CEO. Each team's division had several facilities that manufactured Autolites. To add to the confusion, we were never told what Autolites were. Each team met in its own small conference room where it planned its strategy.

Our first act was to elect a division president, operations manager, sales manager, financial manager, and a manager of capital and construction. I was elected president of our team. I think the group just wanted to watch me squirm. What the hell did I know about managing a division? I felt lost since I didn't have a very good idea what each manager should do. Plus, I felt uneasy bossing older, more experienced people. When we needed to make a decision, they sat looking at me waiting for my verdict. I just looked back.

The two days were divided up into two-hour periods. Each period represented one quarter of a year. During a period, we determined how many Autolites to produce, where to sell them, how much we would charge, and whether to build any new factories or expand existing ones. At the end of the two-hour period, we submitted our quarterly business plan. The information from each of the teams was fed into a computer to determine what happened. We then received a summary listing how many units we had sold, the average price, the cost of production, and other related information. Unfortunately, this information arrived when we were almost halfway through the next quarter.

On the first day, the simulation went from 8:00 a.m. in the morning until 10:00 p.m. at night. In the afternoon of the second day, the competition ended. We then provided a presentation to the board of directors showing our division's performance. We busily prepared flipcharts showing how our sales volume, average selling price, revenue, profit, and cash flow had improved during the game.

Since Costanza was the CEO, we made our presentations to him in the "Board Room." As expected, he was difficult to appease. He asked pointed questions about why we had done certain things. As the division president, I had to answer his questions and try to explain our screw-ups. Despite my incompetence, our team came in second.

The best circus performance occurred during the first presentation. That team had overextended themselves by building new plants and had gone bankrupt. Their president, Gene, tried to put a positive spin on the disaster.

Gene started out, "After some initial setbacks we were able to regroup and..."

Costanza interrupted. "Cut the bullshit. The corporation gave you $2 billion to start your division. How much money have you made for us?"

"As I was saying, after an initial setback we reorganized our efforts and ..."

"I said cut the bullshit. I'll make it easy. What is your net worth right now?"

After some consultation, Gene said, "Our net worth is $400 million."

"You started with $2 billion and now only have $400 million. What the hell are you doing in this room? A bankrupt division is an embarrassment. You dumbasses aren't fit to attend the board meeting. Get the hell out of here."

"Get out?"

"Yes. Get out. I want you and your team to stand in the hall and ponder your stupidity while these competent managers make their presentations."

With that, Gene's team was exiled to the hall in shame.

At the end of the three weeks, I was glad that the seminar was finally over. It was a long time to be away from home and the long days in class limited communication with the outside world. I was anxious to get back and find out what had happened at home and at work in my absence. On the other hand, I had learned a lot during the seminar. It had broadened my knowledge of how corporations functioned and how to deal with tough and complex situations.

Sometimes even dumbasses learn something

My first test of whether I really learned anything occurred a few months later. I was surprised when I was promoted to general superintendent and the group I looked after expanded from 12 to 90 people. All the people related to production, maintenance, technical service, and research reported to me. The heads of the departments were much older than I was. Fortunately, I remembered my experiences at the Burgin mine.

While working at the Burgin, I was exposed to several bosses that followed the Theory X philosophy and I knew how miserable it was to work for them. My experience made me want to be a Theory Y manager which was reinforced during the seminar. I had learned that seeking advice didn't mean you were a weak boss. In some ways, you had to be more confident in yourself to use this style. If Theory Y was used, the boss benefited from others' experience. And at 28 years old I definitely needed all the help I could get. In the end, I would be held accountable for the decisions I made so I might as well get all the help I could. It didn't take long before I was put to the test.

Just after my promotion I was walking from the lab building to the parts warehouse when the maintenance superintendent, Wayne, confronted me. He was twenty years older than me and had spent his whole career in maintenance.

"Well, hotshot, I understand you're my new boss," Wayne said. "I've been waiting for you to come by and tell me what to do."

"What do you mean, Wayne?"

"Since you were promoted over me, it must mean you know more about maintenance than I do. So, I've been waiting for you to take charge and tell me how to run the department."

"Hell, Wayne, who are you trying to kid? You know a lot more about maintenance than I do. That's why you're running the department. I'll be asking you questions about what we should do. My job is to make sure you have the resources you need to get the job done and to stay out of your way."

Wayne appeared startled. Then he said, "Clark, I've never had a boss tell me that. I really appreciate your approach. You can count on me."

I took the same approach with the rest of my team and it worked well. I received their input on problems and discussed with them what was the best way to proceed. And they felt free to point out problems if they thought I was making a bad decision. I genuinely appreciated their help. We worked together as a team and felt free to talk about anything. All of this helped us avoid bad decisions as we figured out the best way forward.

One day, Wayne came to my office and told me we needed to fire Bruce, one of the heavy equipment mechanics. This was surprising since Bruce had previously been a model employee. However, during the last six months he had made several costly mistakes. In one episode, he had forgotten to put oil in the engine of the D-9 dozer after an overhaul. When the engine was started, it froze up, causing nearly $10,000 damage. On another occasion he put his hand on the manifold of a hot diesel engine and was severely burned, even though he had watched the operator shut it down twenty seconds earlier.

Remembering the morning quiz that Costanza flunked, I said, "Wayne, this is out of character for Bruce. Let's see if we can figure out what is going on."

"What do you suggest?"

"If he will agree, let's send Bruce up to the hospital in Salt Lake City for a complete physical. If he is on drugs or has some other problem, we'll find out. Then we can decide what to do."

"I think we're wasting our time, but if you want to do it I'll let him know."

A few weeks later, Wayne was back in my office. "I just heard from Bruce and you were right," he said. "It turns out our errant mechanic has a brain tumor. Apparently, it was causing him to have memory lapses and he'd forget where he was in repairing the equipment. He will undergo surgery to remove the tumor in a few weeks. He will likely be off work for four months but should be as good as new when he returns."

"I'm glad we didn't fire him," I said. "I would have felt terrible when I found out he had a tumor but didn't have any health insurance."

"I feel the same way," Wayne said.

Apparently, Costanza had taught me something after all. I needed to be sure to not do what he would have done.

CHAPTER 19

Disaster Strikes

Just when you feel comfortable, the world tips upside down

I enjoyed being general superintendent at Moab. It gave me the chance to deal with all kinds of production and maintenance problems, plus I still got to look after research. Based on my experience at the Burgin Mine, I didn't want to micromanage everything. Generally, I tried to step back and let my staff deal with things, but if they ran into a particularly difficult problem, I was happy to wade in. Along the way, I learned a lot about day-to-day operations as well as how to develop long-term plans and budgets. By implementing ideas such as how to eliminate the crystallizer, increase efficiency of the product dryer, and improve tailings treatment, Moab was running well and our profits kept increasing. I found it challenging but enjoyed the challenge. I also hoped the experience would improve my chances for becoming general manager when Rudy retired in a few years. I still had a lot to learn but had come a long way in the nearly eight years since college.

As often occurs when you get comfortable with your job, the unexpected happens. My wife answered the phone. It was February 11, 1981, and I was sitting in front of the TV playing Space Invaders. I was surprised when she told me Rudy Higgins was calling. This couldn't be good. He'd only call this late at night if there was a serious problem at the plant.

"Hi, Rudy," I said. "What's up?"

"I just got some terrible news," Rudy said in a shaky voice. "Dick Mollison called to let me know that the corporate jet crashed." Dick was the Vice Chairman of Texasgulf. "Dick said that the chairman, along with several of the senior executives, were on board. It doesn't look like there are any survivors. I will let you know if I hear anything else." We talked for a few more minutes then hung up the phone in case someone called with more information.

I was stunned. I couldn't imagine what the company would be like without the chairman, Dr. Fogarty. He had been instrumental in the company's growth and expansion and had established the company culture. It was comforting to have a CEO who knew our names and was interested in us and our families. The company would be a different place without him.

That night as I watched the evening news it was dominated by the plane crash. Although they didn't have much information about what had happened, they did have pictures of the burning wreckage in a cluster of trees. It made me feel queasy.

Over the next few days, information trickled in and I started to realize the magnitude of the disaster. The accident devastated Texasgulf's senior management team. In addition to losing the CEO, we also lost the treasurer, the VP of Chemicals, and the VP of Research and Engineering. These were people I worked with and considered friends.

Their day started out with a ride on the corporate jet from White Plains, New York, to Toronto, Canada, for a meeting. During the flight to Toronto, the pilots had problems with a generator and lost electric power a couple of times. Although the plane's engines kept running, the pilots had to reset the circuit breakers before they could get the instruments back online. This was a nuisance but didn't create a serious problem while flying at high altitude on a sunny day.

In Toronto, the pilots figured out how to fix the generator while the executives were in the meeting. That evening they decided the risk was minimal since they knew the plane would continue to fly if the generator acted up, and so they headed back to New York. By the time the plane reached White Plains, it was dark and overcast. The clouds extended all the way to the ground. Then, as the plane was on final approach, the electrical system failed again. This distracted the pilots at a critical time. Flying in the fog without the instruments, they didn't realize they were continuing to descend. Suddenly, the plane slammed into the trees instantly killing everyone on board.

The victims' families were completely shocked by the accident. None more so than Al Woodling's wife. Al Woodling, an accountant for Texasgulf, had been in Toronto for an audit. He finished his work early and thought it fortuitous that the corporate jet happened to be there. They offered him a ride to New York so he could get him home early. He didn't call his eight-month pregnant wife since he wanted to surprise her.

Al's wife was sick with dread when she heard about the crash. None of her attempts to reach her husband were successful. She feared the worst but hoped he was just traveling back home on a commercial flight and couldn't be reached. It wasn't until a couple of days later that the investigators found an extra body in the wreckage. It was Al. By this time, the stress had caused his wife to go into labor prematurely. Both baby and mother were okay, but their lives changed drastically due to the plane crash. The men on board that plane were not just corporate executives, but fathers, husbands, brothers, sons, and friends.

My grief was pale compared to what Al's wife was going through. I could not imagine the loss of a spouse like that. But, I was still upset. One of the pilots, Shan Sorenson, was a friend of mine. He had grown up in Utah only eight miles from my hometown. I felt sad and depressed thinking about what had happened to him. And I knew the company would be a different place without Dr. Fogarty. He had provided excellent leadership and had moved the company forward while taking care of the employees.

As the days went by, it became apparent that losing the CEO and several senior members of his team was creating a lot of problems. People were being promoted to positions they weren't ready for. And, it had a trickle-down effect. When one person was promoted, someone then had to fill his old job. The corporate office was distracted as they tried to fill positions and reorganize the office. As a result they weren't getting much of their normal work done. In the meantime, those of us at the plants were just trying to keep everything running.

As things finally started to settle down in late June, I found out there was another problem headed out way. It started when my secretary, Marge, walked into my office.

"There is a gentleman here that insists on seeing Rudy Higgins," she said.

I looked up from my desk. "Tell him Rudy isn't here. He is up in Salt Lake on vacation."

"I explained that, but he insists on seeing whoever is in charge. I think you'd better come talk to him."

I reluctantly got up and walked to the lobby. There, I was surprised to find a gentleman in a suit carrying a briefcase. Most visitors were dressed casually in Levi's and a golf shirt. I introduced myself and asked him how I could help.

"I need to speak to the person in charge."

"Rudy Higgins isn't here. I'm the general superintendent. Rudy left me in charge."

"Do you have any paperwork showing you are in charge?"

"I do. I'll have the secretary get a copy for you. What is this about?" Based on the conversation, the receptionist hurried down the hall to talk to Marge.

"I can't tell you what this is about. All I can tell you is that I am here to serve papers on you."

This alarmed me. I wondered what we had done.

About this time, Marge showed up with a copy of the notice stating that I was in charge during Rudy's absence. The gentleman took the copy of the notice, had me sign a paper saying I received the documents, and then handed me a 3-inch-high stack of papers.

"What am I supposed to do with this?" I asked.

"I can't tell you," he said. "But I would suggest you contact your legal department."

With that he walked out the door.

I took the papers to my office and quickly browsed through them. They didn't seem to make much sense. It appeared that they were protesting a Utah law making it illegal for a foreign company to own natural resources in the state. Since Texasgulf wasn't a foreign company, why would someone file a lawsuit? I tried to call the lawyers in the corporate office but couldn't get through. Their secretary said they were dealing with an emergency and would call back later in the day. She asked me to forward the documents to them by overnight mail. I caught up with Rudy and let him know what had happened, but he was as perplexed as I was. I waited around the office the rest of the day hoping our lawyers would call. They didn't.

It was the afternoon of the next day before I finally got a call. It turned out that a French Company, Societe Nationale Elf Aquitaine, had launched a hostile takeover of Texasgulf. Elf was in the process of buying all the shares of the company. Although the price of the stock had been around $47 per share, Elf was offering $56 per share. Unfortunately, the stockholders couldn't resist an almost 20 percent return on their money. We were crumbling as a company.

After the takeover was complete in late July, the company was restructured. Texasgulf's highly profitable Canadian holdings were sold off to generate cash to pay for the stock. Elf was primarily interested in Texasgulf's Oil and Gas division. Owning this would give them a foothold in the lucrative oil and gas business in the Gulf of Mexico. Thus, Texasgulf's Oil and Gas Division now reported directly to Elf in Paris. The other U.S. mining operations that produced potash, phosphate, soda ash, and sulfur were just a nuisance to them. Elf had almost no experience with these businesses and so was not particularly interested in them. The result of all this was that Texasgulf now had half as many people, was not nearly as diversified, and only had limited funding for exploration to find new ore bodies or develop new mines. On a long-term basis, we were doomed.

It was clear that 1981 was not going to be a fun year.

Waging war with the wrong person. Again.

Initially, Elf didn't mess much with Texasgulf. They were too pre-occupied with expanding the oil and gas production in the Gulf of Mexico. But, after a two-year "getting to know you" period, Elf made the decision in 1983 to restructure the company. As a part of this, the Business Evaluation and Research department, BER, was formed. The group was to work with the various plants to develop a long-term capital spending plan. This was to help assure that capital was spent on projects that provided the most value to the corporation. Without this external overview, the plants tended to spend money on problems that were a local headache and usually didn't consider projects that improved long-term profitability. A Texan, David Crockett Edmiston, was named to head up the group. I was first astounded and then appalled by this. Edmiston and I had a long-running feud.

In the mid-1970s, Dave was the president of the Chemicals Division of Texasgulf which included the Moab facility as well as the Aurora, North Carolina, phosphate complex. Although Dave was smart, in this position he was a major pain in the ass. Authorizations For Expenditures, AFEs, for Moab's larger capital projects had required his signature. However, he would return the AFEs unsigned for arbitrary, non-technical reasons. Sometimes, they were returned because they had been filled out using the wrong type font. Others were returned because he could see that the secretary had used correction fluid to "Wite-Out" a mistake and then typed over it. It was a major offense if we used an incorrect word or misspelled it.

I was not the only person who had problems with him. Since no Texasgulf facility ever had a union, Dave would implement any work rule he chose. He constantly infuriated the employees at the plants. It became bad enough that the employees of the Aurora facility threatened to unionize. The final straw came in 1978. The story I heard while in Moab was that the Aurora residents had voiced concerns about the impact of mining on the quality and availability of their well water. Dave reportedly got up in one of the meetings and told the residents that Texasgulf owned the rights to the ore under their homes and that they had better shut up or he'd have the draglines go right through town. The local newspapers had a field day.

In Texasgulf, if you really screwed up but knew where the skeletons were buried, you were not fired. Instead, you were transferred to special projects and assigned to the regional office in Golden, Colorado. Normally, once you were at the "Leper's Colony" your career was over. Somehow, Dave was receiving a reprieve.

I expressed my concerns about Dave to Rudy Higgins. He suggested we bring it up with the company president, Tom Wright, during the production and marketing meeting to be held in Moab in July. Since it was a couple of weeks away, I would have time to figure out how to best summarize my concerns.

During the first day of the meeting, Rudy asked Tom if we could talk with him about the plan to have Dave head up the new BER group. Tom said that he wanted to talk to us too and suggested he hitch a ride back to the hotel with us and we could discuss our concerns on the way.

As Rudy drove the car to town, he asked me to tell Tom about our fears.

"Tom," I said, "I think it's a serious mistake to promote Dave Edmiston. I know you remember all the problems Dave created in the 1970s at Aurora. He was a major frustration to all of us." I then spent the next few minutes outlining the fiasco with AFEs and other problems. "Based on all this, I can't believe that Dave will once again be given control over the capital spending program."

Tom sat motionless in the car for several seconds as if in deep thought. Finally, Tom said, "It is interesting you brought this up. That is exactly what I wanted to talk to you about. You have done a good job explaining why I need someone to act as a buffer between Dave and the plants. In the case of potash, that person is you."

I was dumbfounded. I couldn't believe he wanted me to go to work for Dave after I had just explained what a pain in the ass he was.

Tom continued. "You will be a manager of the BER group and can look after Moab's interests while investigating ways of expanding potash production at Moab or by acquiring other potash resources. You will also get to relocate to the Raleigh, North Carolina, office."

I was speechless. Going to work for Dave would assure I had a miserable, contentious existence. In addition, moving any further east than Denver was not appealing to me. Riding dirt bikes, hiking, hunting, and fishing were my primary leisure activities. I was flabbergasted.

"Tom, I don't think you can pay me enough to get me to move to Raleigh to work for Dave."

"Well, don't make a hasty decision. I'll send you a formal offer in a few days for your consideration. Besides, if you take the job I will owe you a favor."

A few days after the meeting, I received the offer. It turned out that I could be bought. I thought I was receiving a big pay raise but found out later that they had lowballed me. They expected that I would want to negotiate for more money and were surprised when I took their first offer. Apparently, I hadn't learned anything from my hiring experience in 1973. As it turned out, it would be a few more years before I got it right.

I reported to work at my new job in August of 1983 and the family moved to North Carolina in October. I was not particularly enthusiastic when I started. I had gone from supervising 90 people to looking after a secretary, but at least I would still be involved with Moab and could try to help the people there. And hopefully I could figure out how to expand potash production at Moab and abroad. My intention was to return to Moab in a few years as the plant manager. And since Tom owed me a favor, maybe it would happen sooner rather than later.

CHAPTER 20

Doing Time in Raleigh

Sometimes you're right and you still pay the consequences

I was very apprehensive my first day in the Raleigh office. Although my prior feud with my new boss, Dave, occurred years ago he might still remember it. On top of this, I worried that the company president might have told Dave about the derogatory remarks I'd made during the car ride back to Moab. If he had, I was dead meat.

My new office was located near downtown Raleigh, North Carolina. Texasgulf occupied all three floors of a large, red brick building and on my first day, the office manager took me on a tour. The first floor contained the computer center and a cafeteria which was a significant perk since we were provided an excellent free lunch. The second floor contained the offices for transportation, sales, and the lawyers. The third floor housed accounting, the executive offices for the president and senior VPs along with my department, the business evaluation and research group, isolated in a corner.

Although my office was on the top floor, it was not in the best location. It overlooked the dumpsters at the back of the parking lot. I was disappointed. At Moab I'd been second in command and had a large, well-furnished office in the executive suite. In Raleigh,

I was just a peon with a small plain office. However, I did get to keep my company car.

The fifteen people of the BER group handled market research, customer complaints, and looked after capital spending and long-term planning for phosphate, soda ash, and my specialty, potash. I was to review potash's capital spending and also explore ways to expand potash production at Moab and worldwide.

My apprehension about Dave was soon relieved when he came by my office and welcomed me to the group. Either Dave was good at hiding his feelings or Tom hadn't told him what I'd said. Maybe things wouldn't be so bad after all. Yet as I settled into my new job, I got to know all the people I worked with except for Dave.

Davy Crockett Edmiston was from Texas and as proud of it as you'd expect with a name like that. He started with the company years earlier at a sulfur facility in the Lone Star State. Dave was very aloof, kind of like a sleeping volcano. You didn't know what he was thinking until he erupted. If someone said hello to him in the hallway, he didn't answer. When Dave ate lunch in the cafeteria, he sat alone. If you sat down next to him and tried to strike up a conversation, he just ignored you. He only spoke to me to give me assignments or to give me hell about something I'd done.

One of my initial projects was a continuation of one started while I was still in Moab in 1982. For some reason, one of the few exploration projects our new owner, Elf, was willing to consider was potash. A Texasgulf geologist, Gonzalo Tufino, thought he'd found a potash deposit in Argentina. A large oil field was being developed in the southwest part of that country with the oil located beneath a thick bed of salt 3,000 feet below the surface. Gonzalo reviewed some of the logs the oil company made while drilling the wells and based on this data, he believed he'd found evidence of a potash bed. He convinced Texasgulf to let him drill a few exploration holes. Unfortunately, he had no experience with drilling. That's where I came in.

Disrupting my job to work on someone else's project annoyed me. I had plenty to do at Moab and the exploration project appeared to be a lost cause. Potash is a bulk commodity. In order to make money, you need to sell millions of tons of product

annually. Unfortunately, Gonzalo's potential deposit was located
in the middle of nowhere. The location would not only make it
very expensive to build a large potash facility, but it would make
it necessary to build a 360-mile-long railroad to transport the
product. Even if we found the best possible potash deposit, there
was no way it would make economic sense. Why should I waste
my time on a wild goose chase?

I decided to give Ken Kutz, the vice president in charge of explo-
ration a call. I was nervous discussing this with a senior executive
I hardly knew. Ken listened politely to my concerns and then said,
"My job is to make these kinds of executive decisions. That's why
they pay me the big bucks. Your job is to carry out my decisions.
Now, get to work."

Damn.

I had the impression that my impertinence had really pissed Ken
off. But, despite my lack of enthusiasm, I was to provide technical
assistance *as required*. So I provided Gonzalo with an equipment
list and general instructions for drilling a core hole. I figured the
drilling contractor would know all about coring. I went back to
work on running Moab, but I monitored the drilling program just
in case. I became worried in mid-December when Gonzalo had
been drilling for ninety days and they still weren't close to being
done. That's when I received a phone call from the VP of Exploration, Mister Big Bucks.

"Clark, we need your help at the drill site," Ken said. "The
drilling rate is terrible and they can't figure out how to speed it
up."

I was not excited. "They've been working on this project
for almost three months," I said. "I'd like to celebrate my tenth
wedding anniversary and Christmas in Moab. Delaying my trip a
couple of weeks shouldn't make much difference."

"Unfortunately, the drilling program is really screwed up. We
need your help now. You may recall you are to provide technical
assistance *as required*," he said. "Well, that assistance is required
immediately. We'll make sure you get back home by Christmas
Day."

I was not happy. But then neither was Ken. He seemed even

madder than he had been after our first conversation. In any case, I packed my bags and prepared for the trip. It started with me driving from Moab to Grand Junction followed by flights through Denver, Miami, and Rio de Janeiro to arrive 28 hours later in Buenos Aires. There, I was met by Gonzalo. He'd grown up in Bolivia and was fluent in both Spanish and English. We soon became good friends. He escorted me from the international airport to a Sheraton so I could catch up on my sleep. The next morning, we caught a plane at the domestic airport and flew to Neuquen, and then on to Rincon del Los Sauces in an old four-seat, single engine Cessna. From Rincon, we drove a couple of hours, arriving at the drill site 60 hours after I left Moab. Since I was now in the southern hemisphere, I had gone from the dead of winter to the middle of a hot summer. It took a few days for my body to adjust to the 105-degree heat.

PRC-1 exploration hole being drilled in Argentina

The drill site was located in a desert on the back side of the Andes Mountains. The tall tower of the rig was surrounded by a cluster of water and fuel tanks plus metal racks for storing drill pipes and supplies. House trailers were located on one side of the drill site. Electric power was supplied by a nearby diesel generator. Unfortunately, the trailer where Gonzalo and I stayed was near the generator so we got to listen to it rumble all night. Restroom facilities were provided by a nearby ravine that was deep enough so the workers on the drill rig couldn't see us as we conducted our business.

After settling in, I started to evaluate the drilling problems. The drill rig and surface equipment were marginally adequate but the down hole equipment wasn't. They were just using a drill pipe and a drill bit. Because of this, the hole's direction deviated wildly and there wasn't enough weight on the drill bit for it to penetrate the rock. At a minimum, they needed a three-point and a six-point reamer plus nine drill collars. The reamers would keep the hole going straight. The drill collars were basically heavy duty pieces of drill pipe with 4-inch-thick walls that added the weight needed to push the drill bit through the rock faster. At Moab, we'd call in the order for the drill equipment and a "hot shot" service would deliver it within eight hours. In Argentina, we used their shortwave radio to place the order and were told to expect delivery in thirty days. I couldn't believe it. Thirty days!!

My South American vacation was going to hell.

Although the original agreement was that I could now head home, they "asked" me to stay and optimize their drilling as best I could while waiting for the reamers and drill collars. They would ensure I'd be home by New Year's Day. But when there were more delays in supplies, they asked me to stay until mid-January and then to the end of January. My five-day adventure ended up taking fifty-four days to complete. I finally got home on February 12. So, instead of getting home by Christmas Day as promised, I arrived just before Valentine's Day. And I wasn't much of a Valentine. Betty came to Grand Junction to pick me up. Unfortunately, I hadn't had a chance to bathe for almost a week. We drove back to Moab with the windows down and heater on high to enjoy the "fresh" winter air.

Maybe I wasn't the most naïve traveler!

As I got back to work at my old job, I fervently hoped this was my last trip to Argentina. It wasn't. Only six months later, after joining the BER group in Raleigh, Dave told me I needed to set up a lab in Argentina. He explained that the four exploration wells drilled so far had found that the salt deposit did contain potash. Unfortunately, the potash beds appeared to have large waves like those at Moab which meant they would be difficult to mine. To better evaluate this, they wanted to drill twenty more wells in the hope of finding a place in the deposit where the beds were flat. Once again, I tried to convince them that this was a lost cause. And once again I failed.

Dave explained that they needed a lab in Argentina so they could quickly analyze the core samples. Core samples were columns of rock taken from the geologic formation of interest. They are recovered by using a drill bit shaped like a donut with industrial diamonds embedded in its surface. As the bit drills down, a 4-inch diameter column of rock moves up into the core barrel. After drilling for 20 or 30 feet, the core is retrieved and the process repeated until samples of the entire zone of interest are recovered. Evaluating cores from the first four holes had been very slow because the columns of rock had to be shipped by boat to the U.S. for analysis. Gonzalo chose the small town of Chos Malal for the new lab since it was near the drill rig.

With some apprehension, I decided to have my old prankster from Moab, Reuben, set up the lab and then train locals to do the analytical work. Reuben was a good analyst but prone to getting into mischief unless closely supervised. Ralph Chamness, a geologist from Aurora, would be responsible for examining the cores and measuring the angle of the beds. Arrangements were made for the team to make a week-long trip to Argentina to round up equipment and supplies and find a suitable building for the lab.

Chos Malal was situated in the rain shadow of the Andes Mountains about 680 miles southwest of Buenos Aires. Basically, it was in the middle of nowhere. This was a desert region with very little vegetation. The travel plan was for Reuben and Ralph to meet

up with me in Miami for the flight to Buenos Aires. I suspected
Reuben hadn't traveled much and so I called him to provide a few
tips. It turned out I didn't provide enough. Arriving in Miami, I met
Reuben and Ralph at the gate for the flight to Buenos Aires. We
boarded the plane and settled in for the long flight. Upon arrival
in Buenos Aires, we went down to baggage claim. Ralph and I
claimed our bags, but Reuben's wasn't there. We headed to the
ticket counter where they confirmed his bag was not on the plane.
He filed a claim and was told his bag might be on the flight arriving
the next day. If not, maybe the one after that.

After Reuben grumbled a few nasty remarks at the ticket
counter, we caught a taxi for the ride downtown to the Sheraton.
As I finished checking in, I heard Reuben in a heated discussion
with the desk clerk at the end of the counter.

"Now what's going on, Reuben?"

"The damn clerk wants a credit card."

"Well, give her one."

"I don't have a credit card. I deal strictly in cash."

I was stunned. How could you travel without a credit card?
"You've got to be kidding me," I said. "How much cash did you
bring?"

"Two hundred dollars."

"Two hundred dollars! For a week in Argentina!!"

"Yeah, when me and the old lady go on a week-long vacation
in the camp trailer, we never need more than two hundred dollars."

Needless to say, I should have given Reuben more detailed
information about international travel. I ended up charging
all Reuben's expenses to my credit card. This included his new
wardrobe while he waited to get his bag. It took me a couple of
days back at the office to get our expenses sorted out.

After a week in Argentina, we'd found a good location for the
lab and made arrangements for the lab equipment and reagents.
We flew back to Buenos Aires and arrived at the international
airport to check in. Much to our surprise, Reuben was told his
suitcase was arriving on the next flight from Miami. Maybe he'd
finally caught a break. We hustled down to baggage claim, found
the correct carousel and waited for his suitcase. After a while,

Reuben noticed a sad, beat-up looking suitcase coming around the carousel. It was tattered and the latch had sprung. A pair of nylons was wrapped around the suitcase to hold it shut.

"Look at that sorry piece of shit," Reuben said. "I can't believe anyone would travel with that thing."

"I can't believe anyone would be seen with that thing," I said.

A few seconds later Reuben said, "Wait a second. That's my suitcase."

Reuben grabbed it off the carousel and inspected it. Surprisingly, he still had everything. I asked him about the nylons, but he swore they weren't his. Apparently, the suitcase had sprung open and someone had tied it shut with the pantyhose. He took the suitcase upstairs and rechecked it for the trip home. The airline replaced the nylons with a belt for no additional charge.

Using the groundwork laid by our trip to Argentina, we were soon able to establish a laboratory in Chos Malal. Ralph was responsible for logging in and describing the cores while Reuben's job was to split and analyze the cores to determine the amount of potash and impurities present. Since they soon had everything under control, Dave said I was free to move on to other projects. Thus far, moving to the BER group in Raleigh hadn't been much fun. It had to get better.

Whining about the cold didn't give me the result I'd hoped for

While Reuben and Ralph were at work, I started considering options for Moab. One possibility was to mine a deeper potash bed that was 900 feet below the old mine workings. To get more information on mining potash beds under old mine workings, I decided in late January of 1985 to visit the Allan potash mine located about 60 miles southeast of Saskatoon, Saskatchewan. I knew the people there and Allan was currently mining under their old mine workings and could tell me what to watch out for.

Arriving in February proved to be problematic. My previous trips to Allan had been in the summer or fall. I wasn't prepared for a Canadian winter. I started to shiver on the short walk from the terminal to my rental car. Checking the temperature, I was startled to see it was 32 degrees Fahrenheit below zero. Fortunately, when I got to the car it was idling and warm. I threw my bags in the back seat and headed down the highway. Even with the heater set at maximum, ice was forming on the inside of the windshield. In order to see where I was going, I had to scrape off the frost every ten or fifteen minutes. The drifted snow across the highway added to my concerns.

I spent the day at Allan with my friend, Mike Hawyrluk, touring the mine and discussing rock mechanics. In the late afternoon, I climbed in the rental car to head back to town. The car wouldn't start. Darn. I trudged back in the office to complain about Hertz and get some help.

Mike followed me back out. When we reached the car he said, "You didn't plug the car in."

I was confused by his comment. "The car's not electric," I said.

"No, you dumbass. You have to plug in the block heater or the car won't start."

Mike had me open the trunk and then showed me a short extension cord that was stored there.

"Anywhere you park up here in the winter will have an electrical outlet," Mike said. "Otherwise, if your car sits here for more than 15 minutes you're screwed."

Something else I needed to remember.

I climbed in the car and headed back to Saskatoon scraping frost off the inside of the windshield as I went. I checked in the hotel and was just starting to rest when the phone rang. I answered it and it was company president, Tom Wright.

"I just received a call from the Vice President of Exploration," Tom said. "He needs you in Argentina to straighten out a serious problem."

I was not happy about the thought of going back to Argentina.

"You've got to be kidding me," I said. "Gonzalo is supposed to be running the show. Did he say what the hell was going on?"

"All he said was that they were having problems with Reuben and Ralph. He needs you down there immediately to straighten it out."

"Immediately, like sometime next week?"

"Immediately, like tomorrow," Tom said.

Son-of-a bitch.

"Okay. I'll make arrangements. But this'd better be important."

So I flew from Canada to North Carolina, spent one night in my own bed, and then headed for Argentina the next morning. After flying through the night, I finally arrived in Chos Malal. I was shocked by the 112-degree temperature as I got off the plane. A big change from Saskatoon. As my body warmed up, it felt like I had the flu. It apparently needed a little time to adapt to such a wide temperature swing.

Gonzalo met me at the terminal and told me about his problems with Ralph and Reuben. Ralph was supposed to provide a geologic description of the cores where he noted the thickness and angle of each bed. But he also felt compelled to note that the data indicated that the potash bed was distorted and folded. Gonzalo was not happy about this. He had hoped to find a flat place in the deposit which could be easily mined. If he did, his prestige in the company and with other geologists would increase dramatically. If the potash was distorted, no one would have much interest. Ralph, on the other hand, wanted to make sure that nothing he said would come back to haunt him. His evaluation showed that the deposit was deformed and undulating.

For Reuben's part, he was finding that the potash bed was contaminated with magnesium. This would also lessen the value of the deposit since it would make it much harder to process the potash. Unfortunately, both Ralph and Reuben were expressing their opinions to others in the company and to colleagues on the outside.

Since Gonzalo was the project leader, he and his boss, Ken Kutz, felt they should be the ones interpreting the data and filling management in. That is why I had to make the trip, to rein in Ralph and Reuben.

When I arrived at the lab, I caught up with Ralph and Reuben and told them I needed to have a private meeting with them.

"Ralph, what's going on with you and Gonzalo?"

Ralph was obviously upset and got right to the point. "The deposit isn't flat," he said. "And Gonzalo doesn't want to hear it."

Shit. These guys had a lot to learn. Things that took me a while to learn, too, unfortunately. "Listen," I said, "I'm not asking you to lie. But your job is to record the objective facts."

Ralph stared at me quizzically.

"If you measure a bedding angle in the core to be 20 degrees," I explained, "report it. If someone questions it, they can get the core out and make their own measurement. Just report it. That way you haven't lied and you can feel comfortable putting your name on the report."

I could see that he was starting to understand.

"Let Gonzalo do the extrapolating," I added. "If he wants to say the deposit is flat, it's his ass on the line not yours. Are you okay with that?"

"Yeah. I'm okay with that."

With that matter settled, I turned to Reuben.

"And what's going on with you?" I asked.

"The potash samples have significant magnesium in them," he said. "When I start telling people that the deposit is useless because of the magnesium, Gonzalo gets upset."

"Your job," I said, "is to provide the chemical analysis of the core. As with Ralph, if someone questions your results they can get a core sample and analyze it themselves. But it's not your job to interpret the results and broadcast the information back home. Just do your job. It's Gonzalo's responsibility to let people know the results of the test work."

They both assured me that they would stick to their jobs and try to get along with Gonzalo. At the end of the discussion, I went to bed. My flu like symptoms were worse. I hoped it was just the wild temperature swing combined with the long flight and stress of dealing with a personnel problem. Fortunately, the next morning I did feel better and started on my trip back home. I was pissed off that I'd been forced to make an "emergency" trip for a 15-minute conversation I could have handled over the phone from Saskatoon.

Despite my misgivings, I continued to help with the Argentine potash project for several more months. Then I gradually quit receiving phone calls. I had plenty of other things that needed my attention. Finally, in June of 1986, I was surprised to get a call from Gonzalo. He told me the VP of Exploration, Ken, asked him to let me know that they were pulling the plug on the Argentine project. Even though they had proven the existence of a large potash deposit, it was clear that it would not be developed. Gonzalo said that due to the remote location there was no way a new facility could be economically viable. Thus, the project was being shut down.

I was totally pissed off. Four years of aggravation could have been avoided if Ken had listened to me in 1982 before I took my Christmas vacation in Argentina. As time went on, I thought about what I could have done differently. I realized engineers in general, and me in particular, didn't always do a good job presenting ideas. When I figured out that the project couldn't succeed, I should have spent more time preparing a presentation with graphs, maps, and numbers. And it was clear that I should have provided the presentation to Ken Kutz in person. A trip to New York would have been a lot easier than the trip to Argentina. I also realized that feuding with someone in senior management wasn't very smart. I suspected that the last trip to Argentina was solely to show me it wasn't smart to make a senior executive mad. Unfortunately, I didn't learn that lesson very well.

CHAPTER 21

Trying to Buy a Sinking Ship

*Pay attention to your premonitions; they may be telling you
something important*

Dave Edmiston surprised me one morning in mid-1985 when
he walked into my office. Normally he just stood at his door
and yelled if he needed someone. Clearly something was up.

"I've got a project that needs your immediate attention," Dave
said. "As you know, several months ago PCA's Canadian potash
mines were put on the market. After extended deliberations,
we've decided to make a bid on the mines. They will provide the
expansion in potash we've been looking for. But unfortunately, we
only have thirty days to get the bid together. You need to assemble
a team and inspect the facilities as soon as possible. Because of the
time constraint you will have a company plane at your disposal."

I knew that the Potash Company of America, known as
PCA, was owned by Ideal Basic Industries and had two potash
mines in Canada. One mine was located in west-central Canada
near Saskatoon, while the other was at the eastern edge of New
Brunswick. Unfortunately, Ideal Basic had made some poor
financial decisions and was facing bankruptcy. They wanted to
sell the two Canadian potash mines as soon as possible to satisfy
creditors. It irritated me that Texasgulf management had known

about the sale for months yet didn't decide to submit a bid until the last minute.

Offsetting my irritation was the fact that I had a company plane at my disposal. I'd only ridden on a company plane a few times when I was tagging along with senior management. Clearly, this acquisition was important if they were letting me use a plane to speed up the evaluation. I'd never looked after a project that was even remotely this large before. I guessed that senior management wanted to diversify and expand the company. Combining two large potash mines with Texasgulf's existing Moab potash and Aurora phosphate facilities would make Texasgulf a force to be reckoned with in the fertilizer industry.

Over the next few days, I hurriedly made arrangements to visit the Canadian mines and production facilities. Then, I assembled a team consisting of a mining engineer, geologist, financial analyst, and me. The mining engineer, John, and financial analyst, Conrad, were easy to corral since they were part of BER group. I'd known the geologist, Dave, from when I worked at Moab. His boss readily agreed he could join the team. I would be responsible for assessing the refinery in addition to looking after the team and preparing the final report. I felt overwhelmed and nervous. I had never done this type of evaluation before which made me wonder why I was heading up the team. Although I knew a lot about potash, I knew very little about financial analysis. I felt more comfortable dealing with projects that were strictly engineering. This seemed like another opportunity to get myself fired.

Thus, I was off on a new adventure. The first step was for the team to fly from Raleigh to Saint John, New Brunswick. The adventure began when I pulled into the parking lot of Raleigh's private airport terminal. It seemed unreal to walk in and be greeted by one of the pilots. It reminded me of my trip to Moab in 1973 when I was interviewing for my first job after college. As before, the pilot took my bag and escorted me to the plane. We were airborne 15 minutes later. As the senior executive on the flight, I got to choose where I wanted to sit and what food the pilots were to provide. Four of the seats faced each other so we were able to play cards and visit during the flight. I felt like royalty.

We were met at the Saint John airport by a PCA employee who drove us to the mine. There we received a brief orientation and then divided up so we could make good use of our time. Conrad headed off to look at the books and I headed underground with Dave and John. Although I really should have spent my time in the mill, I jumped at the opportunity to learn about the methods used in a different underground mine.

The mining had started at a low point in the potash bed and they were working their way uphill using continuous miners. They also mined salt and sold it as I'd instigated at Moab. As we continued the mine tour, I realized that even if we weren't the successful bidder the trip was proving very educational. I was gaining a new insight into potash technology. But after a brief mine tour, I had to reluctantly return to the surface to do a detailed review of the mill.

After the plant visit, I huddled up with the team at our hotel for our debriefing. The processing plant was very similar to Moab's and there wasn't much risk that it wouldn't operate efficiently. The big question was the mine's anatomy. As expected, the miners were having a lot of trouble dealing with the distorted potash bed. As a result, the mine costs were high and profitability was low. Unfortunately, this sounded a lot like the problem that had driven Moab to try solution mining. Although the facility was only a few years old, it needed a large influx of capital to get rid of the bottlenecks and improve the mine. For this reason, the New Brunswick facility wasn't worth much.

We spent the night in Saint John and visited the port the next day. There was a large warehouse for storing potash waiting for shipment. The port was unusual in that the daily tides in the Bay of Fundy could be as high as 50 feet. This posed problems for the ships. If they were at the dock when the tide went out they would end up sitting in mud. To keep this from happening, the port authority had dredged out a large basin for each vessel to float in. It was kind of funny at low tide; the ships looked like large toy boats sitting in enormous bathtubs.

Next, we flew across Canada to Saskatoon, 1,829 miles away. While in flight, we played cards and discussed the upcoming mine visit. Flying on a corporate plane was certainly a different experience than flying commercially. We could do what we wanted on the plane and didn't have adjust our work schedule to meet a commercial flight's timetable. We just took as long as we needed to finish our work and knew the plane would be waiting for us when we were ready to go. I could get used to this.

The five-hour flight provided time for me to tell the team what I knew about PCA's Patience Lake mine. One of initial hurdles for mining potash in Saskatchewan was figuring how to sink a shaft through the Blairmore formation. This was a formation about 900 feet below the surface that contained loose sand and a lot of water. When the Patience Lake mine attempted to sink a shaft through this "quicksand" zone in 1958, the Blairmore quickly flooded them out. After a few years working on the problem, they finally figured out that they could use large refrigeration units to freeze the formation. They could then sink the shaft through the ice and equip it with a waterproof liner to keep the water out when they let the formation thaw. After they solved this problem, they were able to mine one of the best and flattest potash beds in the world. This meant relatively easy mining and low production costs. As we finished up our discussions, we landed in Saskatoon and headed to the hotel for a restful evening.

The next morning, we were picked up by a PCA employee and driven to the Patience Lake facility. Again, the team split up to make the best use of our time. As before, I spent a couple of hours on an underground tour and then spent most of the rest of the day looking at the refinery.

Unlike New Brunswick, this was a very profitable operation. Potash production began in 1965 and the facility quickly gained the reputation of being one of the low-cost producers of potash in the world. It was producing almost 10 times as much potash as Moab. There was, however, one thing about the mine that made me uncomfortable. There was a small water flow of about 100 gallons per minute seeping into the mine. Water going into a potash mine was never a good thing. Since potash is water-soluble, this stream could dissolve out a larger channel or undercut a critical support structure. If this happened, the water flow would increase and eventually flood the entire mine. When they explained the water flow situation to me, I felt very uneasy. However, since it had been going on at Patience Lake for 20 years and had not presented any difficulties, the logical part of my brain told me I was being overly cautious. This facility was the gem in PCA's potash portfolio and they didn't seem to be too worried about it.

After two days in Saskatoon we flew back to Raleigh. There we spent several days documenting our trip, preparing a financial analysis, and working out what we thought was a reasonable bid for the two mines. Senior Texasgulf management reviewed and adjusted the bid down to $150 million before it was submitted. A month later, Dave walked into my office.

"I've got some good news and some bad news," he said. "The good news is that we submitted the highest bid for the PCA property. The bad news is that they rejected all the bids and are asking everyone to submit new ones."

My team and I reviewed the information. We decided that we had been overly conservative and adjusted the Texasgulf bid up an additional $20 million. Even with the higher bid, we were not successful. Instead, a company named Rio Algom ended up with the two mines. I wasn't happy. I suspected this might be my last chance to expand potash production for Texasgulf. I was running out of ideas and wasn't sure what I would be doing in the future without any potash projects to work on.

Unfortunately, Rio Algom's celebration for getting the two potash mines was short-lived. A little over a year after acquiring the facilities, the Patience Lake mine began to flood. The water flow I had been nervous about had in fact gotten out of control. So, the mine that was the real moneymaker was in serious trouble. And, to make matters worse, the remaining New Brunswick mine needed an infusion of $150 million before it would be economic. If Texasgulf had been the successful bidder, I would have been in deep trouble. I heaved a sigh of relief that I had dodged that bullet. But I also decided that I should pay more attention to my premonitions.

As it turned out, my dealings with the Patience Lake mine were not over. A few months after learning about the flooding problem,

I was sitting in my office when the phone rang. To my surprise, it was a call from the mine manager of the Patience Lake facility. He remembered I'd made a presentation about Moab's solution mining system several years earlier at a Canadian Institute of Mines meeting. He asked if I would be interested in doing some consulting for them. They would pay me $10,000 for two weeks' work. Since Texasgulf had run out of options for expanding potash production, I naively assumed that the company wouldn't care if I helped the Canadians out. However, with my past track record I thought that I had better not press my luck. I gave Tom Wright a call to hear his thoughts.

"You'd better think again, you dumbass. After all the money we've spent on experiments so you could learn about solution mining, do you think we're going to let you sell your knowledge to someone else? There is no way you can do consulting on the side while you work for us. You had better give me the Patience Lake phone number so that I can make sure they understand."

I gave Tom the contact information and then called the mine manager. I told him that I couldn't do any consulting and that Tom would be calling him shortly. A few days later, Tom called me back. "We worked out a deal with Patience Lake," he said. "I told them they could use your services for a week for $25,000."

"Are they sending me the $25,000 check?"

"Hell, no. They are sending the check to Texasgulf. It will help pay for some of your stupidity."

Screwed again.

A couple of weeks later I found myself at the Patience Lake mine. When I arrived, they explained that the water flow had increased to about 55,000 gallons per minute. I was impressed. They thought that it was critical for me to immediately go underground so I could see firsthand what the water was doing. One of their geologists, Jerry Streisel, was assigned to accompany me and keep me out of trouble.

We changed into coveralls, picked up our hard hats, lamp belts, and mine lamps and headed across the yard toward the No. 1 shaft. As we were walking along we met the hoist man. Jerry told him not to go on break yet since we needed to go underground before the shaft flooded.

"You're too late," he said. "It just flooded and the station is underwater. You had better go down the No. 2 shaft."

Since the deposit had a slight slope, the bottom of the No. 2 shaft was a little higher in elevation. This meant it was still above water, at least for now. We walked over to the No. 2 shaft, climbed in the man cage, and were quickly lowered 3,200 feet down the shaft. When we arrived at the station, my anxiety increased significantly. There was a large concrete bulkhead blocking the entryway to the main mine workings. A 36-inch steel pipe stuck out of the bulkhead with a large valve attached to the end of it. I could see that the valve was closed.

"What's the valve and bulkhead for?" I asked.

"We installed a 40-foot-thick concrete bulkhead to protect the shaft from the water. The high-pressure gate valve allows us to continue to access the mine until the water reaches this level. Then we will close the valve to keep the water out of the shaft."

"You mean we need to crawl through that pipe to get into the mine?"

"You got it. We will need to open the valve to get in and then close it when we're done with our tour."

I was getting nervous. What if someone happened to come by and not knowing we were in the mine, closed the valve?

We opened the valve, crawled through the pipe, and stood up on the other side of the bulkhead. To our right, I could see the water flowing up and around a pillar and then running down an entry into a low area. Since the potash and salt in the mine were water soluble, the water was dissolving the pillars which supported the mine roof. Periodically, a large section of the roof would collapse, causing large waves in the underground lake.

I asked, "Are there any more shafts into the mine?"

"This is it. If the water comes up and submerges the pipe, we're in big trouble."

What in the hell had I gotten myself into? If Texasgulf wasn't going to share the consulting money, maybe I could at least get hazardous duty pay. "Let's make this a quick tour," I said.

We climbed into a battery-powered cart and headed out parallel to the edge of the lake. I noticed that the air seemed stale which, when I thought about it, made sense because there was no longer any way to ventilate the mine. In places, mice and rats could be seen scurrying around. Generally, it was like we were riding along the edge of a lake. But in other places we could see water flowing around a pillar of potash or notice large waves when something collapsed into the lake. I made a few notes and then we headed back. I heaved a sigh of relief when we were finally back through the pipe and on the other side of the bulkhead preparing to be hoisted from the mine.

The rest of the week was much less stressful. It was spent discussing ideas for converting Patience Lake to a solution mining facility. On Friday, I was finally able to head back to my office. As it turned out, Patience Lake was successfully converted to a solution mining facility. It was nice to be involved in a successful potash project even if it was for another company.

Over the years, I thought about my first visit to Patience Lake and my premonition about the water flow. Fortunately, I was lucky and didn't get the company involved in a disaster. But it would have been better if the premonition had led me to evaluate this situation in more detail. I might have realized that the mine was at significant risk and taken that into account during the evaluation. Although it was good to be lucky I couldn't always count on it—it would be better to be both smart and lucky.

CHAPTER 22

How to Piss Off the Boss Without Really Trying

Learn to listen between the lines

For some reason, I've never been very good at sensing others' emotions. This not only created problems with my mother but also with teachers and friends. Unfortunately, it sometimes reared its ugly head while working for Texasgulf. One incident occurred in late 1985 when I was asked to develop Moab's reserve estimate. This "educated guess" of the tons of potash that we would ultimately recover was used by the accounting department in our financial statements. If the Moab facility cost $100 million and was expected to recover 50 million tons of potash, the accountants would divide the cost by the tons and use an amortization rate of $2/ton in their calculations. So if Moab produced one million tons during the year, they would show a cost of $2 million which would go toward repaying a part of the original investment. I was worried about getting crossways with accounting so I spent several weeks developing an estimate I could defend. This also seemed like a good opportunity to show off my extensive knowledge of the solution mining system.

When I completed the analysis, I took it to Dave Edmiston for his review. He told me he was busy, but that I was to present the information at the upcoming production and marketing meeting to be held in Green River, Wyoming. Green River was the site of the Texasgulf soda ash operation. I was looking forward to the trip since I would once again get to fly on the company plane and also visit Green River's underground mine.

Myself and the senior management team flew out the day before the meeting. This gave us a chance to visit with the other attendees during dinner and as we loosened up over drinks in the bar. The next morning we were picked up and given a scenic 20-minute drive to the plant site. The meeting was held in a conference room in the main office building. The 40 attendees were seated around a large conference table with the company president, Tom Wright, at one end and a projector screen at the other.

The meeting went along fairly smoothly as sales forecasts and operating budgets were discussed. Finally, I was called upon to discuss the Moab reserve estimate. I explained that in 1972 when Moab was converted to solution mining, it was estimated 12 million tons of potash would be recovered. Based on my 13 years of experience, it appeared the estimate was overly optimistic. I took great pride in explaining how I'd calculated my reserve estimate. I felt it was very advanced technically and also innovative. Using an overhead projector, I displayed the calculations as I discussed my results. I estimated Moab's remaining reserves to be 2.4 million tons rather than the 10 million tons estimated the previous year.

Tom Wright looked surprised when he heard my estimate.

"That isn't the right number," Tom said. "You're way too low."

I was embarrassed to be standing in front of a large group while the company president pointed out a mistake I'd made. I looked at the numbers but just couldn't figure out where I'd screwed up the math.

"I'm sorry," I said. "I just can't see my mistake."

"Your mistake is that the estimate is way too low."

I still couldn't see any error in my math. Of all the times to screw up a calculation, doing it now was the worst.

"Tom, I can't see a mistake in the math."

"The mistake is that you came up with the wrong number. It should be closer to 10 million tons."

From the look on his face, Tom was getting mad. I kept looking at the screen but couldn't see where I'd screwed up.

In a stroke of stupidity, I said, "Tom, I can't just arbitrarily change the numbers to get an answer."

"You won't need to. Your replacement can. You're fired. Now sit down and shut up."

As I sat down, the people next to me tried to slide away and just stared at their notes. I felt like I had leprosy.

During a break from the meeting, the head of accounting pulled me aside and quietly explained what the problem was. Texasgulf was in the midst of a tough financial year and expected to show a significant loss. My reserve estimate would add to the problem by forcing accounting to write off an additional $40 million. Since Tom was already getting heat about the company's poor performance, he didn't need me adding to his problems. He just wanted me to calculate the reserves the way it had been done before. Damn. I should have just said I'd look into it and sat down.

At the end of the meeting, we were to take a tour of the mine and processing plant. Tom explained that since I was no longer an employee I couldn't participate. I ended up sitting in the waiting room of the office building. When the tour was over, everyone came together to say their goodbyes. Then the senior management team headed for their cars for the trip to the Rock Springs airport. When I tried to climb in, Tom said that since I was no longer an employee I couldn't ride in the company plane. I would have to find my own way back to Raleigh. He suggested that maybe I could hitch a ride to Salt Lake City and take a commercial flight home. I stood outside the office building with my bags feeling dejected as I watched the cars drive off.

After standing there 10 minutes trying to figure out what to do, Roger, the mine manager, came outside and offered to give me a ride to the Rock Springs airport. I hopped in his car and we sped down the highway. Arriving at the airport, I was glad to see the corporate jet still sitting on the tarmac. Now, if I could just get aboard. Stepping out of the car, I could hear one of the plane's engines was running but fortunately the stairs hadn't been retracted. I grabbed my bags, raced to the plane, and climbed on. As I came through the door, I could see the senior management team seated in the back section of the plane. When they saw me they fell silent. I nervously selected a seat and sat down alone near the front of the plane. After a few minutes, the pilot raised the stairs, closed the door, and we took off.

About an hour into the flight, Tom walked up the aisle and stood next to me.

"Don't worry, Clark," he said. "You can come to work tomorrow. I will get someone else to prepare the reserve estimate."

"Thanks. In the future I'll try to listen closer to what you're telling me."

With that he went back to his seat. From this, I should have learned not to cross the boss or any senior manager. But history had shown me to be a slow learner. Offsetting this was my tenacity in solving tough technical problems. My tenacity probably saved me from the consequences of my stupidity.

Lightning strikes again!

One of the perks of working in the BER group was the entertainment provided by the staff meetings. Dave Edmiston held them every Tuesday and Thursday. This was a habit he brought with him when he returned from exile in Golden, Colorado. The meetings started at 7:00 a.m. and ended promptly at 8:00 a.m. regardless of where we were in our discussions. This forced us to come to work early two days a week. And since we were salaried employees we got nothing for it. Not even donuts.

Dave always sat at the head of the table and started the meeting by interrogating the person to his left. When he was done with him, he proceeded around the table clockwise. Dave took as much time as necessary to thoroughly grill the victim before moving on. Thus, we usually ran out of time before everyone had been abused. I learned to arrive early so as to get a seat to Dave's right. Then, I could just sit and watch the entertainment.

Nearly every meeting included an update on the Saltville DFP project. DFP, defluorinated feed phosphate, was used in poultry feed to supply the calcium and phosphate essential to the animals' diet. Texasgulf initially diversified into feed phosphate by acquiring Dical plants in Weeping Water, Nebraska, and later in Kinston, North Carolina. Dical or dicalcium phosphate was different than the DFP we would produce at Saltville. DFP was tricalcium phosphate and much more difficult to manufacture. While expanded operations to produce DFP would add to the company's portfolio, a new plant would cost over $60 million. That was a lot of money in 1983. Texasgulf decided to get creative. In the small, mountainous town of Saltville, Virginia, they found an old, abandoned manufacturing plant. A study was conducted that showed the plant could be converted to produce DFP for $10 million, significantly lower than the $60 million for a new plant. Texasgulf naturally jumped at it. To sweeten the deal, Virginia offered to fund the project as long as the cost didn't exceed $10 million. They wanted to lower their high unemployment, and Texasgulf wanted to save some money. With this new acquisition, the company could expand into the DFP business for free, which made the project too good to pass up.

I wondered if the company was making a mistake. Since a DFP plant needed both phosphate rock and phosphoric acid for raw materials, most DFP plants were located at a phosphate mine. This eliminated the need to ship the raw materials and reduced the production costs. It seemed like shipping the raw materials 320 miles to Saltville would put the plant at a disadvantage. However, since it wasn't my project I didn't worry about it.

During the entertainment at the staff meeting, it quickly became apparent that the project manager didn't know what he was doing. The decision was soon made to add someone with DFP experience to the group. It was a good call. Steve Auman was a chemical engineer who had worked at a competitor's DFP plant in Florida. He had spent several years improving efficiency and resolving technical problems. With Steve's experience, he was a good resource for the Saltville project. He quickly became known for his technical expertise and for being frugal. He drove a beat up, rusted out orange van to work.

What Steve didn't know when he joined the group was that

he'd be in the hot seat explaining the latest fiasco to Dave. I didn't envy him. The project manager often ignored Steve's advice, so that even though he had no control of the project, he was continually catching hell for the latest screw up. The circus at Saltville went on for almost two years. Nothing went well. The rail spur serving the site collapsed into a large sink hole. This meant everything needed to be trucked to the plant which added to operating costs. On closer inspection, it was found that the plant's equipment needed significant repairs. Not a surprise for a plant that had sat unused for years. On top of this, Steve pointed out changes that had to be made based on his previous DFP experience. All of this pushed up the project cost.

Things came to a head in April 1985. As usual, Steve was sitting to Dave's left. When Dave asked Steve how the Saltville project was going, Steve reluctantly admitted they had a problem. A recent estimate showed that that project was going to cost about $14 million instead of the $10 million budgeted. Dave exploded. This was the first he had heard about the overrun. Dave explained to Steve that if the project exceeded $10 million, Texasgulf would lose all of the funding from Virginia. Thus, the project would cost Texasgulf $14 million rather than getting it for free. At the end of Dave's tirade, he told Steve to get on the phone and tell those jackasses at Saltville that they needed to cut whatever was necessary to get the project down to $10 million. If they didn't, they were all fired.

The discussion of Saltville took the entire hour. As the meeting broke up and Steve headed to his office, I told him I greatly appreciated the entertainment he provided.

He was not amused.

The Saltville project was finally completed in late October of 1985. They had cut costs everywhere they could think of, and the project still came in at $15 million. Virginia withdrew their funding and Texasgulf had to pay the entire bill. Although Steve survived, the project manager didn't. On top of this, they were having a very tough time producing salable product. They had cut too many corners trying to reduce costs. If they were going to overrun the budget anyway, they should have spent enough money to run a reasonably reliable plant. In early 1986 they had the plant operating, occasionally. I was glad I hadn't had anything to do with such a screwed-up mess.

My primary job in the BER group was to find a way to expand potash production. I'd helped explore for potash in Argentina, evaluated the option of buying two Canadian mines, and looked at ways to significantly expand potash production at Moab. Unfortunately, by 1986 I still hadn't achieved my goal and was worried I was running out of time. Thus, I was surprised one April morning when Steve Auman stepped in my office and told me Tom Wright wanted to see me. It seemed strange that Steve delivered the message since he didn't have anything to do with potash. I walked down the hall with Steve to the executive suite where we were met by Tom Wright and Dave Edmiston.

"Clark," Tom said, "I want you to go from here directly to Saltville to deal with a serious issue with the kiln scrubber."

I was taken aback by this. I hadn't had anything to do with Saltville and only vaguely knew of the scrubber problems from the staff meetings. "Tom, I don't know anything about Saltville's scrubber," I said. "Are you sure you want me to try to deal with this? The engineers at Aurora that work with phosphate all the time would be a better choice," I said.

"Dammit, you need to listen. I want you and Steve to walk down the stairs, get in Steve's van and head to Saltville NOW."

I looked over at Dave, but he just shrugged his shoulders. Steve was staring at the floor.

"I need to know more about what I'm getting into."

"Steve can fill you in during the four-hour drive to Saltville. You can buy any clothes or personal items you need when you get there. Now get the hell out of here and on your way."

Once again, I'd pissed off Tom. At least he didn't fire me this time. As we drove toward Saltville I was grumpy. I wasn't happy going to work at a manufacturing plant in a business suit. And with time running out on my quest to expand potash production, I didn't need this distraction.

Fortunately, Steve broke the silence and started to explain the Saltville scrubber problem. Unlike the other feed phosphate products, DFP was produced by reacting phosphate rock and soda ash in a high temperature kiln. Unfortunately, producing DFP was trickier than expected. Although the plant started up in October 1985, it was still having problems producing salable product in early 1986. The current problem was related to the scrubber that cleaned the exhaust gases from the kiln.

Saltville produced DFP using a nine-foot diameter rotary kiln that was 280 feet long. The kiln was basically a very large rotating pipe that was lined with bricks so it could withstand the 2,500-degree Fahrenheit operating temperature. The kiln was tilted so that feed added to the uphill end gradually tumbled downhill to the discharge point. As the feed moved down the kiln, it met a long, hot flame created by burning pulverized coal that was blown into the lower end and ignited. The hot exhaust gases tended to carry the burnt coal ash out of the kiln to the scrubber. Once at the scrubber, the gasses were sprayed with a caustic solution made using quick lime and water that absorbed toxic gases and removed particulate matter. The solids were then filtered out of the scrubber solution. Ideally, the filter cake should be non-toxic with the consistency of thick cookie dough. This would allow it to be hauled to the local landfill for disposal. The problem was that for some reason the filter cake was not passing the EPA's toxicity test and couldn't be taken to the landfill. Unfortunately, I knew nothing about dealing with this problem.

After our four-hour drive, we finally reached the plant and drove through the gate. On the way to the office building, Steve pointed out the scrubber and the piles of filter cake waiting for disposal. At the office building, we were met by the plant manager, Joe Rose, and escorted to the conference room where I was introduced to the operations superintendent, maintenance superintendent, and the manager of technical services. Just as we started to discuss the details of the scrubber problem, the receptionist came in and whispered something to Joe. He left the room and came back in a few minutes with two men in suits.

"These two gentlemen are from the EPA," Joe said. "They insist that the scrubber sludge stockpiled in the yard is a hazardous waste. Since we don't have a permit to store hazardous material, they plan to shut the plant down. I told them that an expert from our corporate office just arrived. Clark, would you please tell them how you plan to fix the problem."

I was stunned. I didn't have any idea what was causing the problem or how to fix it. I had just arrived at the plant 30 minutes earlier. And, although I was 35 years old, I wasn't known for thinking well on my feet or being diplomatic. The fiasco in Wyoming was a good example of how I could screw things up. I was nervous that anything I said might cause me or the company serious trouble. However, since I still had my suit on, I probably looked more important than I was.

The Saltville facility: the scrubber is next to the tall smokestack on the left and the kiln is behind the five silos in the center of the photo

After several seconds and a little stuttering, I said, "Texasgulf has a large technical staff at its Aurora, North Carolina, facility that is supporting the effort to find a solution to the problem. In addition, Texasgulf has several excellent engineering companies under contract that will lend support. You can rest assured that Texasgulf considers solving this problem a top priority. We would greatly appreciate it if you would give us some time to resolve this unexpected difficulty."

Surprisingly, they agreed to give us two months. However, if the problem wasn't solved by then, Saltville would be shut down and Texasgulf fined $10,000 per day for each day it had operated out of compliance. In my 13 years with Texasgulf, this was the worst mess I had been in. And for a change, I hadn't created it. Thus began my troubled and co-dependent relationship with the Saltville facility.

After the meeting and a tour of the plant, Steve took me to buy some work clothes and we checked in at a local motel. The next morning we started to work on the scrubber problem in earnest. Unfortunately, we weren't alone. Due to the seriousness of the problem, Bob Forest, the VP of Feed Operations, had traveled to Saltville from Omaha, Nebraska, and was there in the morning. He didn't want one of his plants shut down if he could help it. He thought the problem could be resolved by using finely ground quicklime and increasing the reaction temperature. On the other hand, his boss, Frank Robinson, believed that a special, more reactive quicklime from Pennsylvania would do the trick. The lowly manager of Saltville, Joe, believed that we needed to add reaction vessels and change the flow pattern in the scrubber. The company president, Tom Wright, even pitched in with some ideas for modifying the scrubber vessel.

Unfortunately, due to the time crunch, everyone insisted on testing their ideas simultaneously. The net result was utter chaos. It was impossible to tell if any idea was working since we were changing so many variables at once. When I suggested we test one thing at a time, they reminded me I was low man on the totem pole and they would do what they wanted. After two weeks of this nonsense, I decided I was wasting my time and hitched a ride back to Raleigh. If they didn't want my help the bosses could fight it out among themselves.

The next morning, I was sitting at my desk in the office when Dave Edmiston walked past my door. When he saw me out of the corner of his eye, he stopped and backed up.

"What are you doing here? Is the Saltville scrubber fixed?"

"Not hardly. It's a three-ring circus up there. They already have too many cooks in the kitchen. I just added to the confusion."

I then explained to Dave what was going on. Dave stomped out of my office and headed down the hall to see Tom Wright. About fifteen minutes later, Tom Wright's secretary, Nelda Watkins, called me.

"Mr. Wright would like to see you in his office immediately, if not sooner," she said.

This didn't sound good. With some trepidation, I walked down the hall to Tom's office. He was waiting at the door when I arrived. Not a good sign. As I walked in, he slammed the door and tore into me.

"I sent you to Saltville to take care of the scrubber. Now I find you ignored my orders and came back to Raleigh even though the damn scrubber isn't fixed."

Oh shit. I am in serious trouble this time.

My heart was racing. "Tom, I couldn't fix the scrubber because there were too many people working on it at the same time."

"Yeah, Dave told me you didn't think I, or anyone in senior management, was smart enough to fix it. I want you to know I was an engineer when you were still shitting yourself in diapers. What makes you think you know more about scrubbers than I do?"

This was not going well.

"Tom, I am sure if you were at Saltville you could quickly fix the problem. You are smart enough and have the authority to take control of the situation. But your job is here running the company. I can't fix it because I don't have any authority. Why not let Frank or Bob take care of it since they're vice presidents?"

I waited nervously while Tom considered this for a few seconds. The silence was killing me.

Finally, he said, "Okay, smart-ass. You have absolute control over the scrubber. Whatever you say goes. But you don't have control over anything else at Saltville, just the scrubber. And you've two weeks to fix it. If you don't, you're fired and this time it will stick. Now get back up there and fix the damn thing." Tom looked at me a few seconds and then said, "I mean now. Get your ass in gear."

I headed back down the hall, picked up my briefcase, and headed back to Saltville. Along the way, I decided to press my luck and stopped by my house to change clothes and get my suitcase.

As I drove back to Virginia, I wondered if I would survive this. It started to dawn on me that I needed to learn to be more diplomatic. At this point in my career I was still not very aware of people's egos or corporate politics.

Upon arrival at Saltville, I headed directly to the scrubber and started to give the operators instructions. Suddenly, Bob Forest appeared and told the operators to ignore my instructions and he gave them different orders. Since he was the VP responsible for Saltville, they did what he said.

Not wanting to make a scene I said, "Bob, let's go outside and discuss this. There are some things you need to know."

"To hell with that. I am in charge of the feed plants and the operators will do what I say."

"But, Bob, it would be better to discuss this outside."

"Bullshit. What I say goes. I don't have to listen to a damned incompetent engineer."

That's when I lost my temper. "Bob, I am responsible for fixing the damn scrubber and I only have two weeks to do it. I don't have time for any wild goose chases. I need to fix it before all hell breaks loose."

"Hell's already broke loose. I'll give Tom Wright a call and get your dumb ass straightened out."

With that, Bob headed up the hill to the manager's office with me trailing two steps behind him. When we arrived, Bob plopped down in the manager's chair, picked up the phone, and dialed Raleigh.

"Hello, Nelda. This is Bob Forest. I would like to speak to Mr. Wright." Bob listened for a few seconds. "I don't care if he is in an important meeting, I need to talk to him right now." After a several more seconds Bob said, "Hello, Tom. This is Bob Forest. I have your so-called scrubber expert here and ... but Tom... yeah, but ... yes, sir. I understand, sir. Yes, sir. I will make sure he gets everything he needs. Yes, sir. I'm sorry I bothered you. Goodbye."

With that he slammed the phone down, looked at me and said, "Go to hell, you son-of-a bitch." He then stomped out of the office, climbed in his car, and headed for the hotel. Now I was really in deep shit. I had managed to piss off the company president and a vice president all in the same day.

Fortunately, I had technical support from the Aurora facility and Steve Auman. We went to work on the scrubber and within a few days had the situation under control. It turned out that the operators were only taking samples and monitoring the scrubber's chemistry once a shift. On top of this, they were being frugal with the quicklime additions to save money. After changing to hourly chemistry checks and raising the pH target, the solids from the scrubber were found to be acceptable for disposal in the landfill. They were no longer considered a hazardous waste. I had avoided being fired, but just barely.

I heaved a sigh of relief when the Saltville fiasco was finally over. This time when I returned to Raleigh, Tom Wright came by my office and told me he appreciated what I had done. He said I wasn't fired and that I'd convinced him that I was good at solving problems. However, he did point out that my diplomacy did need a little work.

Although I'd once again survived my stupidity, I could see that I needed to think about why people acted the way they did. I also needed to consider their egos and show more respect, particularly to those in senior management. I could see that the Argentina fiasco might have gone better if I had approached Ken Kutz differently and shown more respect for his position. It was becoming clear that I needed to listen to Tom and think about what he was saying. If I didn't, I might just end up permanently fired next time.

CHAPTER 23

Marseilles Acquisition

Some of the best entertainment is free

One morning a few weeks after the Saltville fiasco, I was surprised when Tom Wright stopped by my office. He asked me to attend a meeting in the boardroom in twenty minutes. I told him I'd be there, but he walked off before I could find out what the meeting was about. This seemed strange. Maybe I was going to get chewed out for something I'd done. But when I walked in the boardroom, a large group was already seated at the table. I had to negotiate my way to a vacant seat on the far side. Looking around I saw my arch nemesis, the VP of Feed Production, Bob Forest, sitting on the opposite side near the end of the table. Seated next to me was the head of technical services at Weeping Water, Gregg Perrault, and across from me was the VP of Feed Sales, Fred Stephens. There was also an assortment of market research and other feed production people. This made me wonder why I was there in the first place. I didn't have anything to do with feed phosphates.

A few minutes later, Tom Wright walked in and sat down at the head of the table and at the opposite end from Bob Forest. He opened the meeting with a few introductions and then got down to business. The purpose of the meeting was to discuss the lackluster sales of Dical, a feed phosphate. Dical was produced at the Weeping Water, Nebraska, and Kinston, North Carolina, plants. Texasgulf wanted to increase their feed phosphate sales to be more diversified and less dependent on their fertilizer business. Plus, feed sales yielded a higher profit per ton of phosphate than fertilizer. In order to increase sales, Fred Stephens had been hired a year earlier and made the VP of Feed Phosphate Sales. Unfortunately, Fred said he was having difficulty expanding Texasgulf's feed business due to our product quality. However, the feed production team didn't believe quality was the issue. They were of the opinion that Fred was an incompetent salesman trying to blame them for his poor performance. After the initial discussion, Tom Wright asked Fred to present his case.

Fred started off by comparing Texasgulf's product to that of our competitors. He explained that it was difficult to gain market share with an inferior product. Texasgulf's product had more fines and dust in it and a lower bulk density than the other products on the market. The bulk density was a problem since customers mixed our product with other feed materials and packaged it in fifty-pound bags. Since our product was lower in density than the product they had been using, they had to buy larger bags. It was similar to the difference in the size of a bag required to hold a pound of popcorn versus a pound of marbles. The fines were a problem for the customers since any time they handled our product it created an unwanted dust cloud and made a mess.

When Fred sat down it was Bob's turn.

"We've collected numerous samples of our product and our competitors' product," Bob said. "Our product is 90 percent larger than 0.15 millimeters, while our competitors is at 99 percent. By the same token, our bulk density is 51 pounds per cubic foot versus their 60 pounds. The data shows there is no statistically meaningful difference between the two products." Bob looked around the room and then continued. "Despite what our so-called expert, Mr. Stephens, says, our customers are perfectly happy with our product."

Attacking Fred was probably not a good decision. Fred could

hold his own in an argument plus Tom Wright had been part of the team that hired him.

Fred responded, "Our existing customers are happy because they have never received good product. The problem is that potential new customers have received good product from our competitors and aren't interested in purchasing crap from Texasgulf, at least not for the same price. If we don't improve our product quality, the only way we can get their business is to slash our price."

Bob interrupted. "As shown by our statistical analysis, the amount of dust and the bulk density of our product are not statistically different than our competitors."

Fred seemed annoyed. "Regardless of what you say, there is a hell of a lot of difference between one percent and 10 percent dust and 51 versus 60 pounds bulk density."

"I am telling you that the difference isn't statistically meaningful."

At this point, Tom had heard all he could stand. "Bob, I'm impressed with your statistical analysis. If I was looking for a statistician, I'd hire you. Unfortunately, I'm looking for the VP of Feed Production to solve a production problem. Your job is to get off your ass and start manufacturing a quality product."

"Tom, there is no reason to get upset," Bob said.

Based on my experience with Tom, this wasn't a smart thing to say. I tried to slide back from the table so as to not get caught up in the crossfire.

"Upset?" Tom asked. "*Upset?*"

I slid lower in my chair. Oh, shit. This was about to get ugly.

"I'll show you upset, you dumb son-of-a-bitch. I've had about all the statistics I can *stand*. I thought you were in charge of production," Tom said. "You had better figure out how to make quality product. And it had better be soon." He didn't even pause for dramatic effect. "We're going to have a meeting in a month. If your team hasn't figured out how to produce quality product by then, there will be a whole new cast of characters sitting around this table."

The room was quiet for a few seconds.

For some reason Greg Perrault apparently felt it was time for technical services to chime in. "Uh," he said, "Tom? I don't want to be the person to tell you—"

Don't say whatever you're thinking of saying.

"That it's going to cost $300,000 to fix the problem," Greg finished.

"Greg," Tom said, "you don't need to tell me that. Your replacement can. This goddamn meeting is adjourned."

Tom then stood up and walked out of the room. I was surprised by the abrupt end of the meeting. We all just sat there looking at each other for several seconds, then gradually got up and dispersed.

As I walked back to my office, I still didn't know why I had been invited to the meeting. I was just an outsider enjoying the entertainment and trying not to get caught in the crossfire. What I didn't know was Dave Edmiston and senior management were in the middle of negotiations with Beker Industries to purchase their Marseilles, Illinois Dical plant. Beker was in bankruptcy and had to liquidate their facilities. Texasgulf had made an offer that was only a fourth of Beker's asking price. Beker said they wanted some time to think about it. Dave suspected they were looking around trying to find someone that would pay more. While Beker looked for another buyer, they agreed that Texasgulf could send someone to the Marseilles plant to do a more detailed evaluation of the facility.

In May of 1986, Dave Edmiston visited me in my office. I was always nervous when he came to see me.

"Clark, I want you to go to Marseilles, Illinois, for a couple of months."

"What's in Marseilles?" I asked.

"I want you to inspect the Beker facility."

"Inspect it for a couple of months? It won't take me a couple of months to check the plant out. What else do you want me to do?"

"Nothing."

"Nothing? You want me to go to Marseilles and just sit on my butt?"

"Yup."

I sat there looking at Dave in disbelief. This didn't make sense.

Finally, I said, "Dave, there is something you aren't telling me. I need to understand why I'll be sitting there."

Dave stood looking at me for several seconds. "You are not to ever repeat this," Dave said, "but I don't trust Beker. While we're waiting for their decision, I am afraid they will start selling off the plant's equipment. Your job is to make sure nothing leaves the property. But I don't want the people at Marseilles to know what you are doing. Just act like you're checking things out."

Maybe having me sit in on the heated Dical meeting was to give me some background on feed phosphates and the people involved in its manufacture and sale. In any case, I headed for Marseilles the next day. When I arrived, I found there were four Beker employees still at the site including the plant manager, Dick Bacon, the office supervisor, Gene, the head of the electrical department, Cliff, and the head of mechanical maintenance, Shorty. They greeted me and took me to a local restaurant for lunch. After lunch, we wandered around the plant inspecting equipment. At the end of the day, they were surprised when I announced that I would be back the next morning.

The next day, Dick and I did a much more detailed inspection of the facility. This continued again the next day. And the next. At the end of the week, they were surprised to hear that I would be back on Monday. As the days and weeks went by, we explored the plant, watched the barges go up and down the Illinois River and sat in the office and talked about our experiences. Eventually, we started golfing every other day to kill time. On some Fridays I would head home and return the next Monday. But sometimes I'd spend the weekend in Illinois just in case Beker was planning something. Like me, Dick and his team didn't have much to do except sit around in case Beker needed them to show the plant to someone. The wait was pretty boring for all of us.

After six weeks of this "demanding" duty, Texasgulf finalized the deal to purchase Marseilles. The final price was a surprising $2.25 million. Beker had almost given the plant away. I was preparing to head home when Dave called.

"I heard from the travel department you're making arrangements to fly home," Dave said.

"Yeah. I thought I would get back to work on the potash project."

"You need to cancel those plans. You are now the Marseilles project manager. You are responsible for restarting the Marseilles facility as quickly as you can. However, you are not to spend more than $1.5 million on the startup. You can either keep the former Beker employees or hire new people as you see fit."

"Dave, I don't know anything about Dical production."

"Well, you'd better learn. The startup is your responsibility. Let me know when you have an expected startup date."

Marseilles facility: the office is on the right with the plant on the left

This was an entirely new experience for me. I had never been involved in a plant startup. I didn't know anything about hiring operators nor did I know anyone who could help me. On top of that, I knew almost nothing about Dical production. It was a completely different process than was used at Saltville. It didn't involve a high temperature kiln. Instead, Dical was made by reacting phosphoric acid with limestone. How in the world had I gotten myself into this mess? I also wondered why Bob Forest wasn't more involved. He was the VP of Feed Phosphate production. The plant would eventually be his responsibility and the manager of Marseilles would eventually report to him. It seemed like he would want to have a say in who that manager would be. Based on our confrontation at Saltville, I couldn't understand why Bob let me be involved.

I thought about what to do first. It seemed that since Dick Bacon had managed the plant for several years, it made sense to immediately hire him and make him the plant manager. He would know which positions needed filling and who should fill them. He would also know what equipment needed to be replaced and what needed to be done to get the plant ready to run. I forwarded Raleigh a request to hire Dick and it was quickly approved.

On Dick's first day as a Texasgulf employee we sat down to discuss our path forward to get the plant ready to run as quickly as possible.

"So what do you want me to do first?" Dick asked.

"What do you think we should do?" I responded.

Dick look at me perplexed. "Since you're my boss, I thought you would provide the details of what to do."

"Dick, you are the expert in running and maintaining this plant. That is what I want you to do. I don't know anything about running Marseilles. Instead, my job is to make sure you have the resources to get the plant up and running. I will want to be kept in the loop so I know what is going on and how I can help. I also think it would be good for the two of us to tour the plant at least once per week to discuss any problems that come up."

Dick sat thinking for a few seconds then he said, "Clark, I appreciate your confidence in me and I won't let you down."

Dick's first act was to hire Gene, Shorty, and Cliff, the three other people Becker had kept while searching for a buyer. Next, Dick re-hired the best of the maintenance crew so they could start getting the plant ready to operate. On our weekly plant tours, he explained the production process to me and I sometimes suggested a few plant modifications to him. I also had to occasionally encourage Dick to upgrade the equipment. He was used to the spending restraints imposed by Becker during their financial problems. I explained to Dick it was better to have a reliable plant than to try to save a few bucks and end up losing a bunch of money due to lost sales.

Even with all the work Dick was doing, I was staying very busy. I spent a lot of time with Dick's team helping them understand Texasgulf policies and who to contact to set up bank accounts and obtain operating permits. In some cases I had to do a little research myself when I didn't know who to contact.

In early September, Dick and I were invited to a budget meeting in Raleigh. The sales group was first on the agenda. It was their job to tell the plants how much they could sell so the plants knew how much to produce. When asked, Fred Stephens said he could sell everything that the feed phosphate plants could make. At the time the Weeping Water facility was struggling to make 60,000 tons per year of product. This was somewhat of an embarrassment since a competitor had a plant that reportedly produced more than 200,000 tons per year.

At this point, Tom Wright asked, "Bob, what is the maximum production you can get out of Weeping Water?"

Bob Forest thought for a few seconds. "I think we will eventually get up to 90,000 tons per year, but we probably should only budget 70,000 tons for next year."

"How many tons do you think you can get out of Marseilles?"

"That plant is just a piece of shit," Bob said. "I doubt it will ever produce more than 60,000 or 70,000 tons per year."

"Do you agree with that, Mr. Bacon?" Tom asked.

Dick Bacon sat for several seconds pondering the situation. On the one hand, Bob Forest would be his new boss as soon as the plant started up. On the other hand, he didn't want his plant to be second to Weeping Water.

"I think Marseilles can do at least 125,000 tons per year."

Bob jumped to his feet. "Bullshit. That plant will never exceed the production of Weeping Water."

"Sorry, Mr. Forest. I was just offering my opinion."

Dick was already getting in trouble with his future boss. Later I asked Dick how sure he was about producing 125,000 tons per year. He told me he was positive. Before Beker closed the plant, it had produced over 150,000 tons per year. He had lowered it to 125,000 just to be safe.

By mid-October, Marseilles was nearly ready to start production. It only required a few finishing touches. Having Dick Bacon on board with his years of experience at Marseilles was proving to be a major benefit. On top of that, he had worked for Beker during the difficult time proceeding their bankruptcy. He knew how to get things done cheap. It was a refreshing change. Usually, I had to get after people for spending too much money on a project.

By the end of October, Marseilles was up and running. It had started up on schedule and with each day the plant was disproving Bob Forest's opinion that it was just a piece of junk. As time went on, it continued to ramp up production rates while making the highest quality product in the industry. Bob Forest's pride and joy, Weeping Water, still hadn't figured out how to do this.

I heaved a sigh of relief that the startup had gone so well. Along the way, I had learned a lot. Finding good people, trustworthy people, and then letting them do their jobs had been critical to the success of the project. I learned that just because you were the boss, you didn't have to control everything. If I had tried to direct all the work with my limited knowledge of the process, it would have been a disaster. By relying on and empowering others, the plant had been brought into production on schedule and below budget. These were all traits that I'd learned from the bad experiences at the Burgin mine coupled with the good experiences I'd had after the management course in Hershey, Pennsylvania. Apparently, I could occasionally learn something after all.

CHAPTER 24

Adventures at Weeping Water

Being the new kid on the block

In late September, while working on the Marseilles startup, Frank Robinson, the VP of Operations, gave me a call. He said Bob Forest was having serious health issues and that Tom Wright thought it would be best to relieve some of his workload. Tom wanted me to take over managing Weeping Water. Unfortunately for me, I would report to Bob who would remain the VP of Feed Phosphate Production. Based on his parting shot at me at the end of the Saltville scrubber fiasco, I suspected Bob didn't know about the offer.

"Has Bob agreed to this?" I asked. "I don't think he has a very high opinion of me."

"I haven't discussed it with him," Frank said. "I didn't think there was any reason to upset him until I knew whether you were interested."

Great. This sounded like a train wreck in slow motion.

"What about the Moab expansion?"

"It doesn't look like it is going to happen. The potential gain is not worth the risk and cost of developing the new technology."

The news about Moab was depressing. Despite that, at least I would still have a job. I thanked Frank for the offer and told him I'd get back to him in a few days.

The Weeping Water facility was located 25 miles south of Omaha, Nebraska. It was Texasgulf's first effort at diversifying into feed phosphate products. Since Bob Forest had spearheaded the effort to acquire the facility in the mid-1970s, it was his pride and joy.

After considerable thought, I decided to take the job. It was agreed that I would continue work at Marseilles until the plant had completed its startup. Then I would take over as the manager of Weeping Water and relocate from Raleigh to Omaha, Nebraska. I had been selected because Tom wanted the product quality issues resolved and for some reason thought I could do it.

The whole thing seemed strange. Despite infuriating senior management several times in two years, I was being promoted. On top of that, I'd spent the first 13 years of my professional career becoming a potash expert. As a reward, I was made manager of a feed phosphate plant. Although I knew a little about the technology, it stressed me out that I needed to quickly improve product quality. Plus, my new boss hated me.

What have I gotten myself into?

By November 3, 1986, the Marseilles startup was complete and I was on my way to Nebraska to start my new job. Initially, I would stay in a hotel in Omaha until I found a new home. From there, Weeping Water was only a 30-minute drive south. As I was waiting for my flight to Nebraska, I thought about a problem that had worried me for several weeks. No one had told Bob Forest I was the new manager of Weeping Water. To make matters worse, Bob was in the hospital with leukemia. Since Frank was Bob's boss, he should have told him of the change, but so far he hadn't done it. He kept telling me that he didn't have the time to make a 15-minute phone call. I suspected Frank was just wimping out since he knew Bob and the management team at Weeping Water would be pissed off. While waiting at the airport for my flight, I decided to call Frank Robinson one last time.

"Frank, you've got to let Bob Forest know about the management change," I pleaded. "I'm sitting at the airport getting ready to fly to Omaha to take charge."

"Clark, I'm real busy today," Frank said. "I would appreciate it if you would just go ahead and take care of it."

"But it won't take you that long. If you really don't have time, maybe you could get Tom Wright to do it."

"There's no reason to bother Tom. Since you will be there in a couple of hours, it will be easy for you to swing by the hospital and tell Bob yourself."

Damn. I couldn't believe Frank wouldn't take care of this.

After I hung up, I pondered which would be the best way to handle the situation. Although it might look like I was chickening out, I was sure it would be less stressful for Bob if John Groesser, office supervisor, let him know. It also seemed like it would be better for Weeping Water's management team to learn I was their new boss from a private meeting rather than when I walked in the office tomorrow. I called John Groesser and informed him I was flying to Omaha and needed to meet up with him, the general superintendent, Eddy Gegg, and the technical supervisor, Gregg Perrault, at my hotel at 5:00 p.m. He said he had other plans, but with my persistence he finally agreed to get Eddy and Gregg and meet me. He was curious about what was going on, but I just said we needed to have a face-to-face discussion.

When they arrived, I met them in the hotel lobby and escorted them up to my room. I could tell they were nervous. Small talk didn't seem like a good idea, so I just charged ahead with the news.

"This probably isn't the best way for you to find out but I've been appointed the manager of Weeping Water."

There was just silence as they looked at each other in shock. Gradually, their disbelief turned to anger and disappointment. John was the first to speak up.

"You've got to be kidding me. After all the time I've spent taking care of the Feed group, they would treat me like this. I know it isn't your fault, but I'm really pissed off."

Eddy wasn't happy either. "This is the stupidest thing I've ever heard," he said. "They should have chosen someone like me with feed phosphate experience. Instead of working on the quality issues, I now get to spend my time teaching you about the plant."

I could understand their frustration. They had assumed that one of them would be made manager. Now, out of the blue, they learn an outsider has been promoted to the job. As they talked, I remembered what I had learned at Hershey and at Moab when I was promoted to general superintendent. Based on that experience, I told them I was as surprised as they were by management's decision and that Eddy was right—I would have to rely on them. But together we could resolve Weeping Water's problems. If they could figure out what they needed, I would make sure they got it. At the end of our discussion, I asked John to arrange for a staff meeting the next morning to let the rest of the team know.

The next day, I was very nervous as I walked into the staff meeting. I needn't have worried. Everyone was already aware of the management change. Apparently, someone had leaked the news. I told the group I was excited to be working with them and would appreciate their support as we resolved the product quality issues.

When the meeting was over, the next item on the agenda was to let Bob Forest know of the change. I asked John to step into my office.

"I know you and Bob are close and I think he'll take it better if you go by the hospital and let him know."

"Gee, Clark, I really don't want to. I understand what you're saying, but he probably won't take this well at all. He'll feel like he's been cut out of the management loop."

We sat in my office and discussed it for a while. John felt that since I was the manager he shouldn't have to do it. But he gradually came around and could see it would be best if he took care it. John visited Bob that evening and let him know. He said that Bob had accepted the news gracefully. Sadly, Bob didn't have long to live. He passed away six weeks later, just after the Weeping Water Christmas party.

The next order of business was for me to learn about the Weeping Water facility and help solve the product quality issues. Weeping Water produced dicalcium phosphate known as Dical and monocalcium phosphate, or Monocal. These are mineral supplements used by livestock producers to assure animals such as hogs and cattle have sufficient calcium phosphate in their diets for bone construction and cell development.

Dical and Monocal are produced by reacting limestone with phosphoric acid. Diversifying into this business provided Texasgulf with another source of income from phosphoric acid other than the fertilizer business. The acid was produced at the Aurora, North Carolina, facility. Weeping Water was also unique among Dical plants in that it had its own limestone mine just a half mile from the plant. This gave Weeping Water a cost advantage over its competitors and gave me the chance to be back in the mining business.

In touring the mine, I was pleasantly surprised to see that a stream had cut a valley deep enough to expose the 14-foot-thick limestone bed. Thus, we didn't have to sink a shaft but could just drive in the mine. The portal looked like a tunnel for a small roadway making it easy for trucks and equipment to drive into the mine which was kind of like driving into a large parking garage. This was completely different than the hot, dangerous Burgin mine where I'd worked.

Underground, the mine entries were laid out in a grid pattern like streets in a small town. They were spaced 80 feet apart and were 40 feet wide. The limestone was broken loose using explosives and then loaded into dump trucks using a front-end loader. The trucks transported the limestone from the mine to the plant where it was stockpiled. There, it was crushed, dried, and ground to the consistency of flour so it could easily react with the acid.

Phosphoric acid from the Aurora facility was railed to Weeping Water in tank cars and unloaded into two large rubber-lined tanks. The acid was then pumped to the production facility where it was mixed with the limestone. The ensuing reaction neutralized the acid and produced carbon dioxide. Depending on the ratio of phosphoric acid to limestone, either Dical or Monocal was produced. The product was then dried in a rotary dryer, screened to remove the dust and oversized material, and placed into storage. Although some of the product was shipped by rail, most was shipped to customers by truck. As I learned about the plant, I also learned about the surrounding community.

Not surprisingly, the Weeping Water facility was located near the small, rural town of Weeping Water, Nebraska. In 1986 the population was just over a thousand. It was even smaller than Spanish Fork had been when I grew up. But it had the same atmosphere. Most families had lived there for generations. Everyone knew everyone else. You were considered an outsider unless you had been born there. The local businesses survived due to the patronage of the farmers from the surrounding area. Life in Weeping Water was pretty laid back. A favorite form of entertainment was to watch a Little League baseball game in the summer or a basketball game in the winter. Surprisingly, Eddy Gegg was the town mayor. I considered moving the family to Weeping Water but due to the lack of a hospital and the small size of the school, my family decided to live in Omaha.

As I settled into my new job, I learned that preparations needed to be made for the company Christmas party and that I was in charge of organizing the shindig. The employees and their spouses were invited along with corporate executives from out of town. When the date neared, I became very apprehensive. As the plant manager, I was expected to introduce guests and make a speech as dinner was served. Fortunately, I had John Groesser available to look after the details of the party to make sure it was suitable for our illustrious guests.

I was glad John selected a first-class restaurant in Omaha for the party. The festivities would begin with cocktails and hors d'oeuvres. Next, the guests would be served the dinner of their choice along with dessert. After dinner, the group would visit and share a few more drinks or show off their moves on the dance floor.

On the evening of the celebration, several corporate guests, including the president of Elf Aquitane's U.S. operations, Gino Giusti, and his wife, Ruth, arrived. They had taken time from their busy schedule and flown in from New York. Initially, the party seem to be going well. As the crowd mingled, they ate hors d'oeuvres, some of which were unique to the Midwest. Gino and

Ruth were sampling some deep-fried tidbits served with cocktail sauce that they found particularly tasty.

After eating several, Gino asked what they were. I replied, "They are Rocky Mountain oysters. It's a regional delicacy."

"I have never heard of oysters in this part of the country."

"Ah, they aren't really oysters."

"Then what are they?"

I leaned over and whispered, "They are calf testicles that have been deep fried."

The color drained from Gino's face. "You've got to be kidding me."

"I wish I was."

Gino leaned over and whispered to his wife. At first, she was incredulous. After I confirmed what Gino had said, Ruth made a mad dash to the restroom. Maybe I should have taken the time to check out the menu or warned the guests.

As the cocktail hour drew to a close, it was apparent several people had taken full advantage of the free drinks. The crowd was getting loud and boisterous. Finally, we sat down for dinner. As the food was served, I stood up and welcomed everyone to the party and introduced our special guests. As I was introducing Gino and Ruth, Rob Burby, one of the mill operators, passed out and fell face-first into his food. His wife, being concerned for his well-being, turned his face to the side so that he wouldn't suffocate on the mashed potatoes and gravy.

My hope that nothing else would happen was quickly dashed. When Gino stood and started to make a few remarks, another operator got sick and had to run to the bathroom. We could hear him throwing up in the background as Gino was talking. Unfortunately, the heavy drinking by some party goers continued after dinner and resulted in a few more problems, including a near fight.

I was very aggravated and stressed out by the end of the evening. Between the Rocky Mountain oysters and people passing out in their food, I suspected I hadn't favorably impressed corporate management. Clearly, I needed to pay attention to more than just the operation of the plant. This was not a very illustrious start for a new manager. The next Christmas party had a few changes in the menu and a strict, two-drink limit.

General view of the Weeping Water facility

As I settled into my new job, I began to take daily tours of the plant. I wanted to talk with the people and get their insights into things, and I also wanted to make sure the plant was being properly maintained. The operators were surprised to see me and I was surprised by the atrocious housekeeping. It turned out Bob Forest had seldom toured the plant. He would occasionally visit the control room but that was about it. With my daily visits, the operators quickly learned to clean up their spills, pick up the hoses, and vacuum up the dust.

Wandering around the plant, I thought about how to deal with my top priority: improving product quality. As was pointed out several months earlier in the boardroom meeting in Raleigh, Weeping Water's products contained excessive dust and a low bulk density of only 50 pounds per cubic foot. The density needed to be 60 or better. I knew that I needed to make progress on this quickly or Tom Wright might lose his sense of humor. Fortunately, I had an ace in the hole: Dick Bacon.

While getting Marseilles ready for startup, I spoke to Dick Bacon about Weeping Water's problem. Marseilles was known for having quality product. Dick explained that to achieve high bulk density, they used a high-speed mixer to combine the limestone and phosphoric acid. This speeded up the reaction so it released the carbon dioxide gas before the material entered the pug mill where it would be granulated. The pug mill was a four-foot-wide metal box that was 12 feet long and had two solid metal shafts running parallel to each other along the bottom. Each shaft was about 8 inches in diameter with 8-inch-long paddles that were angled to push the slurry along and granulate it as the shafts rotated. This meant that Marseilles' pug mill could ball up the material into smooth, dense granules that were kind of like small BBs.

Weeping Water, on the other hand, used a pug mill to both blend the acid and limestone together and to granulate the product. This meant the mixture was bubbling out carbon dioxide gas as it was granulating, not before. The result was small voids, or pockets, in the granules which reduced the bulk density. It also made the product more friable and thus, more dusty.

Like many things, once I understood what was going on I couldn't believe I hadn't figured it out sooner. It wasn't rocket science. By adding a high-speed mixer, the product quality problem at Weeping Water would be solved, I hoped.

I decided the best way to get the project started was to arrange for Eddy Gegg and Gregg Perrault to accompany me to Marseilles. There, we toured the facility and paid special attention to the high-speed mixer. It was like a very large kitchen blender except it was open on the bottom. This allowed the material that entered at the top to be rapidly mixed by the blades on the vertical shaft before exiting out the bottom. The throat on the blender was 32 inches in diameter and the blades were turned by a 40-horsepower motor. You could make a hell of a milkshake with it.

After we returned, we quickly designed a high-speed mixer and sent it to a local shop for fabrication. While that was underway, we started to work on the pug mill. We replaced the logs and started to add more paddles. Unfortunately, Weeping Water had previously pulled down their product inventory due to their low production rate. Thus, we had to get as much work done as quickly as possible during the outage. This added to my stress.

One afternoon, we were adding paddles to the pug mill. Carl, an operator, was pulling on the drive belts that looped over the motor and pug mill drive. As he moved the belts, the logs in the pug mill slowly rotated to a position that allowed for the installation of the next set of paddles. To see if I could help speed up the work, I reached inside the pug mill and pulled on the paddles to help rotate the logs. The logs did rotate more quickly, but it was accompanied by a scream of pain. I ran to see what had happened and found Carl holding up his right hand. His index finger was broken. When the pug mill unexpectedly rotated easier and faster than expected, he was slow letting go of the drive belt. His finger had been caught between the belt and pulley.

Carl looked nervous. He knew I'd stressed that Weeping Water had better not have any more reportable injuries. Initially I was upset and wanted to give Carl hell, but then I remembered what it had been like at the Burgin mine. If the foreman told us to do something and someone was hurt, he'd yell at us even if we'd followed his instructions to the letter. He'd never admit he'd screwed up. I didn't want to be like that. I wanted those around me to see that I'd take responsibly if I made a mistake. I took a deep breath and apologized to Carl for unintentionally causing the accident. I acknowledged that I should have let him know what I was going to do. I also said that I'd make sure that, other than the pain, it wouldn't impact him negatively. The troops seemed surprised by my attitude. Over the next few days several of them let me know that they appreciated my honesty and willingness to accept responsibility.

As I headed back to my office, I realized that my record at Weeping Water was not looking good. In addition to the Christmas party fiasco, I hadn't yet resolved the quality issues, was behind on production, and was now responsible for a reportable injury. I hoped I didn't get a call from Tom Wright.

When we finally finished modifying the plant, including the addition of the high-speed mixer, product quality immediately improved. The salesmen were ecstatic, at least for a couple of weeks. Yet we were still not keeping up with sales, particularly since the improved product led to increased demand. On top of this, we had a rash of back injuries. Most were brought on by improper lifting. Since back injuries were difficult for doctors to diagnose, I suspected some were faked. And since Texasgulf considered safety a high priority, I wasn't sure my career could tolerate this on top of everything else.

In an attempt to improve our safety record, I had the plant shut down one morning for an all-employee safety meeting. The meeting was held in the large conference room above the offices and I even provided refreshments. As part of the meeting, I showed a video that illustrated the proper way to lift heavy objects and how to avoid back injuries.

At the end of the meeting, I stood up and addressed the group.

"There is no reason for all these back injuries," I said. "I don't want to hear any more excuses. You won't get hurt if you lift properly."

The group looked at each other. I didn't get the feeling that they were buying into this.

"What do you mean?" Bill asked. "Sometimes if you pick up something heavy your back can slip out even if you do everything right."

"Not if you're lifting properly. You need to crouch down and lift with your legs like they showed in the video."

"But even doing that, a person can sometimes get hurt. We aren't all spring chickens."

"Then get someone to help. There is no reason for an injury unless you're doing something wrong. Any more questions?"

There were no more questions. There was, however, a little grumbling when they left.

As the group meandered off, I spoke with a few of the stragglers and answered their questions. It seemed like they understood the importance of safety and lifting properly. When everyone had left, I decided to check on the inventory of product in the large, storage dome. The salesmen were getting testy about us getting behind on shipments and I was worried we were about to run out. As I drove along, I thought about the safety meeting and hoped I had put the fear of God into them. There had better not be any more back injuries.

Reaching the dome, I climbed out of the car to open the large garage-style door that provided access to the dome. This was a manual door that needed to be lifted. I was still thinking about the morning's meeting as I bent over, grabbed the handle, and gave it a jerk. It didn't budge, but my back did. I went right to my knees.

The pain was excruciating. When I looked to the right side of the door, I saw that a dead bolt was holding the door rigidly in place. Unfortunately, instead of bending my knees and using my legs to lift the door, I had bent my back and lifted in exactly the manner that the video had warned against. I was flabbergasted that 30 minutes after the safety meeting I managed to do exactly what I'd warned the operators against.

Oh, shit. I will never hear the end of this.

Although I could get back onto my feet, I couldn't stand upright. I shuffled over to a low wall to the left of the door. By grabbing the top, I was able to gradually straighten up. I no longer gave a damn what the inventory was in the dome. Shuffling over to my car, I looked like the Hunchback of Notre Dame. I opened the door, but I couldn't bend over to get in.

After a few minutes, the spasms in my back eased up a little and I was able to gingerly sit down. I drove back to the office where I had the same problem getting out of the car. Fortunately, there was no one around. I then shuffled into the building and down the back hallway. When I reached my desk, I stood there trying to figure out how to sit down. The damn chair had wheels and kept trying to scoot away from me. I thought I had made it in without being detected when my secretary and John Groesser showed up.

"Are you okay?" John asked. "You look like you're in a lot of pain."

"I'm fine. Just leave me alone and get back to your work."

"You don't look too good."

"Speak for yourself. Just do me a favor and close the door on your way out."

They looked at each other, shrugged, and finally left me alone. With some effort and pain, I was finally able to sit down. Rummaging through the desk drawers, I found some aspirin and took twice the recommended dosage. If it helped at all, it wasn't much.

I sat at my desk the rest of the day waiting for quitting time. Finally, I couldn't hear anyone in the building. I managed to get up from my desk and peeked out of my office. Everyone had left. I shuffled out to my car and headed home.

Although it took three weeks for my back to heal, I tried to carry on as if there was no problem. The troops may have been suspicious, but they didn't say anything. However, I was definitely more sympathetic the next time there was a back injury.

When you're the boss, you're the boss

By June of 1987, I was starting to feel optimistic. The product quality was excellent and production rates had improved as we learned more about running the modified plant. We were building inventory and might be able to set a new production record for the year. I was pondering all of this as I drove to work on June 12. My route took me past the plant on the way to the office building. As I approached the maintenance shop, I noticed a large group of people standing near the railroad tracks by the plant where the new product storage silo had recently been completed. Although I just got a quick glimpse, something didn't look right.

Ah, shit. What's happened now?

I stopped the car and backed up to get a better look. I couldn't believe my eyes. The new 450-ton silo, put into service yesterday, had collapsed. When built, the bottom of the silo was 24 feet in the air so railcars could pass under it. It was held in the air by four large steel columns. Oddly enough, instead of tipping over, the silo had fallen straight down. The cone on the bottom of the silo had completely imbedded itself in the ground. Now, all that was visible was its upper portion. It looked like a huge ground-level tank surrounded by four columns. I parked the car and walked over to the gathering crowd.

"Did anyone get hurt?" I asked.

The maintenance foreman, Bill, answered somewhat sheepishly, "There were no serious injuries. I did get skinned up a little and have footprints up my back."

That seemed a little strange.

"What happened?"

"Just after I got to work, I received a call saying there was something wrong with the silo. I gathered up a few mechanics and headed over to check it out."

"What did you see?"

"It appeared that the support columns were under stress. We walked under the silo so we could look straight up the columns to see what was going on."

I was incredulous. Why in the world would anyone walk under a 450-ton silo that was having problems?

"You did what?"

"Yeah, I wasn't too bright. As we were standing there, we heard a loud bang and took off running."

"Everyone made it okay?"

"Yeah. But, unfortunately, I was at the front of the line and the slowest runner. Buck was behind me and in his haste knocked me down and ran right across my back. The rest of the group followed. Fortunately, I was out from under the silo when it happened."

"What a mess. I'm glad no one was hurt."

Building the new silo had been approved in early 1986 before I was appointed manager. By the time I started at Weeping Water, the columns were up and the silo was under construction. Since the design was complete and the contract for construction issued, I hadn't paid much attention to the project. Instead, I put most of my effort into dealing with the product quality issues.

After a couple of delays while waiting for materials, the silo was finally put into service on June 11. As the silo filled, the load cells faithfully reported the weight of the material. Things were progressing well through the evening. However, early in the morning, the control room operator noticed that the load cells were counting backwards. He raced from the control room to the silo but couldn't see anything wrong. He decided that it must just be an instrumentation error.

The operators continued to monitor the silo until morning.

They also couldn't see anything wrong but did hear strange noises and groaning from the steel. When the maintenance crew showed up in the morning for work, the operators called and told them about their concerns.

Bill gathered up his maintenance crew and walked over to see what was going on. They were so engrossed in troubleshooting, they didn't think about the danger they were putting themselves in. They were extremely lucky that no one was seriously hurt or killed when the silo came down.

Collapsed Dical silo at Weeping Water

An independent engineering firm was hired to determine what had gone wrong. After several months of investigation, it was found that the engineer working on the project had made a mistake. The engineer's design supported the silo using four "L" shaped brackets. The flat, horizontal part of each bracket rested on a column. Unfortunately, the steel plate where the bracket was attached to the silo's shell wasn't strong enough to support the load. When the silo was filled, the 450 tons caused the brackets to tear pieces out of the silo shell and the whole thing collapsed. When we finally sorted out the problem, I asked Eddy to contact the engineering company to find out what they planned to do. Later in the day, Eddy walked into my office. I could tell there was a problem.

"What did the engineering company say?" I asked.

"They reminded me that they had been swamped with work

when the silo was designed. Rather than delay the project, they suggested that we hire the recently retired head of their engineering department to do the design work."

"So, what's the problem?"

"We hired him directly rather than through the engineering firm. Although the engineering firm has insurance, the retiree does not. We can sue him, but other than causing him to go bankrupt we won't accomplish much."

"You mean we're going to get stuck for the cost of this fiasco?"

"Yep."

"How much are we going to have to write off?"

"We had approval to spend $400,000. Unfortunately, we spent $600,000. But the corporate office doesn't yet know about the overrun."

"You mean I've got to tell senior management that we have to eat the $400,000 approved for constructing the silo plus an additional $200,000 to cover the overrun?"

Eddy just stood there and looked at the floor.

I called Raleigh and let them know about the situation. To say they were unhappy would be a major understatement. Unfortunately, a few weeks later I had to travel to Raleigh for a preliminary budget meeting. As part of the meeting, the group had dinner in a private room at the Angus Barn restaurant.

During dinner, Tom Wright looked over at me and in a loud voice said, "Clark, I am very disappointed that Texasgulf paid $600,000 for a bunch of scrap steel and a hole in the ground. I hope for your sake nothing like this happens again."

Before I could say anything, Clyde Davis, the VP of Transportation, spoke up. "Tom, I think it's unfair to hold Clark responsible for the silo fiasco. He wasn't even at Weeping Water when the project was approved. Construction was well underway by the time he arrived."

Tom stared at Clyde for a few seconds and then said, "If you're the boss, you're the boss. Sometimes you get lucky and get credit for good things you had nothing to do with. Sometimes, you are unlucky and inherit disasters. But if you are the manager, you are responsible for your plant. Clark, nothing else had better happen at Weeping Water."

It was not a very enjoyable dinner for me.

Fortunately, the remainder of the year was fairly routine. We cleaned up the mess around the silo and disposed of all the steel. The year was closed out without any major incidents. The Christmas party even went well and the group was much better behaved, although there was a grumbling about the two-drink limit. As the New Year began, I was beginning to feel like things were under control and I could ease up a little.

I had learned a lot during my first year as the manager of Weeping Water. Spending time in the plant talking to the operators provided a lot of insight into how to improve things. It had also been important to listen to the management team's ideas. Arranging for my staff to visit the Marseilles facility had not only resolved the product quality issue, but it also provided ideas for improving other areas of the plant. Admitting when I had made a mistake not only improved morale but also improved communications so that people would let me know if I was making an error or causing a problem. And, despite the screwup on the silo, I had survived the year and was looking forward to a less hectic 1988.

CHAPTER 25

Saltville Revelations

It's a good idea to keep your eye on your people

After a crazy year resolving Weeping Water's problems, the first weeks in 1988 were relatively sane. Weeping Water was producing quality product at a record rate. I was learning to deal with and even enjoy the cold Nebraska winters. The family had adjusted to our location and had formed new friendships. I was enjoying work and the people I worked with. But, I should have known it wouldn't last. On February 2, my secretary walked into my office and told me my boss, Frank Robinson, was on the phone.

"Clark," Frank said, "I need you to go to Saltville and manage the facility for a few weeks."

"What's going on?"

"Unfortunately, Jacoby slipped and hurt himself." Dave Jacoby was the plant manager Bob Forest had selected to run Saltville after the EPA fiasco in early 1986. Frank continued. "Dave was shoveling the snow off his porch when he fell and cracked his tailbone. He managed to get an infection and is going to be laid up in the hospital for a while. Unfortunately, there isn't anyone at Saltville capable of looking after things."

"Frank, I've got plenty to do here in Weeping Water. Isn't there someone else that can handle this?"

"Tom Wright said he wanted you. Besides, it shouldn't take longer than a few weeks."

Darn. I suspected this was going to take longer than a few weeks. But it looked like I was going whether I wanted to or not. The logistics would be aggravating. I would effectively be responsible for two plants separated by over 800 miles. Although Weeping Water was doing well and had a good management team, I was still worried. The assignment was also stressful on a personal level. I would have to spend most of my time in Saltville while my family remained behind in Omaha. I wouldn't be around to help out and would only see them a few days each month. This didn't seem like it would be much fun.

I expected managing Saltville would be a major challenge. I'd heard it wasn't doing well financially. It seemed strange they'd bring in an outsider—me—to try to fix things. Since I only had a year's experience as a plant manager, someone else with more experience would've been a smarter choice for handling things. To try to get a better idea about what was going on, I decided to call my old buddies in Raleigh. They said there were rumors Dave Jacoby had been up to some shenanigans. Although he had a reputation for solving tough, mechanical problems, he also had a reputation for ignoring the rules, particularly safety and accounting rules. My contacts confirmed that Saltville had financial problems. Despite spending over a million dollars on improvements during the past two years, Saltville was producing a very limited amount of salable product. With little product to sell, they were losing money big time. How had I managed to inherit this headache?

As I traveled to Saltville to begin my temporary assignment, I reflected on my last visit to Saltville in 1986. Tom Wright had let the plant manager go and was searching for a replacement. Bob Forest had been given the option of appointing either Dave Jacoby or me to be the new manager. Unfortunately, this was only a month after the scrubber incident when Bob got mad and told me to go to hell. Bob went through the motions as if he was really considering me; I even traveled to Saltville to be interviewed, but in the end, he chose Jacoby. Despite that, I still wanted Saltville to be successful and convinced them to have Dale Jensen transfer from

Texasgulf's Wyoming facility to Saltville. I had met Dale a couple of years earlier and was impressed with his abilities. Now I would unexpectedly have the benefit of Dale to help me solve Saltville's problems.

Upon arrival, I asked Dale Jensen to take me on a tour of the facility. I wanted to see what had changed since my last visit. As we walked along, Jacoby's love for fixing things became evident. He'd made improvements to all kinds of equipment including the kiln drive, the scrubber's filter press, and the product cooler. Unfortunately, I also saw some things that seemed odd. I found that a narrow-gauge railroad was under construction. Dale explained that it was to transport the filter cake from the scrubber to the kiln for drying. The filter cake needed to sit under the kiln for a few days to allow the radiant heat from the hot kiln shell to dry it. Otherwise, the landfill wouldn't accept it. I was highly skeptical that this was a cost-effective approach. I knew that Dave Jacoby was a model train enthusiast. He had built a railroad in his house that traveled through the rooms on the main floor. His wife used it to send him food and drinks as he watched TV. I suspected Jacoby just wanted another railroad to play with. I didn't want to have any involvement in this boondoggle. I could get into plenty of trouble on my own.

Further along on during the tour, I noticed the maintenance department was tearing down an old unused building. It seemed to me that their time would be better spent improving kiln reliability rather than improving the appearance of the plant. There was no use having a good-looking plant if it ended up shut down. As I watched them my heart started to pound.

"Ah, did anyone think to have the building checked for asbestos?" I asked Dale.

"Not that I am aware of," he answered.

I suspected that they were removing asbestos and hauling it to the landfill without proper protection for the workers or with the landfill's knowledge. Not good. We could be cited for exposing the workers and might have to pay to dig up the asbestos at the landfill for proper disposal. I remembered Tom Wright telling me that when I was the boss, I was the boss and would be responsible for whatever happened.

After the tour, I told the maintenance superintendent, Neal, to immediately stop work on the railroad and to discontinue dismantling the old building. Neal said he was concerned that Jacoby would fire him if he didn't finish these projects. I told him I would make sure he wasn't penalized for following my orders. I had worked for bosses that didn't take responsibility for their actions. When it happened to me at the Burgin, it made me mad and I lost respect for my chickenshit boss. I wouldn't do that to Neal.

When I got back to the office, I thought some more about the potential asbestos problem. In the early 1900s, asbestos was found to be an excellent fireproof insulation. More recently, however, it had been determined asbestos dust could cause serious lung problems and possible death. For this reason, it was now illegal to handle or remove asbestos unless proper safety precautions were taken. Clearly, I needed to know whether the old building contained any asbestos, but I didn't want to get anyone needlessly upset. I spoke to Raleigh and they arranged for an inspector to visit the plant. It turned out that there was asbestos all over the old building and we needed to hire a special crew to remove it. The question was what to tell the Saltville employees as well as the landfill.

I called my boss, Frank Robinson, and told him about the asbestos fiasco.

"You don't need to tell the maintenance department what's going on," Frank said. "We'll just have the special crew come in and clean up the mess."

"I don't think that's going to work," I said. "The maintenance crew is going to be suspicious when contractors show up to remove the asbestos dressed like they're ready for a spacewalk."

"What do you recommend?" Frank asked.

I thought about it for a few seconds then continued. "We need to be up front with the workers and tell them what happened. They need to know that Texasgulf will look after them. They will do a better job if they know the company is trustworthy and looking after their safety. Besides, it's the right thing to do."

"What about the landfill?"

"We need to tell them too. Otherwise, it could get messy and the community won't trust us."

Frank reluctantly agreed and we proceeded on that basis. I brought in an asbestos specialist to talk to the employees. He told them that their risk was minimal. Normally, people developed problems only after years of exposure to asbestos. After the meeting, several people came up and thanked me for the company's honesty. Fortunately, years later no one developed any health issues from their limited exposure.

When I told the landfill they were initially upset. I was afraid they would tell us we had to dig it up and dispose of it in a proper facility. That would be expensive. They thought about it for a few days and then told me they appreciated Texasgulf's honesty. They said we could just leave it where it was since it wouldn't be a risk buried under all the dirt. It would be a greater risk to dig it up since the exposed asbestos could become airborne. But they warned me that there would be significant fines if we ever did it again.

After the first few weeks at Saltville, I was beginning to feel battleworn. Shutting down work on the railroad and dealing with the asbestos fiasco was trying. I wondered what other headaches were lurking out there waiting to spring on me. I decided that now would be a good time to look at Saltville's operating costs. I wondered if Dave had been getting creative there as well.

In reviewing Saltville's costs, I didn't see any obvious shenanigans. I was surprised, however, to see that Saltville's costs were almost 65 percent fixed. This meant they spent almost the same amount of money whether they were running and producing product or not. Thus, if they were only producing salable product 30 percent of the time, their cost per ton would go through the roof. With their poor production rate, it was clear why they weren't making any money. They should have concentrated on this rather than building a railroad or tearing down an old building. The production rate needed to be dealt with, and quickly. But, I wasn't sure that I was up to the task. I didn't know much about DFP production and even less about kiln operations. How in the world was I going to fix this problem?

To figure out what was screwing up production, I needed to spend more time in the plant with Dale and the operators. Unfortunately, there was a lot of office work and administrative issues to deal with. But, despite this, at 4:00 p.m., I would lay the paperwork aside and go down to the control room and talk with the troops. I would often stay until 9 or 10 p.m. It was not only a productive use of my time, but since I didn't have a family to go home to, it was more interesting than sitting in a motel room watching TV.

At first, the operators were quiet when I was with them. But after a while, they started to feel comfortable around me and began to talk. We'd walk around the plant and they would give me their opinion about what was going on. They often had good ideas about how to deal with problems and would let me know about unusual things they observed. The information provided invaluable insights into improving operations. With my technical background, I could understand the underlying principles of what was happening and could also sort out bad ideas that weren't theoretically feasible. I then reviewed these ideas with Dale and Neal. If we all agreed, they'd make the necessary changes. The three of us made a good team.

The modifications we made significantly improved the plant performance. We were producing more tonnage and the plant was much more reliable. Unfortunately, we were still having trouble making a sellable product.

Saltville was trying to produce defluorinated phosphate rock which was known as DFP and used by the poultry industry. Unfortunately, the birds couldn't tolerate much fluorine. DFP was produced by mixing phosphoric acid, sodium carbonate, and phosphate rock together. The mixture was then heated to 2400 degrees to drive off the fluorine. Dale had found that the defluorination process wouldn't work if the rock contained too much silica. Unfortunately, the rock provided by Texasgulf's Aurora facility contained variable amounts of silica that was almost always higher than the kiln could tolerate. Thus, the kiln was mostly producing off-grade product.

Based on the information provided by Dale, I called Aurora and told them we would not accept any phosphate rock with more than 2.7 percent silica. I suggested that they check each rail car before they shipped it. Otherwise, any cars that didn't meet this specification would be shipped back to them, at their expense.

They weren't happy about this and told me to go to hell. However, they reconsidered when I pointed out I could let Tom Wright know Saltville's poor performance was their fault. When the plant went bankrupt, they could explain to Tom why checking the rail cars was inconvenient. They decided it wasn't such a bad idea after all. I just hoped Dale was right.

Fortunately, the kiln responded favorably to the low silica rock. However, just as I started to take a breather, Tom Wright gave me a call.

"Clark, how are the AFEs coming along for the projects to repair Saltville's equipment?" Tom asked.

Tom's question made me cringe. My history with AFEs during my solution mining tests at Moab was not the best.

"What specific AFEs are you interested in?" I asked.

"The AFE for the new kiln drive, the one for the new instrumentation system, and the AFE for the scrubber improvements," he said.

"Ah, Tom, I think those projects have been completed."

"What?! Goddamn it, you'd better be kidding me. Are you telling me that money has been spent without corporate approval?"

Maybe I had better check this out before Tom gets any more upset.

"Um, let me investigate this and I'll get back to you."

Maybe I should have looked at capital spending when reviewing Saltville's books.

After I hung up the phone, I yelled down the hall and asked John Conner to come to my office. John was the office supervisor. He looked after human resources, purchasing, and accounting.

When John walked in my office, I asked, "What do you know about the AFEs for the kiln drive, instrumentation, and scrubber projects?"

"What do you mean by 'what do I know?'"

"Well, were the AFEs for these projects approved?"

John stood in the doorway for several seconds. He had the

look of a trapped animal. "The AFEs were never written for those projects."

"How the hell did you pay for them?"

"We paid the bills and booked the charges in a suspense account."

"In a suspense account! You mean there are thousands of dollars that are hanging out there?"

"I think we have a little over a million in that account. I was just following Dave's orders."

"What the hell were you going to do if you were audited? You're supposed to make sure that the corporate accounting procedures are followed."

"Yeah, an audit would have presented a problem. But if I didn't do it, Dave would fire me. I decided to take my chances with the auditors."

"Ah, shit. I need to think about this."

I pondered the situation for a while. On the one hand, I didn't want to get John Conner or Dave Jacoby fired. On the other hand, I didn't want to get fired for someone else's stupidity. I finally decided I'd better call Tom.

"Tom, I think we may have a little problem," I said.

"What's that?" Tom asked. The tone in his voice made me think he was expecting the worst and getting ready to explode.

"The projects you asked about have already been completed. They booked the money for them in a suspense account."

"In a suspense account. What in the hell were they thinking?"

"I think they planned to submit the AFEs and then move the costs to the proper accounts when the AFEs were approved."

"Well, you need to immediately get the AFEs prepared and sent to Raleigh. In the meantime, I need to think about this a little more."

The next day the auditors arrived.

I was really beginning to miss Weeping Water.

Fortunately, the auditors only found a few additional, and luckily, small projects requiring AFEs. The office staff and I, along with Dale, spent the next few weeks preparing AFEs. At least our cost estimates for the projects were easy to calculate since the money had already been spent. I heaved a sigh of relief when they were finally forwarded to Raleigh for approval.

While I was distracted, Dale continued to resolve the process problems. With the strict enforcement of the silica specification, the plant stayed on grade most of the time. Just when I started to think things were under control, a new headache popped up. My secretary, Susan, walked into my office to let me know that Tom was on the phone again.

"Clark, what do you know about Jacoby selling tools and supplies to Saltville?"

"I haven't heard anything about it."

"Well, check it out and get back to me."

What had Dave done now?

Once again, I yelled down the hall and John came scurrying into my office. "Do you know anything about Dave selling tools to Saltville?"

"Yeah, he sold the plant quite a bit of stuff including a lot of tools."

"Why in the hell did he do that?"

"Well, when Dave first arrived, the maintenance shop didn't have hardly anything. This was because the initial cost of the plant was more than anticipated and they wanted to stay under the budget of $10 million. Rather than try to get approval to purchase equipment, Dave decided it would be easier to just sell the plant equipment he already had like drill presses, arc welders, a metal lathe, and assorted other tools and supplies."

"Where the hell did Dave come up with all this stuff?"

John began to look a little nervous. "He said that he had previously purchased them over the years from the salvage yard at Aurora. He had planned to set up a shop in his garage to give him something to do in his spare time."

"So you're telling me he bought equipment from Texasgulf at Aurora and sold it to Texasgulf at Saltville? And this didn't seem strange? How much did he charge Saltville?"

"He charged Saltville a flat $10,000."

"You mean to tell me that the plant manager sold his own

facility $10,000 worth of maintenance equipment? Who approved the payment?"

Now John was really looking uncomfortable. "Dave did."

"Dave signed the authorization to pay himself $10,000?"

"Yup."

"Did he at least write an AFE for it?"

"Nope."

I called Tom back and relayed the information to him. The auditors were back the next day to inventory the equipment and assign a value. I was starting to get suspicious that someone was calling Tom on the company hotline. I wished Dave Jacoby would get well so he could deal with this. I was catching hell for someone else's stupidity. I could get in enough trouble on my own. However, Dave was still struggling to fight off the infection, or so he said. I was beginning to wonder if he was just pretending to be sick.

Despite the distraction caused by Dave's accounting shenanigans, the plant was doing much better. We set a production record in April and were on track to set another one in May. With the improved production, Saltville was finally generating a positive cash flow. I was just starting to feel optimistic about things when, you guessed it, Susan once again appeared in my office. She announced that Tom was on the phone. As I picked up the receiver, John Conner walked into my office. He had started to pay close attention to incoming calls. I put Tom on the speaker phone.

"Clark, do you know anything about blacksmithing equipment?"

"I don't, but John Conner just happens to be here. Maybe he knows something about it."

John heaved a sigh. "I was wondering if this might come up. Dave bought about $5,000 worth of blacksmithing tools and equipment. He put them in the old parts warehouse. Sometimes, he liked to unwind by working with iron."

"You mean Texasgulf spent $5,000 to help Jacoby unwind? How the hell did he justify that?" From the tone in his voice, Tom seemed to be skeptical of this expenditure.

"Dave would set up the equipment at the city park on July 4th and make trinkets for the townspeople. They seemed to appreciate it. It was kind of a goodwill gesture to the community."

Tom was not happy. However, I was learning something. If I was ever responsible for multiple plants, I needed to visit them once in a while to make sure nothing inappropriate was going on. It might be good to spend a little time wandering around without the manager so I could visit with the troops. You never knew what you might find out.

During the next few months, John Conner and I fielded additional inquiries about a hunting rifle, a model train set, and assorted other irregularities. In late May, I received another call from Tom. On this occasion, Tom Wright said that when Dave recovered from his illness, he was going to be transferred back to Aurora. They needed him to help with problems in the mine there. Plus, they could watch him a lot closer. Also, Aurora would not allow Saltville to transfer Jacoby's cash advances to their books.

"I am not sure I understand what you're saying, Tom," I said.

"Rumor has it that Dave has been getting regular cash advances during the two years he has been at Saltville. However, he hasn't turned in any expense reports to offset these advances."

At that time, it was normal for an employee who was taking a company trip to get a cash advance. This was meant to cover the cost of incidentals such as taxis and parking fees.

I asked John about the advances. He said that Dave had received several advances while he was plant manager. I asked John for more details. "What were the advances for?"

"They were for all kinds of things. Sometimes, he would run down to the hardware store for some bolts. Sometimes, he needed to pick up some weed spray or other miscellaneous items."

"So Dave was signing for his own cash advances?"

"Well, the plant manager can sign for all advances at his plant."

"Dave's cash advances were supposed to be forwarded to Raleigh for review. A plant manager can't approve his own cash advances. How much does he have on the books?"

"A little less than $20,000."

"You've got to be kidding me! Where the hell are the receipts?"

"They are in that large chest on the floor at the end of his desk."

I walked over and lifted the lid on the chest. It was completely full of receipts, paper bags, and miscellaneous items such as gloves, a box of screws, and even a couple of pairs of women's panties. I didn't even want to guess what the panties were for.

"John, I hate to tell you this. Since Dave isn't here, you're going to need to fill out the expense reports for him."

Although John wasn't happy about it, he dragged the chest to his office and waded into it. It took him almost two weeks to sort it out. We disallowed the expenses for ladies' underwear. At the end, John could account for about $15,000. Dave had to make up the difference from his personal checking account.

In early June, Tom called to ask if I was interested in managing Saltville. I told him that I appreciated the offer, but that it was just a lateral move, not a promotion. I wasn't about to drag my family 800 miles without a good reason. He told me he understood and they'd find someone else. I asked that they hurry. I hadn't spent much time with my family since early February.

Finally in mid-June, the company announced that the new manager would be John Gray. John had worked at Aurora for several years and was looking for an opportunity to expand his experience. When John took over I was greatly relieved to end my temporary two-week assignment that had lasted almost four and a half months.

Dave Jacoby returned to Aurora. I was astounded that he hadn't been fired. He must have had pictures of someone in senior management in a compromising situation. However, at Aurora, Dave helped resolve some major problems. He worked out an ingenious system for dewatering and stabilizing the mine. He later was instrumental in resolving issues with other areas of the plant and became much more safety conscious. He did well, as long as there was someone around to keep him in check.

I returned to Weeping Water a little worse for wear. By now, Weeping Water seemed like an alternate universe. Being away from home for nearly five months working long hours and solving difficult problems had taken its toll. I felt like I needed a vacation.

But, I had learned a lot while in Saltville. It had definitely turned out that being honest with the workers and landfill about the asbestos fiasco had been the right thing to do. Lying to people about important issues could create a lot of problems. It was also clear that the plant manager must give critical issues top priority. To add a narrow-gauge railroad or tear down an old building while the plant was losing money was crazy. It was also clear that Dave Jacoby's boss, Frank Robinson, should have been visiting the plant regularly. Dave had demonstrated that a plant manager at a remote location could easily get out of control. No one at the plant dared cross him. Thus, it was easy for his power to corrupt his judgment. Absolute power corrupted absolutely, or so I'd heard. As I thought about it, I realized I was in the same situation at Weeping Water as Jacoby had been. No one from senior management ever came by to check on me. And, despite all the infractions, they hadn't fired Jacoby.

CHAPTER 26

Learning the Value of Money

Never trust me around a computer

Although I enjoyed the people in Saltville, it was good to get back home to Nebraska. It was June of 1988 and I had been living in a cheap motel for five months. It was not much fun. I was glad to finally be sleeping in my own bed. Plus, it was good to be back with the family. In my absence the kids had learned a lot and become more independent. I knew it was demanding on Betty to look after the family without my help, and she was certainly glad to have me back but not necessarily happy to have my input on some things. She had come to enjoy her freedom.

As I drove down to the plant on my first day back, I was curious to see what the troops had been up to in my absence. Saltville had taught me that people sometimes get lax about taking care of things when no one's checking on them. Arriving at the office, I chatted with the staff for a few minutes before sitting down at my desk. I was surprised at how much paperwork had piled up. Although I was going to need to spend more time than normal at my desk, it would give me the chance to see how the staff was getting along with the new computer system.

Today it is hard to imagine what accounting was like in the mid-1980s. When I first started work at Weeping Water, the accounting ledgers were kept manually and checks were handwritten. However, in 1987, I spearheaded the effort to move Weeping Water's accounting to a local file server. Raleigh took care of providing the equipment and software. Our new server was set up in a specially fabricated room just outside my office. Although the room was surrounded by the office building, for some reason it had windows making it easy to see who was working in there. The server made it much faster and easier to complete our month-end closing so our financial data could be quickly sent to Raleigh. This was done using a dial-up phone line and a 1,200-baud modem. Although by today's standards it was unimaginably slow; back in the 1980s this was innovative technology.

With the new system, Raleigh stressed that it was critical that we back up the server on a weekly basis. If the server crashed, it would be very time consuming to reconstruct the accounting records. If it happened at month end it would be a disaster. The corporate office needed our data to close out the books at month end. Without it, the closing would be delayed and senior management would get testy while waiting for the results. Unfortunately, in watching the activity in the office, I became convinced the troops were not backing up the server. I suspected that they had become lazy in my absence. This seemed like an ideal time to play a practical joke while also teaching them a lesson.

Since college, I'd continually messed with computers. At Moab, I had been instrumental in acquiring computers and writing programs to track the plant's performance. I even developed a game called Planet War that my cohorts and I played after work. Our wives were pissed off when they found out the true reason we were late getting home. From this, I'd learned that when the server was turned on it was initially dumb. All it could do was look at a specific spot on the hard drive for instructions and these instructions normally told it where to look to load the operating system. Knowing this, I prepared a new series of commands that interrupted the startup process and displayed a message. I tested this on my computer and then waited for a good time to spring my trap.

The opportunity arrived a week later when the accountants were preparing for the month-end closing. As was typical, they were stressed up due to the limited time they had to close the books and get the information to Raleigh. I waited until the office staff had gone home for the day and then restarted the file server. After logging in as an administrator, I transferred my new set of instructions to the server and shut it back down.

The next morning, Bob Startzer, one of the accountants, arrived at work and booted up the file server. Watching from my office, I saw his eyes open wide in surprise when the server wouldn't boot up. This was followed by a frown when his continued efforts to start the server were frustrated. After a few attempts, he dashed out of the room and got John Groesser. The two of them charged back into the computer room and started to mess with the server. Watching from my office, it was hard not to laugh at their desperate efforts. Finally, after a hushed conversation, they headed to my office.

"We've got a problem with the file server," John said. "We can't get it to boot up. All we get is an error message saying that it can't read the hard drive."

I looked up from the work I was pretending to do. "That doesn't sound good. Are you sure it has a problem?"

"We tried to boot it up several times but just keep getting the same message."

"Darn, and it's the end of the month. I'm glad we've got a backup copy. It sounds like we'll have to get the computer serviced and then restore the files."

They looked at each other with guilty expressions. Finally, John spoke up. "Well, we probably haven't been as diligent backing up the files as we should have."

I gave them my best PO'd face. "Oh, shit. When was the last time you backed them up?"

"I think it was mid-February."

About the time I left for Saltville.

"What are you going to do?" I asked.

They stood looking at each other for a few seconds. Finally, John said, "If we get the drive replaced, we can restore the files to February. Then we'll have to reenter everything for all the weeks since then. Working 16-hour days, it will take at least two weeks to get it done."

"Darn. Raleigh isn't going to be happy about that. They'll need to close the books before then. We're going to catch hell if we're the reason they don't get it done. Let me take a look at the server."

We headed into the file room and turned on the server. After a few seconds, the message came up.

> Hard drive C: unreadable
>
> Unable to load DOS operating system
>
> No input/output possible

I looked at the screen for a few seconds. "This doesn't look good," I said. John acknowledged the message.

"Do you know where the computer manuals are?" I asked.

While John and Bob were distracted, I quickly pressed the "C" and then the "H" keys. This signaled the server to replace my program with the original one and then erase my program from the drive.

"Before we call the serviceman, why don't we try booting it up one last time?"

Bob dutifully switched it off and then powered it back up. Much to their amazement and relief, the server started up without a hitch.

I pretended to be surprised by the turn of events. "It looks like we dodged a bullet this time. But we need to be more diligent in the future. I don't want to catch hell for you two screwing up."

They both agreed, but later in the day I saw them in a hushed discussion in Bob's office. I thought they might be suspicious of the miraculous repair of the server. As it turned out, they were more than suspicious. They were plotting their revenge and it would include my arch adversary: golf.

The Greater Omaha Ag Business Association planned to hold their annual golf outing in a couple of weeks. In preparation for the outing, I thought it would be a good idea if John Groesser and I shot a practice round at the Oak Hills Country Club. As the plant manager, Texasgulf provided me a membership. Since I hadn't been playing much golf, I hoped this would refresh my skills.

The practice round of golf was a disaster. I hit balls in the water hazards. I couldn't get out of a sand trap on a bet. I even managed to hit a house, much to the dismay of the homeowner. But the worst shot was on the fifth hole when I managed to hit a golf ball onto nearby Interstate 80. As the ball merrily bounced down the westbound lane, the cars had to dodge it to avoid being hit. I couldn't believe how poorly I had played.

The next Saturday was the Ag Business golf outing. With some trepidation, I teed off on the first hole. Although this round of golf wasn't quite as bad as my practice one, it was still a disaster. I became aggravated by the amount of time I spent in the rough. My attitude didn't improve when I was awarded a box of twelve golf balls for hitting the most balls into the water.

Arriving home that evening, I was not in a good mood. I am a competitive person and my performance on the golf course was humiliating. As I started to get ready for bed, Betty said she had something to show me.

"Before I give this to you," she said, "I want you to promise not to get mad."

This did not help my attitude. "What do you mean, 'don't get mad?'"

"You need to settle down. This isn't anything to get upset about."

"Don't tell me not to get upset. Show me whatever it is you need to show me."

She pulled out an envelope. The return address said it was from the Oak Hills Country Club. Inside was a letter addressed to me. As I read it, my heart started to pound.

Dear Mr. Huff,

Based on your recent round of golf at the country club, we are compelled to revoke your golfing privileges until you have shown that you have a basic understand of the rules of golf and are no longer a risk to the adjoining homeowners and your fellow golfers. When you are ready, you can make an appointment with the club pro to demonstrate your improved golf technique. Until that time, please feel free to continue using the dining facilities.

The letter was signed by the club manager. To say that I was mad would be a gross understatement.

"I am going down to the country club tomorrow," I said, "and shove my putter up the golf pro's ass. I don't need to put up with this bullshit."

"Before you do anything drastic," Betty said, "look closer at the letter."

It was good she suggested this. Previous letters from Oak Hills were on special stationery that used brown ink for the letterhead. The letterhead on this one used black ink. Based on the faint lines on the letter, it looked like the letterhead was a copy of the original. The envelope also looked like a copy.

"I think someone is trying to pull a joke on you," Betty said.

I couldn't argue with that.

"I think they got me with this one," I said.

"Got you!" Betty said. "I was the one that spent all day agonizing about how you were going to take this."

At this point, I reverted back to my days at school in Spanish Fork. I had learned to never let someone bully or tease me. Despite being an adult, I still couldn't just let this one go. I wanted revenge.

"I will take care of this Monday morning. Give me a call at 10:00 a.m. and then listen. You don't need to talk."

Monday morning, I was sitting at my desk when my secretary, Pam, came in to tell me that Betty was on the phone. She looked a little worried. I picked up.

"Hello, Betty. How are you doing?" I asked. I pretended to listen for several seconds and then said, "They did what? I can't believe that, and you did what? Aw, shit, you shouldn't have gotten them involved... no, don't do anything else... look, I'll take care of it when I get home. Goodbye." I slammed the phone down and started back to work.

Since Pam's desk was just outside my office and John's was next door, they could clearly hear my side of conversation. The two of them huddled up for a few minutes and then John came into my office. "How are things going, Clark?"

"The plant is doing pretty good. However, I am pissed off at Betty."

"Why? What happened?"

"Well," I said, "she received a letter from the Oak Hills Country Club on Saturday."

He tried to play it cool, but I knew I'd eventually have him. I pressed on.

"The letter said that they were revoking my golfing privileges based on my poor performance last week. She was afraid of how I would react so she didn't show me the letter."

Still no response from John. But he kept glancing at Pam as she stared at her desk.

"Instead, this morning Betty went down to the country club to cancel our membership!" John started to look nervous. "When she arrived," I continued, "they said they didn't know anything about the letter. They said that the other country clubs in the area were hurting for members. They thought that one of them had sent the letter in an attempt to get me to cancel my club membership so that I might join their club."

John's face looked like he was really alarmed by this news.

"Oak Hills was so upset," I said, "that they took the letter to the post office and filed a complaint. Apparently," I leaned in as if it was serious, "the FBI now has the letter and is investigating the whole mess as mail fraud."

Panic flashed across John's face. I had him. I only wished Betty was here to see it.

John hurried to his office where he was joined by the rest of the office staff. I could hear them discussing the situation in hushed tones.

Finally, John, Pam, and the rest of the group came into my office. "Clark," John said, "we sent that letter to you as a practical joke. You need to get the investigation stopped."

"But it looked like it was on Oak Hills stationery," I said. "Who did that?"

Pam looked intently at her feet. "I copied the letterhead, but I was just following John's instructions."

"The envelope had an Omaha postmark. How did that happen?"

Another staff member said, "I took the letter to Omaha to mail it. John said to do it."

Apparently, the rats were abandoning the sinking ship.

John looked down the line at his accomplices. "We need to get the investigation stopped. We definitely don't want the FBI involved in this."

"John, Betty was pretty upset about this. I think it would be a good idea if you called and apologized to her."

John immediately left my office and called Betty. After a few minutes, he returned to my office. "I apologized and asked her to get the letter back to me. She listened to my apology and then said I should talk to you."

John and the office staff were surprised and relieved when I told them the truth. They were particularly glad that the FBI wasn't involved. They told me that they would absolutely never try another practical joke on me. They had learned their lesson. When I got home that evening, Betty said that John's apology was the best she had ever heard and maybe I should take notes.

I figured that they had learned a lesson. It was not a good idea to play practical jokes on me. Even if I deserved it. But I also learned something. Never react to a situation when you are mad. I should have remembered that from when I wrestled with my mom after the rock throwing contest. If Betty had not calmed me down, I would have made an embarrassing scene at the country club. I made a mental note to remember that in the future. It proved beneficial on several occasions.

Despite the distraction of my golfing misadventure, I was always interested in improving the plant performance and its appearance. Even with my limited presence at Weeping Water, Raleigh had approved funding to add more screens which improved the product quality. They also approved the installation of a new dryer fan and bag house which increased production rates. As the plant appearance improved, the operators took more pride in the facility and the sales group started showing the plant off to their customers.

As it turned out, the enhanced product quality combined with better plant appearance caused a problem. We couldn't keep up with demand. Based on my experience at Saltville, I knew Weeping Water's profits would soar if we could satisfy this surge in sales. Unfortunately, there weren't any opportunities in the existing plant we hadn't already taken. Building a new plant seemed out of the question. After some research, I came up with a plan that would increase production and reward the employees at the same time.

The proposed plan shared the value of productivity improvements with employees. During the base period, we would keep track of how many man-hours were required to produce a ton of product. These numbers would be the base factors. Then each month we would use the base factors to determine how many man-hours would have been required at our original production rate. If the actual man-hours were less, a bonus would be paid to the employees. The bonus would be half of the calculated labor savings. In simple terms, the company would split the labor savings 50/50 with the employees.

One way to reduce labor was to reduce the head count. However, this wasn't what I was after. At Weeping Water, a better way to earn a bonus was to increase production rates. The increased production would dilute labor costs and the employees would get a big bonus. At the same time, the company would be happy because it would not only get half of the labor savings but all the energy savings plus the income from the additional sales.

This type of plan had never been tried at Texasgulf before, but I made the pitch to senior management anyway. When I showed how much money the company could save, they were interested. When I talked about the ability to increase sales, they were convinced but with a couple of conditions. We could only utilize the plan for two years. I would need to let the employees know that there would be no bonuses after that. The other condition was that John Groesser, Eddie Gegg, Gregg Perrault, and I would not be part of the plan. It was our job to make sure that safety, environmental compliance, product quality and plant appearance were maintained.

In mid-1988, I presented the plan to the employees. I explained how the calculations would be done and made sure they understood it would only last for two years. I then fielded a few questions. At the end of the discussion, I explained it was up to them. I was giving them this option and there would be no hard feelings if they didn't want to do it. They were overwhelmingly in favor of it. They couldn't see how they could lose. At worst, they would only make the same amount of money they were making now. But if they did good, they would receive handsome, quarterly bonuses.

Based on the employees' response, we immediately implemented the plan. Morale and productivity began to improve. To some extent, they were working harder. However, they were also working smarter. They came up with innovative ideas for improving efficiency. Although this sometimes required a capital expenditure, Texasgulf didn't object.

By the end of 1988, I was surprised by how much an improved employee attitude increased the production rate. My biggest headaches were making sure everything was done safely and that the product met specifications. During the next year, production rates increased by over 40 percent. The employees were happy because they were getting significant bonuses. The company was ecstatic. The increased production was diluting the cost required to produce a ton of product. At the same time, they were selling significantly more tonnage, which meant that Weeping Water was generating 40 percent more profit.

After another year we were still doing well. However, there was trouble on the horizon. The producers of livestock in our market area were changing their feed formulations. This meant that they needed less Dical and Monocal. The sales started slumping off and the quarterly bonus declined and eventually ended. Although the employees missed receiving the bonus, they were not mad at me or the company. They understood that external forces were causing the problem and were happy to have received the bonuses they did get.

As 1989 was coming to a close, I felt I could step back and

enjoy life. Weeping Water was doing well and the problems I had been sent to fix were resolved. I was glad that the Christmas season was approaching. It would give me a chance to spend time with the family while the kids were out of school.

Then on the morning of December 6, Fred Stephens gave me a call. Fred was the VP of Feed Sales in 1986 when he brought up Weeping Water's quality issues to Tom Wright. Recently, he had been promoted to VP over all aspects of feed phosphate including production. I now reported to Fred and he was once again causing me a headache. Fred explained that Saltville was having serious problems.

"Clark, Tom Wright and I would like you to go to Saltville and see if you can get their production rate up," Fred said. "They are losing money and won't survive unless things are turned around. We thought you could help them out."

Ah, shit. This is the 1986 scrubber fiasco all over again.

"Fred, that won't work. I went through this before at Saltville. You can only have one person calling the shots."

"All you need to do is help them get the plant straightened out."

I had known for some time that Saltville wasn't doing well and tried to help them out, but they wouldn't listen. On top of this, Dale Jensen had accepted a job with another company at a soda ash facility in Wyoming. I wasn't sure what had happened, but Saltville needed him. During my previous visit, he had been instrumental in figuring out how to get the kiln on grade.

I continued. "I've already talked to the manager, John Gray, about Saltville's poor performance. But he has his own ideas about what needs done. Since he is the plant manager, he will do what he thinks is best. Even if he follows my suggestions while I'm there, he will go back to doing things his own way as soon as I leave."

"But something needs to be done now," Fred said. "Things are getting critical."

"Maybe, but I have my own plant to look after. Besides, it will just be a waste of time for me to go there. History has shown you can only have one person calling the shots. The company is better served if I stayed in Weeping Water and looked after it."

"I'll go talk to Tom Wright and see what he thinks."

I hoped Tom would see my point of view and leave me in Weeping Water. Besides, although I liked the people at Saltville, I didn't want to have to spend a lot of time dealing with their production issues. I wanted to have a nice Christmas with my family in Nebraska.

Just after lunch, Fred called me back. "I just finished talking with Tom Wright and he agrees with you."

I heaved a sigh of relief. I thought I'd dodged a bullet.

Fred continued. "Tom said that effective immediately you are in charge of Saltville."

I was stunned.

"I absolutely don't want to go to Saltville to manage it. I am happy here in Weeping Water. I am already a plant manager. Going to Saltville would just be a lateral move."

"I don't think Tom was asking whether you wanted to go. He made it very plain that you are in charge of Saltville and to get your ass up there as soon as you can."

"What about Weeping Water?"

"Eddy Gegg can look after the plant in your absence."

"What are they going to do with John Gray?"

"That will be decided later. For now, he can hang around the plant and help out as long as it doesn't create a problem."

"That will be a little awkward. Someone needs to tell John that I'm coming."

"Tom told Frank Robinson to give John a call."

Ah, shit. Here we go again. Based on my move to Weeping Water, Frank will never give John the bad news.

When I hung up the phone I was sick to my stomach. I didn't want to leave my family and spend months at Saltville straightening out someone else's screw up. Especially since I had just come back from there eighteen months ago. And it was almost Christmas. When I called my wife to let her know of the change of plans, she wasn't very happy about it either.

Later in the day, I was sitting at my desk when John Gray called. "I understand that you are on your way to Saltville."

"Yup. They gave me my marching orders a couple of hours ago," I said.

"Well, it will be good to get your advice on how to improve performance."

Advice? Frank didn't tell him!

"Is that all Frank told you? That I would be there to give you advice?"

"Yeah, he said you were going to review operations and make some recommendations."

"John, I think you had better call Frank back. I received a completely different message. I don't think Frank is being honest with you. Please, give him a call and then call me back."

Just before I headed home, John called back. "I finally caught up with Frank. He said that I had understood him correctly. You would just be coming to Saltville to provide advice."

"John, one of us is mistaken. Based on past experience, I would suggest that you call Tom Wright directly and find out what's going on and then give me a call."

John seemed puzzled by my response, but reluctantly agreed to call Tom. A little while later, he called me back sharing that he knew I'd be calling the shots. I felt bad he had been given the runaround—if it were up to me, I would have told him exactly what was going on in the first place.

Thus began a new Saltville adventure. I wondered what they'd done to the plant this time. It seemed strange that they were once again having production problems. I really hated to be starting on a new undertaking that would take me away from my family for months, particularly during Christmas. But regardless of my feelings, I was off to Saltville for the holidays.

CHAPTER 27

Saltville's Troubles Continue

Sometimes you need to step back and look at the big picture

As I headed home from the office, I thought about my earlier conversation with Fred Stephens. I couldn't believe I had to help with Saltville again. I was getting tired of this nonsense. I was the manager of Weeping Water. Saltville wasn't my responsibility. And, to top it all off, this fiasco was going to disrupt my Christmas plans for 1989. In retaliation, I decided to upgrade my accommodations. Instead of staying at the Salina Motel in Saltville for $35 per night, I would stay at the Martha Washington Hotel in Abington for $105 per night. If senior management didn't like it, they could send me home.

Tom surprised me with a call to my house that evening.

"Clark," he said, "you need to fly to Saltville tonight."

This surprised me. "I can't get out of town this late at night. Besides, what's so critical that it can't wait a few days?" I still hoped to put off this fiasco until after Christmas.

"The plant isn't producing anything salable. As a result, they're losing money big time. Unless things turn around soon, I'm going to be forced to close the facility."

Damn.

So early the next morning, I was once again on my way to

Saltville. I arrived at the plant a little after lunchtime. As I drove through the gate, I was surprised to see a large concrete silo and a new loadout system for trucks. I couldn't believe they'd spent hundreds of thousands of dollars on these projects. Maybe they should have thought about spending the money on improving plant operations. It seemed they'd put the buggy before the horse.

When I arrived at the office, John Gray greeted me and said they were just getting ready for a staff meeting. The purpose of the meeting was to discuss ideas for reducing costs. John said that he would use this opportunity to let them know that I was the temporary manager.

I took a seat at the conference table and looked around. John Gray had included the purchasing agent, office supervisor, maintenance and production foremen plus a couple of people I didn't know.

Who was running the plant?

Noticeably absent was Dale Jensen.

After a few minutes, John Gray called the meeting to order.

"First, I'd like to welcome Clark Huff and let you know he is the temporary plant manager. He will hold this position for the next few months while the production problems are worked out."

"It's good to see all of you again," I said. "I wish the circumstances were different."

Although I enjoyed the people, I couldn't bring myself to say I was happy to be there.

"Since it has been one and a half years since my last visit, I will need to rely on you to bring me up to speed on what's going on. But I'm sure we can get things sorted out quickly so I can get out of your hair."

I then turned the meeting back over to John Gray.

John Gray said, "As you all know, the plant is losing money. We need to do everything we can to reduce costs. I have a requisition here for a case of light bulbs. Are you sure that we need a full case?"

"I think we get a discount if we order a case," the office supervisor, John Conner, said.

"Can you check and see how much the discount is?"

"Sure. I'll have Herb look into it."

"Next, I have a requisition for an assortment of nuts and bolts. Do we really need to keep all this in inventory? Couldn't we just go down to the hardware store and pick them up?"

"Sometimes, we need to make repairs at night," said the maintenance foreman, Neal Barrett. "If we don't have the parts it might take the plant down."

This is crazy. How can they worry about a few light bulbs when they aren't making any product? They must not understand the plant's economics.

"Next, we have a requisition for an assortment of stainless steel welding rod. Do we really need all this?"

At this point, I stood up and started to leave.

"Clark, where are you going?" John Gray asked.

"This is a waste of time. I am heading down to the plant."

"Don't you want to help reduce costs?"

"If I remember correctly, Saltville's fixed costs are almost $400,000 per month. You can't save enough on lightbulbs to offset that. The plant has to start making salable product. If it doesn't, Saltville has no income and can't survive."

I can't believe a dumbass engineer like me is explaining economics to anyone. What a mess.

The group sitting around the table looked at each other in surprise.

I continued. "We should reconvene the meeting down in the control room so we can start figuring out what's gone wrong."

With that, we all headed to the plant. The control room operator was surprised to see all of us, and a little concerned. Once again I was at a facility where management didn't normally visit the plant.

In my previous assignments, senior management seemed to think I was technically smart enough to figure out how to fix any problem. I kept telling them I wasn't. During my trips to Saltville and as manager of Weeping Water, I had to put my ego aside and talk to the people in the plant. Many in management wouldn't do this. They didn't want the underlings to find out that the boss didn't know everything. Instead, they sat in the office handling paperwork and attending meetings. But I wasn't worried about impressing anyone. I figured senior management would be happy to have the problem solved. They wouldn't care whose idea it was.

Yet when I talked to the operators, I didn't take anything I was told for granted. I figured it was my job to sort out the good ideas from the bad based on engineering principles. It was then my responsibility to make the resources available to fix the problem. As the troops learned that I would listen and act on their ideas, they appreciated it and felt more comfortable talking to me. This lifted a heavy burden from my shoulders because I didn't have to solve all the problems myself.

I was also surprised some managers didn't spend time in the plant, particularly if there wasn't a problem. Operations and maintenance got lax if no one came around to check on things. Some managers tried to get input from the workers in a formal meeting. It seldom worked. The workers felt nervous about being tormented by their peers if they said anything and so they clammed up. I understood that. I tended to be the same way. I hated to express my opinions to a group. However, most people would open up during casual conversations in their work area.

As I stayed late in the evenings wandering around the plant, I unexpectedly had company. My old companion from the Raleigh BER group, Steve Auman, came to Saltville to help out. He, Neal Barrett, and I spent many long nights checking out the plant while talking to people. It soon became apparent that some of the critical operating parameters were not being properly controlled. Some of this was because the plant was using old, obsolete equipment. Saltville would have done better if it had spent money upgrading the plant rather than building a product silo. But as we resolved the mechanical problems, it became clear that the most significant problem was the poor quality of the phosphate rock. The silica level was bouncing around again. Saltville seemed to have forgotten that it was critical to have stable, low silica rock. No wonder they weren't producing much.

John Gray should have made sure that the phosphate rock met Saltville's standards. But since he wasn't at Saltville when we figured it out the first time, he didn't realize how critical it was.

I had to get after Aurora once again to closely control the silica in the phosphate rock shipped to Saltville. In doing this, things improved enough by February that a new production record was set. It surpassed the old record, set by me in May of 1988, by 400 tons. Saltville also turned a profit for the first time in almost a year. Although it wasn't easy, we kept working at it and production continued to improve.

There's more than one way to fix a problem

While working in Saltville it was interesting to learn about the people. They were certainly different than most people I'd known. I'd been around avid hunters before but hadn't known people that kept moonshine stills hidden in the hills. There were also occasional family feuds that cropped up. I soon got an appreciation of how strong family ties were among the mountain people from two brothers who worked at the plant. One brother, Steve, was a mix plant operator. He was a model employee. He took pride in his work and kept the mix plant spotless. If something needed to be fixed, he would take care of it himself if at all possible. He didn't want those dirty mechanics making a mess in his area.

Steve's brother, Doug, worked on a production crew. Unfortunately, he tended to get into mischief and while I was in Saltville, he was disciplined for sleeping on the job. He let it be known that he was going to retaliate. Soon acts of sabotage were discovered in his work area near the kiln and the sabotage always occurred near one of the kiln rollers. The kiln was essentially a 280-foot long, 9.5-foot diameter steel pipe supported by four, 11-foot diameter steel tires. The thick steel shell of the kiln, combined with the 9-inch-thick refractory bricks inside, meant that each of the four tires had to support 350,000 pounds. Each tire rested between two rollers, called trunnions, that were about five feet apart. The trunnions allowed the kiln to rotate while supporting it and keeping it aligned. Thus, each trunnion supported about 175,000 pounds.

For amusement, someone started placing items between the tire and trunnion. The object would be agonizingly smashed by the tremendous weight as the kiln slowly rotated. Placing a lunch bucket in the pinch point resulted in a metal clad sandwich about a quarter of an inch thick. The lunch box owner wasn't happy when he discovered it.

Photo of a 9.5-foot diamater kiln; damaged items were placed between the tire and trunnion

After the first incident, something was smashed every two to three days. Many of the items were only an annoyance such as trash cans and lunch boxes, but others were more of a problem. One of the electrician's multi-meters was hardly recognizable when it was discovered. An employee's wedding band stolen from the change house was just a paper-thin, weird-shaped donut. Besides the value of the ruined items, we were also concerned about the stress on the kiln bearings. Sometimes the saboteur would run pieces of angle iron or other steel objects between the tire and the trunnion. Taking an outage to replace damaged bearings would be expensive and a horrible waste of time.

As the incidents piled up, we noticed that they always happened when Doug's crew was working the afternoon or night shift. We suspected that this was so there wouldn't be any witnesses. Next, we noticed that the incidents occurred at a trunnion close to where Doug was working during that shift. But no matter how hard we tried we could never catch him. After almost twenty incidents, I'd had enough. Although the evidence was circumstantial, it was overwhelming. I spoke with the legal department. They said I couldn't fire Doug for the sabotage since he hadn't been caught red-handed. However, I could let him go if I told him his services were no longer needed. I spoke with office supervisor, John Connor, and then had the foreman send Doug to the conference room.

When Doug arrived, he was seated at one side of the table with John and I opposite him.

"Doug, I am sorry, but we are going to have to let you go," I said.

"You can't fire me. No one ever caught me putting anything on the kiln trunnion," Doug said smugly.

"I am not saying that you did. But you work here at the company's discretion. I'm not saying that you did anything wrong. I am just saying that we no longer need your services."

Doug looked confounded. "You can't fire me unless you can prove I did something wrong."

"We aren't saying you did anything. We're just saying that we no longer need your services."

Doug looked back and forth between John and me. The smugness was slowly replaced with rage. Suddenly, Doug jumped up. "I am going to kick the shit out of both of you."

John and I also jumped up. We were both surprised. Fortunately for me, Doug started around John's side of the table. I headed out the door and called for help. A couple of mechanics were nearby and came rushing in. I was glad that Doug quickly settled down and no one was hurt. I told him we would pay him three months' severance pay and had him escorted to the change house to clean out his locker.

However, this wasn't the end of it. A little while later, as I sat at my desk, I saw his brother, Steve, walking across the yard carrying a box. This seemed odd since it wasn't quitting time yet. I walked out the door and caught up with him.

"What's going on, Steve?" I asked.

"I'm just cleaning out my locker."

"How come you're doing that?

"I heard you fired Doug and so I figured I'd be next since you'd want to get rid of all of the family."

"That's not the way things work here, Steve. You're doing a good job for the company. We don't want to lose you. Just because we had to let your brother go doesn't mean we are going to hold that against you."

Steve looked surprised. "That's not the way it normally works around here. If somebody gets mad at one member of the family then they hold it against the whole clan."

"I'm not like that. Go put your stuff away and get back to work."

"Thanks. You won't be disappointed."

And I wasn't.

As the weeks rolled on, Saltville continued to produce DFP at record levels. By early March, I was hoping that they would turn the plant back over to John Gray and let me go home. As I sat in the Saltville office pondering this, John Gray phoned me.

"Fred Stephens just called," John said. "He wants me to meet him at the Tri-Cities airport in a couple of hours. Do you have any idea what this is about?"

"I don't know. I'm not in the loop on whatever it is," I said. "Maybe he just wants to talk about plant improvements or something."

"Well, I just thought I'd check. I'll give you a call when I get back."

After I hung up the phone, I thought about what might be going on. I was suspicious Fred was going to let John know that he was being replaced as plant manager. I wondered who the new manager might be. Later that evening, John called me at the hotel and confirmed my suspicions. That didn't surprise me. However, he went on to say that he would be leaving the company. I felt bad about the news. John and I were friends. I suspected they might replace him as a manager but had thought they would find a new job for him at the Aurora facility where he had come from.

By late March, I started to relax. Production continued at

record rates and the plant was making money. Although there were a few problems that needed to be worked out, most of the serious ones had been resolved. I assumed that a new Saltville manager would be named at any time and that I could head back to Weeping Water.

Maybe I learned something from the silo fiasco after all

As I drove into the plant one morning, I noticed a group of people standing by the kiln. On closer inspection, I could see that the kiln shell had a 10-foot-long split in it. As the kiln slowly rotated, bricks and red-hot product fell from the split. Despite this, they couldn't quit rotating the kiln yet. If the rotation stopped before the kiln had cooled down, the kiln shell would sag and become warped. This would be a major problem. Unfortunately, it took almost 18 hours for the kiln to get cool enough so that the rotation could be stopped.

When we could finally inspect the kiln, we found the split was in an 80-foot-long section of the kiln shell that was too thin. The shell was originally made from three-quarter-inch steel plate. The worst of the "thin" section was only a quarter inch thick. It turned out that corrosive gases liberated during DFP production had been getting behind the refractory and corroding the steel shell. We needed to replace the thin section of the kiln before we could resume production.

Herb, the purchasing agent, called around trying find a replacement for the thin kiln shell. However, there were few shops in the United States that could roll three-quarter-inch steel plate into a 9-1/2-foot diameter pipe. The quickest that a replacement section of kiln shell could be delivered was in six months. Having the kiln down for six months would be a disaster for Saltville. We needed to find a way to quickly get back into production.

In reviewing the thickness measurements, we found that worst section was about 20 feet long. The thickness then gradually increased in both directions until the full thickness was reached. If we could find a way to strengthen the worst 20 feet, maybe we could resume production until the replacement kiln shell showed up.

In consulting with an engineering firm, they said that just wielding a piece of steel plate to the kiln shell wouldn't work. In operation, the kiln shell would expand significantly when it heated up to 900 degrees. The steel plate welded to the outside of the kiln shell would be much cooler and wouldn't expand as much. This would cause enough stress between the kiln shell and the added steel plate to break the welds and the plate would just fall off.

Fortunately, I had learned something while investigating the silo collapse at Weeping Water. That failure had been caused when the welds attaching the support plate to the silo body were torn loose. They had only welded along the edge of the plate like we had hoped to do at Saltville. The engineer investigating the failure explained that this was inadequate. He said that they should have also plug-welded the plate to the silo. In a plug weld, holes are cut in the support plate every foot or so. The new plate is then welded to the old at each of these "plugs." This additional attachment, combined with the welds along the edges of the plate, would hopefully make the whole system strong enough to stand this stress.

I called the engineering firm and asked if we could solve Saltville's problem by wrapping the kiln with one-half-inch plate that was attached to the kiln shell using plug welds. They said they would consider it and call back the next day.

"It looks like 3-inch plug welds will work," the engineer said. "They should be about 14 inches apart in a random pattern. However, we can't recommend you do this since we've never seen it done before on a kiln and the company doesn't want to risk being sued."

I thought about it and then talked with senior management. I told them it would cost around $100,000 to temporarily fix the kiln using the plug-welded steel plate. It would take about three weeks to prepare for the test. The project was quickly approved since if it worked, we would be back in production and avoid losing several million dollars. If it didn't work, we would have just wasted a little money.

Fortunately, it did work. We were back in production in

three weeks and able to run a year before shutting down for the permanent repair. By then we had the replacement kiln shell on site and the plant was only down for two weeks.

By early April, I had been at Saltville for four months and was getting tired of it. Living 800 miles from home and only seeing the family a few times during the month was depressing. I called Fred and asked him when they were going to find a permanent manager.

"Clark, we already have a hell of a manager picked out," Fred said.

"Good, I'm ready to get back to Weeping Water. Who have you picked out?"

"You."

"Me? You've got to be out of your mind."

What the hell have I done?

"Every time you have looked after Saltville, performance has improved and problems have been solved. For whatever reason, you seem to be able to get the job done. We need you to look after the plant. Weeping Water seems to be pretty stable now and doesn't need much of your attention.

"Well, that might be good for Texasgulf, but it would just be a lateral move for me. I am not uprooting my family again for a lateral move. I am happy as the manager of Weeping Water. You will need to find someone else."

"I'll tell Tom Wright about your decision. But I know he isn't going to be happy."

I hung up the phone and nervously went about my normal routine. But I knew Tom had a way of getting what he wanted.

The next morning, I was sitting at my desk when the phone rang. When I answered and heard Tom Wright's voice, I sat up straight.

"I understand that you won't accept the transfer to Saltville."

"That's right. It doesn't make sense to disrupt my family just to make a lateral move."

"Well, I've taken care of that. You are the new General Manager of Feed Phosphate Production. You are responsible for all of the feed plants including Saltville. The promotion should help you feel better about relocating your family to Raleigh."

"What about the vacant manager position at Saltville?"

"That's your problem. You're the GM. You take care of it. In your spare time, you can also figure out who you want to manage Weeping Water. Although it will be tomorrow before we make the official announcement, you might as well start your new job immediately. Let me know how soon you can move to Raleigh. I don't want you procrastinating and working from Weeping Water for more than a couple of weeks. Your office in Raleigh is waiting."

I had been snookered again.

CHAPTER 28

Return to Raleigh

How to create a mid-life crisis

I hated leaving Weeping Water. I felt like a king there. Granted, it was a small kingdom, but since management seldom visited, I could generally do what I wanted and not worry about having to justify it. Plus, the people at Weeping Water were like my extended family. Although we occasionally argued, we generally got along and enjoyed each other's company.

Returning to Raleigh evoked a sense of dread. I wasn't fond of the heat and humidity, nor of living in a flat area choked with tall trees. It made me feel claustrophobic. Instead, I enjoyed the low humidity and wide-open spaces where I'd grown up. Where I could actually see the stars and planets. The mountain peaks I could view in the distance kept me oriented as I traveled from one place to another. On top of this, during the last four years I had really enjoyed the opportunity to use logic and science to solve tough technical problems. However, now as a general manager I would mostly be caught up in paperwork and personnel problems. The whole situation caused me to become very depressed.

Why had I made such a stupid decision?

The more I thought about it, the more I started to second-guess my decision to accept the promotion. Granted, Tom Wright, the company president, hadn't given me many options. But as the depression overtook me, my performance at work suffered and I just muddled along. I thought I'd get over it if I just toughed it out but I was mistaken. I started make dumb decisions because I just didn't care what happened.

My new boss, Fred Stephens, who was the VP of the Feed Phosphate and Potash division, could sense I wasn't happy. He told me I could return to Weeping Water if I really wanted to. I considered this but realized it wouldn't be fair to my family. The kids had already moved to Raleigh and started school. To accept a demotion and force them to relocate again in such a short time seemed mean. And it would probably doom my career.

Despite my misgivings, I was now looking after five production facilities. Three of these were Dical plants located in Weeping Water, Nebraska; Marseilles, Illinois; and, Kinston, North Carolina. I also got to look after the DFP plant located in Saltville, Virginia, and the Moab, Utah, potash facility. I was glad to look after the Moab facility since it gave me an excuse to see my old friends, but it didn't really fit in with the feed phosphate plants. Maybe Tom thought I might as well look after it since I'd spent ten years there. Overseeing plants spread over much of the U.S. meant that I got to do a lot of traveling, whether I liked it or not. At least it wasn't overseas.

With the promotion, I was assigned a corner office and a secretary, Sandra Stafford. She had a wealth of experience in the corporate world and took it upon herself to try to keep me out of trouble. She'd let me know about headaches coming my way long before I was informed through official channels. She also worked to help me understand corporate protocol. Sandra was very astute in handling people and provided me with subtle hints when I needed them.

The first order of business in my new job was to find managers for Weeping Water and Saltville. Until I took care of this, most of my time would be spent looking after these facilities. Based on his strong performance as general foreman at Marseilles, Bill Donohue was an obvious candidate to manage Weeping Water. Saltville was a little more problematic since it used unique technology, and experience had shown that not everyone could successfully manage the facility. Luckily, I was able to persuade my old friend Dale Jensen to return from Wyoming to look after the plant. With Dale's previous experience at Saltville, he knew the people and understood the plant's technology. Plus, he had a strong work ethic. I was fortunate to already have strong, seasoned managers at Kinston, Marseilles, and Moab.

In addition to getting to know the people at the feed plants, I also had to establish relationships with the Raleigh workforce. Two of the most interesting fellows were Gary Redshaw and Marty Schwartz. They worked in IT and had to visit the feed plants every few months to upgrade the servers and perform maintenance on the communications system. Since it was only a four-hour drive from Raleigh to Saltville, I found it strange when they asked if they could ride with me when I next visited the facility.

Due to its precarious financial situation, I visited Saltville on a regular basis. On my next trip, I honored Gary and Marty's request and let them tag along. It seemed a little unusual when Gary insisted that he take a turn driving at the beginning of the trip. I went along with his request since it was easier to ride than drive. We headed west from Raleigh until we reached Winston-Salem, and then we headed north toward Mt. Airy. Soon we started to angle our way up the flank of the Blue Ridge Mountains.

After we merged onto I-77, we headed north where there were breaks in the trees and we could look out to the east over the plains of North Carolina. As we drove along, we saw a sign welcoming us to Virginia. Gary looked nervously at Marty and then pulled into a rest area just across the border.

"I think it's better if you drive now, Clark," Gary said as he handed me the keys.

"Not a problem," I said. "But is there a reason you want to change drivers here?"

Gary looked at Marty again. "Let's just say that it wouldn't be good for either Marty or I to get caught driving in Virginia."

"You mean you hitched a ride with me so you wouldn't have to drive in Virginia? What did you guys do?"

"We aren't saying. Believe me, the less you know the happier you'll be."

I climbed into the driver's seat and we headed up the interstate. Although I tried to get them to tell me what they had done, they wouldn't even give me a hint.

Several months later, Gary and Marty visited the Moab facility as they continued upgrading the servers at the various plants. They were also taking the opportunity to enjoy themselves. Early one morning I received a phone call from Rick, the manager of the Moab facility.

"Clark, I need some advice."

"What's going on, Rick?"

"I just talked to the police. Gary and Marty are in jail and need to be bailed out."

"You have got to be kidding me. What did they do?"

"They were partying most of the night at the Wagon Wheel. When the bar closed, they took their party to their motel. Apparently, they and some of the local girls were drinking and skinny-dipping in the swimming pool. The other guests thought that this was more educational than their kids needed and complained to the front desk. Despite several warnings, they continued with their shenanigans. The police eventually arrived and took them into custody. To bail them out of jail, we will need to deposit $1,000 cash with the court. I've never run into this problem before and wanted to discuss it with you."

"We had better go ahead and bail them out. Make sure they understand that they need to pay the company back and that it had better not happen again."

When they returned to Raleigh they kept a low profile. Fortunately, I found that the friendship with the two of them would work both ways. Being depressed and somewhat bored allowed me to regress to my past. I occasionally did things that I shouldn't have done to relieve my boredom. One problem was related to my interest in computer games. A decade earlier, while I worked at Moab, I developed a computer game called Planet War. It was patterned after the board game Risk and pitted players on different computers against each other for world domination. Since we were using computers, we didn't have to take turns and could battle each other continuously. It was a lot of fun. While in Raleigh, I continued to modify and improve the program. Although the game required the use of the company's internal network and one of the servers, I decided to go ahead and install it anyway.

One afternoon, several of my coworkers came by and suggested we play Planet War that evening after work. I told them it sounded like fun and I would make a few adjustments to the program. During previous games, I found that the system wasn't updating the players' computers often enough. In the current version of the game, each of the players' computers was only updated every four seconds. In the heat of battle, this was not quick enough. I decided to change the timer to update everything once per second.

I completed the changes to the program and at 4:15 p.m. I decided to have a trial run before the main competition started. When I launched the program, my computer seemed to quit functioning. While I was messing with it, Sandra came in and said that her computer went down. Several other people walked out of their offices and said that it looked like network was down.

Shit, what had I done?

I rushed back into my office and pulled up the Planet War program. When I looked at the code, I found that the rate I was refreshing the satellite computers was screwed up. Instead of refreshing them once per second, it was refreshing all the computers every millisecond. Although it was a simple coding mistake, the increased traffic on the network caused it to collapse. I promptly shut off my computer and told the rest of the troops there would be no games this evening. I headed home with the belief that no one knew who had brought the network down.

I was sitting at my desk the next morning when Gary walked in. I could tell by the look on his face he was not happy.

"You are probably aware that the network went down yesterday just before quitting time," Gary said.

"Yeah, I saw that. I hope it wasn't too much trouble," I said.

"Unfortunately, it was. Joann in the tax department threw a fit. She had been working on a critical project all day. Since she hadn't saved her work, she lost everything when the system went down. She was mad as hell and let us know it."

"Did you tell her that most people are smart enough to save their work regularly?"

"It didn't seem like the time to bring it to her attention. And she wasn't the only one to come by and bitch. In any case, I wanted to let you know that we worked late but eventually figured out what happened. In the future, it might be a good idea to play Planet War after quitting time. We won't cover your butt if this happens again."

I assured him that I'd take care of it. And to show my appreciation, I forwarded him two bottles of first-class tequila provided to me by a customer from Mexico. Surprisingly, Gary, Marty, and some friends drank both bottles that evening. They were seriously hungover the next day and spent the morning in the back of the computer room asleep. But it was good to have friends who would bail me out in an emergency. As it turned out, I would need someone else to bail me out of another mess that started months earlier.

Before I left Weeping Water, I made a contentious decision. I built a loadout shelter without approval. Most of the product shipped from the plant was in the customers' trucks. However, the Weeping Water loadout system was out in the open so loading had to be suspended anytime it rained or snowed. Otherwise, the product would get wet and set up in the truck. This aggravated the trucking companies and customers.

Over a two-year period, I tried on several occasions to get funds to build a roof over the loadout system. Since this would be a capital project, it required the approval of senior management. However, every time I tried to get the project approved Tom Wright vetoed it. He said that it wasn't costing Texasgulf much to settle the few claims submitted by the customers and he didn't care whether the trucking companies were happy or not.

I took pride in the Weeping Water facility and wanted to provide first-class service. This wasn't possible with the poor loadout system. After considering the problem for a while, I decided to act. I knew that Texasgulf management normally only looked to see whether the cost per ton of product each month was below the budget. If it was, they were happy. Since much of the cost for operating the facility was fixed, an increase in the production rate automatically reduced the cost per ton. Basically, the costs were spread over more tons.

Since we were producing far more tonnage than was budgeted, our cost per ton was almost $10 below budget. I instructed my accountant to start accruing an extra $5 per ton when booking the costs. We were still $5/ton below budget so Raleigh was happy. Although this stressed up the accountant, he dutifully started to accrue the additional $5 per ton and labeled it under "unusual maintenance" services. Since we were producing about 10,000 tons per month, the amount in the slush fund started to add up. This continued even after I moved to Raleigh and Bill Donohue became manager.

Finally, there was almost $600,000 in the fund. This was enough to build the loadout shelter and add some screens to help remove any lumps that might have formed in storage. I instructed Bill to go ahead and build the shelter. Since he was new at the job, he didn't fully comprehend that he was breaking company rules. He completed the project by late summer, 1990. Several of the trucking companies and customers commented on how happy they were with the new addition.

Unfortunately, a few months later Tom Wright escorted the CEO on a tour of the facilities. When they visited Weeping Water, Tom was more observant than I had thought. He immediately noticed the changes to the loadout. Since Bill didn't fully appreciate the problem, he freely described to Tom the innovative way that the project had been financed. Tom was not amused. In fact, Tom was reportedly very vocal in his displeasure about the project, how it had been financed, and the person responsible for it. At the first opportunity, he called to let me know that I was fired.

"Dammit, Clark, you knew that was against company policy. On top of that, you knew that I wouldn't approve the project. Despite that, you went ahead and built the goddamn shelter. What were you thinking? That I would never visit Weeping Water?"

That was exactly what I was thinking. But I said, "I thought that if you could actually see the line of trucks waiting in the rain to load you would approve the project."

"Like hell I would. I don't give a damn how long the truckers have to wait. It only rains once in a while in Nebraska. Why spend money for the one percent of the time they are inconvenienced?"

"The truckers and customers have been very appreciative of the improvement."

"Well, you can see if they are appreciative enough to give you a job. You're fired." With that he slammed the phone down.

I sat in my office in silence pondering my next move. It wasn't silent for long. After a few minutes, my boss, Fred Stephens, yelled down the hall. "Huff, you dumb son-of-a-bitch, get your ass down here."

I headed down the hallway and walked into his office. "I'm guessing that Tom gave you a call," I said.

"You're damn right he did and he isn't very happy. I personally think the loadout shelter was a good idea. Several of the customers have said how much they appreciate it. However, Tom told me to fire you. I can probably talk him out of it, but you need to keep a low profile. Is there anything else I need to know?"

"Not that I can think of."

My reprieve didn't last long. The next stop on Tom's tour was the Marseilles facility. The next day, as he drove into the facility, he noticed a "new" Texasgulf building on the left side of the entry road. It was an old fertilizer blend plant that was part of the deal when we purchased the property. It had sat unused for years. Tom had driven by it before but hadn't noticed it due to its unassuming appearance. However, a couple of months earlier an unused bucket elevator in the building had tipped over and damaged one of the walls. Since we had started to use the building to store maintenance parts, we went ahead and fixed the wall. As part of the repairs, Marseilles had spent $15,000 to put aluminum siding on the building so that it wasn't such an eye sore.

Based on what he'd discovered in Weeping Water, Tom was unusually attentive as he drove into the Marseilles plant. He immediately noticed the "new" building that was apparently built without approval. Despite Dick Bacon's assurances to the contrary, Tom was convinced that I had once again violated company policy.

He immediately got on the phone. "Clark, you dumb son-of-a-bitch, you are really fired this time."

With no advance notice, I had no idea what he was talking about. "What are you firing me for?"

"I just discovered that you built a damn parts warehouse at Marseilles without approval. Fred isn't going to save your ass this time."

I was totally confused. "Tom, I honestly don't have any idea what you're talking about."

"I'm talking about the parts warehouse on the side of the access road to the plant. How did you think you could get away with that?"

I still couldn't figure out what Tom was talking about. I tried to come up with something we had built contrary to company rules. Nothing came to mind. "We didn't build a new parts warehouse."

"Then what the hell is that building on the east side of the access road? A mirage?"

Finally it dawned on me. "That's the old blend plant. It was there when we bought the property. All we did is fix a damaged wall and put a little siding on it."

"That's bullshit. You're not going to talk your way out of this one. Unless you can provide evidence that the building was there, you are really going to be fired this time." With that, he slammed down the phone.

About five minutes later I heard Fred's voice bellowing down the hall. "Clark, get your ass in my office."

I headed down the hall.

"Why didn't you tell me about the parts warehouse? Dammit, Clark, I can't help you if you don't tell me what is going on."

"I didn't tell you because there wasn't anything inappropriate about the project. It was just a minor repair project. We fixed a hole in the wall of a wood building and threw some siding on it."

"Tom thinks it's a big deal."

"Yeah, I kind of got that impression."

"Probably the only way to put this to rest is to find a picture of the old building and the picture better not come from you. I don't think Tom is feeling very trusting."

Fortunately, Dick Bacon was able to find a picture and forwarded it directly to Tom. Tom was still skeptical and had them find another picture plus the list of assets when Texasgulf bought the property. Tom grudgingly admitted that we hadn't done anything wrong at Marseilles. He did, however, keep a close eye on me after that.

Despite Tom's close scrutiny, I did find the opportunity for a few pranks. Occasionally, the people at the feed plants and I played practical jokes on each other. This helped to relieve the tension and bonded us together as friends. Sometimes, however, things got out of hand. One day, the head of payroll, Dick Littlefield, walked into my office. He said that John Conner, the office supervisor at Saltville, was creating a problem. John and Dick often didn't get along and looked for faults in each other's work. However, this time, he seemed to have a valid complaint. Anytime the office staff was late returning from lunch, John would have them put in a vacation request for 15 minutes to cover the extra time taken. He did the same thing if someone left for a few minutes to pick up their kid from school. Several times Dick came by my office to bitch about processing all the 15-minute vacation requests from Saltville.

I called Dale and told him that John needed to be more reasonable with the troops. He assured me that he would talk to John. After I hung up, I started to think about John. He and his first wife, Sandra, had divorced several years earlier. Since then, they had fought a running battle. Sandra was convinced that Texasgulf was giving John big pay increases and she wanted her share. She continually filed complaints that landed them in court once or twice a year.

This seemed like a golden opportunity to play a practical joke on both John and Dick. I typed up a memo to John that read:

Date: February 4, 1992
To: John Conner
From: Dick Littlefield
Subject: **Garnishment of Wages**

As per court order VA-4371256 recorded by the superior court of Smyth County, Virginia, it will be necessary to deduct an additional $2,500 per month from your paycheck. These funds will be forwarded to your former wife, Sandra Fillmore. The additional funds are an adjustment to the alimony and child support payments that you currently make to her.

The increased amount was justified based on the large pay increases she says you have received from Texasgulf combined with the additional expenses for caring for the children from your marriage, plus the children Sandra has had since the divorce and children that she plans to have in the future.

Since the court order was received in January, but your January check was issued before we processed the order, Texasgulf will need to deduct $5,000 from your February paycheck.

Let me know if you have any questions.

I knew that the company fax machines were located by the receptionist's desk and that she monitored who was using the machine. To protect myself, I prepared a valid fax that I needed to send the next day. First thing in the morning, I sent the practical joke fax to John along with a valid fax to Weeping Water. Then I waited for the explosion.

Saltville's fax machine was located in the hallway outside of John Conner's office. This made it easy for him to monitor it to assure the staff wasn't using it for personal reasons. When my fax was transmitted, John heard the machine start up and walked out to see what was coming in. As he read the fax he exploded.

"That damn bitch has done it again!" John yelled. "How the hell did she get the judge to agree to this bullshit? I'll bet when the court sent the notice to my dumbass lawyer, he lost it and the court entered a summary judgment. I'm going to call him and chew his ass out and then call that damn Littlefield."

John was yelling loud enough that everyone in the building could hear him. When he called his lawyer from his office, he was still yelling. However, the lawyer swore that he hadn't received anything but would check with the court.

Next, John called Dick Littlefield's office. The office staff could still hear John yelling.

"What do you mean he isn't in the office? ... Then how the hell did he send a fax? ... Just because he is moving doesn't mean he can't talk to me. I'll give him a call at home." Then he slammed down the phone.

By this time, John was frustrated and angry. When he called Dick's house, Dick was at the store. So in frustration, he vented his rage on Dick Littlefield's wife. When Dick came back and she told him what John had said, he was pissed off. He called up John and told him that he was going to drive up to Saltville and kick his ass. No one was going to talk to his wife that way. John told him to come on up. He was pissed that Dick hadn't told him about the wage garnishment. Dick told John he didn't know what the hell he was talking about and hadn't sent any fax. Possibly someone else in the payroll group had prepared the memo in his absence and just put his name on it.

The inquisition was now on. John wanted to know whether the court order was real. He was pressing both his lawyer and the payroll group to produce the letter. When it wasn't forthcoming, both John and Dick finally realized it was a hoax.

They were adamant that they wanted revenge.

Bob Bowen was the office supervisor in Raleigh responsible for the office staff and equipment. He got a list of those using the fax machine from the receptionist. Then he started to interview the appropriate people.

When Bob stopped by my office later that day he looked tired and agitated.

"I understand you sent a fax this morning," he said.

"Yup. I had to send a fax to Weeping Water about a customer complaint," I said.

"Do you have a copy of the fax?"

"Sure. Let me dig it out." I dug through a pile of papers and fished out the fax. He looked it over and handed it back to me.

"Have you sent any other faxes?"

"No. That's it. Why the interest in the faxes?"

"Someone sent a bogus fax to Saltville. You would be amazed at the fiasco it created."

He was right. I was amazed. I had thought the statement that the court was awarding John's former wife additional child support for children she was thinking about having would have tipped them off. But, as I had observed personally, when someone gets upset they lose track of reality.

By 1994, four years after moving from Nebraska to Raleigh, I was pretty much over my depression. I finally realized that I was acting stupid. After I made a decision, I needed to move forward and not look back. Instead of wallowing in my misery, I should have figured out how to make the best of my promotion to general manager. I could have delegated the paperwork to someone else and continued to work with the plants to deal with tricky technical problems. I gradually realized I'd made the best decision but then acted stupidly.

I also started to realize that I had misjudged Fred Stephens. He had stood up for me when Tom Wright wanted to fire me. Over the years, I came to appreciate Fred and realized he was one of the best bosses that I ever worked for. He would ask questions and help me realize if I was making a mistake. But at the same time, he would defend me if others questioned what I was doing.

Despite my stupidity, I learned a lot during my first years in my new job. However, by the end of 1994, it was becoming clear that things were going to change. The owner of the company, Elf Aquitaine, wanted to concentrate on the petroleum business. As a consequence, they were going to need to do something with Texasgulf.

CHAPTER 29

The End of Texasgulf

Nothing lasts forever

The crash of the company plane in 1981 decimated the senior management team and was a turning point for Texasgulf. We not only lost friends but also employees critical to the company's survival. While distracted by the task of filling the vacant management seats, the French oil company, Elf Aquitaine, used the opportunity to take over Texasgulf. Elf was primarily after Texasgulf's Oil and Gas Division. Texasgulf's other facilities were mainly involved in mineral production and so were of limited interest to Elf. For this reason, Elf allowed them to mostly operate independently and retain the Texasgulf name.

Unfortunately, the 1980s were not a good time for the phosphate business. Worldwide phosphate capacity far exceeded consumption. The net result was that prices plummeted and phosphate producers lost money. To further aggravate Elf, at the time of the takeover, Texasgulf's phosphate facility was in the middle of a major revamp. Thus, Elf not only had to send millions of dollars to cover production costs, they also had to send millions more to pay for a major construction project. Elf was not happy.

In the early 1990s, phosphate demand finally overtook supply and prices improved. But, it was short-lived. As soon as prices went up, the producers debottlenecked their plants and drove the price back down. Elf had had enough. Near the end of 1994, they decided to get rid of Texasgulf by splitting it off as a separate company and selling its stock on the open market. To be an independent company, Texasgulf needed to create and fill key executive positions. Tom Wright was selected to fill the CEO position. Surprisingly, I was promoted to Vice President of Feed Phosphate Production. I couldn't believe it. At the age of only 44, I'd finally been made a vice president.

The initial public offering of stock, known as an IPO, was planned for March 6, 1995. To prepare for this, the new management team concentrated on developing financial forecasts and slide presentations for potential investors. They then spent a couple of months visiting leading investment firms to try and generate interest in Texasgulf.

After a distracted weekend, I headed to the office the Monday morning of the IPO expecting to have an exciting day. I wasn't disappointed. As I pulled into the parking lot, I was curious as to why Tom Wright's car was sitting in its reserved parking space. Tom was supposed to be in New York.

What had happened?

Entering the office building, I got a cup of coffee and sat down at my desk. Since the stock market hadn't opened yet, I made a halfhearted attempt to finish my monthly report. I was shocked when Tom Wright walked into my office. His face was pale and he had bags under his eyes.

"The IPO is off," Tom said. His voice was a little quieter than normal. "Over the weekend, PCS came to terms with Elf and bought Texasgulf."

I was stunned. "What do we do while we're waiting for the sale to be finalized?"

"Not much, and to be honest, I don't really give a shit."

With that, he walked out of my office and headed down the hall to give others the news. As soon as he left, my secretary, Sandra, bolted into the room.

"Did Tom just say that the IPO was off?"

"Yup. It sounds like we are the proud possession of PCS."

"Who are they?"

I explained to Sandra that when I worked at Moab, I'd learned all about PCS which stood for Potash Corporation of Saskatchewan. It came into existence because the Province of Saskatchewan thought that the private potash companies were taking advantage of it. Due to the flat, high grade potash beds in Saskatchewan, the potash companies there were the low-cost producers in the world and making a fortune. The province felt that it was unfair for the companies to get rich exploiting their natural resource. Saskatchewan was only receiving a small royalty from the potash companies, and because the government couldn't change the royalty, they decided to form PCS in 1975 and nationalize five of the potash mines. This made PCS the largest producer of potash in the world.

As might be expected, the government couldn't manage the mines worth a darn. It was hard for PCS to negotiate with the unions since their members were voters. Politicians' friends and family were put in key management positions. The net result was that costs skyrocketed and PCS started losing money big time. Finally, in 1987, the Saskatchewan government had had enough. So they opted to hire Chuck Childers, a senior executive at the mining company IMC, to fix things. Chuck took over PCS with the understanding he would have a free hand in straightening things out. He quickly brought on board another IMC executive, Bill Doyle, to handle sales. Under their leadership PCS was privatized in 1989. They quickly filled key positions with qualified individuals and had a major manpower reduction. The result was that production costs plummeted and profits soared.

I told Sandra that it appeared PCS had decided to diversify by adding another fertilizer ingredient to their portfolio. By purchasing Texasgulf's phosphate operations, they now had two of the three primary fertilizer ingredients. As Sandra and I discussed the situation, others gathered in my office to speculate about how this would affect us. It was unclear what, if any, role we would have in the new organization. And since PCS's main office was in Saskatoon, Canada, we also worried about the fate of the Raleigh office.

It turned out that the completion of the acquisition was delayed a couple of months. The U.S. government wanted to review the deal to determine whether this would form an unfair monopoly. In the meantime, we continued on as employees of Elf. As usual, I was always looking for a way to take advantage of a situation. After some thought, I decided this would be a good time for me to take my plant managers on a paid vacation disguised as a production meeting. I walked into Tom Wright's office to discuss this.

"That sounds like a good idea to me."

"Do you care where I have the meeting?"

"Not really."

"How about if I have a week-long meeting at Disney in Florida?"

He sat up a little straighter in his chair. Tom normally wouldn't tolerate such shenanigans. "Why there?"

"Since Elf still owns us, any money I spend will go against them. They probably won't catch this unusual expense and if they do, by then we will be PCS employees anyway."

"Clark, I like your thinking. Your meeting is approved. In fact, there may be a few unusual expenses of my own that need taken care of."

With that, my managers and their wives joined me and my wife for a week at Disney courtesy of Elf. We did have a couple of business meetings, but most of our time was spent just enjoying ourselves. Plus, it kept us from worrying too much about the future.

In late April the government approved the acquisition and PCS began to interact with Texasgulf. We quickly found out that Texasgulf would cease to exist. All the facilities would now carry the PCS name. In addition, the structure of the former Texasgulf organization was completely overhauled. Most of the people promoted when the IPO was underway were moved back to their original positions. Fortunately, I was able to retain my vice president title.

I was soon impressed with PCS's handling of the company. They held a "getting to know you" meeting in early July of 1995. Senior management from all of the divisions of PCS met at a resort in Phoenix, Arizona, for several days of presentations, golf, and other activities. This "love-in" let us meet our counterparts from the other divisions and provided the opportunity for our new owner to tell us about PCS. Since I was now a VP I was invited. I felt a little uneasy being around all these senior managers.

The first morning of the meeting was for presentations from the main divisions within PCS. John Gugulyn, the VP of Human Relations, was the first speaker and later would act as the emcee. John was another member of the management team who had been hired away from IMC. The meeting room was arrayed with long tables and chairs that faced the podium. The former Texasgulf employees tended to group together. Surprisingly, our spouses were invited to attend the meeting. We were nervously visiting while we waited for the meeting to begin.

John Gugulyn walked to the podium. We found our seats and the room fell silent. Gugulyn looked over the crowd for a few seconds until he had everyone's attention. Then he shouted, "Are you ready to rumble, IMC?" There was dead silence. We looked at each other in puzzlement. John stood there with a confused look on his face. He apparently expected us to respond back with a resounding "YES!" Finally, someone walked over and whispered in his ear. He immediately turned red. He took several steps away from the microphone and turned his back to the audience while he regained his composure. Finally, he stepped back to the microphone and said, "In the excitement I reverted back to my former life. Let me rephrase this. Are you ready to rumble, PCS?"

"YES!" we yelled.

Although this was an unexpected start to the meeting, it did have one benefit. Everyone had loosened up. It would be hard for us to screw up much worse than John had. Maybe I could fit in with this group after all. There were other embarrassing mistakes and comments made during the next few days. However, the meeting did help us to get to know each other better and break the ice. As I headed home after the meeting, I felt a lot more comfortable with my new employer.

After returning to Raleigh, I spent several days thinking about the meeting in Arizona. Most of the participants were older and more experienced than I was. This made me feel unsure of myself. I became more alarmed when Elf moved the Moab potash facility from me to the potash group. Although it made sense, it added to my concern. Hoping not to lose any more facilities, I was anxious that the feed plants performed well and stayed out of trouble.

As I sat at my desk a couple of weeks after the meeting in Phoenix, Dale Jensen called.

"Clark, we've had a bad accident at Saltville," Dale said. By the tone of his voice he sounded upset.

"What happened?" I asked.

It turned out that the accident was a result of a procedure Dave Jacoby implemented when he was plant manager. From my Saltville experience, I knew that the dirty, high temperature gas flowing from the kiln gradually built up a layer of very hard dust on the walls of the four-foot diameter duct. Over time, the dust layer eventually restricted the gas flow and had to be removed. Dave did this using a lance to inject water into the interface between the dust layer and the duct. Since the duct was 900 degrees Fahrenheit, the water would flash to steam and blow pieces of the fused dust loose. The pieces then dropped 15 feet down a chute into a large steel box. Later, the operators would open a door on the box to remove the hundreds of pounds of dust for disposal.

Dale explained that today the operators began cleaning the duct but had to stop to empty the box before continuing. After closing the door on the box, they took a short break and then started back on the removal project. Unknown to them, a valve on the water lance had been leaking which created a pool of water in the bottom of the box. When the lance broke off a large slab of the 900-degree dust, it dropped down the chute into the pool of water. The water flashed into super-heated steam and blew back up the duct and out the door scalding the five operators.

"Oh, shit. What's their situation now?"

"They've all been transported to the hospital and we've notified their families. The area is roped off and an accident investigation underway. Since we know what happened, the investigation shouldn't take long. We should be able to bring the kiln back online late tonight. We need the production since our inventories are low."

"Dale, you need to leave the kiln down."

"Why's that?"

"With what has happened, some of the employees may be in shock or distracted. This could cause another accident. We need to give everyone time to settle down and digest what's happened. The most important thing is to be sure no one else gets hurt."

"I hadn't thought of that. Anything else?"

"We'll need to notify OSHA. They'll probably want to conduct their own investigation. While the plant is down just give the workers mundane tasks to do."

"That's probably a good idea. I'll take care of it."

"Also, just to let you know, I'll be headed your way in case there is anything I can do to help out."

After hanging up the phone, I let the corporate safety and the legal departments know what had happened and then hurried over to Tom's office. He was understandably concerned about the injured employees. But he wasn't happy to have to let the Saskatoon office know about the accident. Although the burns were serious, the injured workers would fortunately eventually recover. At the same time, I worried about my future. To have the most serious accident of my career happen just after the company was taken over was very unsettling.

Luckily, things died down for the rest of the summer and fall. In October, we were surprised to learn that PCS was buying White Springs, the phosphate division of Occidental Petroleum. The White Springs facility was located about 65 miles west of Jacksonville, Florida. It produced phosphate fertilizer and animal feed products. Also included in the deal were port facilities located in Jacksonville and a feed phosphate plant in Davenport, Iowa. The feed plant would be merged into my group.

With the completion of the White Springs acquisition, I occasionally visited there to learn about their technology. The operations manager, Sherrill Williams, looked after all aspects of the production facilities. Sherrill was a good ole boy who had grown up in the area. He was a big man who loved the outdoors and had spent a lot of time boating in the Florida swamps and lakes.

On one visit to White Springs, I was working with Sherrill in his office on some ideas for the feed plants. As noon approached, he suggested that we jump in his pickup and head to a local restaurant for lunch. We had just started down the road when he received a phone call from one of the technicians.

"We are going to need to make a short detour," Sherrill said as we turned onto a dirt road. "One of the technicians is having a little trouble getting a water sample from the drainage ditch."

As with any production facility, accidental contamination of the environment was a big concern. To make sure this wasn't happening, water samples were collected and analyzed for a wide assortment of possible contaminates. After about a mile, we pulled alongside a pickup parked by a large drainage ditch.

"What's the problem?" Sherrill asked the technician.

"Take a look for yourself."

We peered over the side of the 15-foot-deep ditch. The steep sides of the ditch were covered in long grass and weeds. The bottom of the ditch was covered with about 14 inches of muddy water that contained an 11-foot-long alligator. The alligator seemed to be smiling at us.

"So what's the problem?" Sherrill asked the technician.

"You don't pay me enough to get me to climb down in a ditch with a gator in it."

"There's no reason to be a sissy. Just climb down behind him. He can't turn around fast in that ditch."

"The hell with that. I'm not going down in that ditch for a water sample."

"Give me the bottle and I'll take care of it, you big sissy."

With that, Sherrill took the bottle and climbed down into the ditch well behind the alligator. The alligator turned a little sideways to keep his eye on Sherrill, but calmly watched as the water sample was collected. Sherrill then climbed back out of the ditch and handed the bottle to the technician.

"Don't call me the next time you have a trivial problem. Just develop the guts to take care of it yourself." With that, we climbed back in the pickup and headed for lunch. I was learning all kinds of unexpected things from the plants acquired by PCS. They certainly had different problems and ways of dealing with them in Florida. But it wasn't over yet.

In early 1997, PCS acquired Arcadian which produced nitrogen products. Nitrogen was the third major component in fertilizers along with potash and phosphate. Arcadian had several facilities scattered across the U.S. and one in Trinidad. Their main office was in Memphis, Tennessee.

PCS's acquisition of all these facilities provided several synergies. One of the synergies of acquiring White Springs was their production of black super phosphoric acid known as BSPA. Previously, they had trouble finding buyers for the acid. However, we soon found it worked well in our feed phosphate plants. This provided a large internal demand for the acid which loaded up the White Springs facility so that it operated near capacity and generated a good profit. Fortuitously, about this time a feed phosphate customer in Venezuela asked if we had any defluorinated phosphoric acid for sale. Since the BSPA was naturally defluorinated, the salesman, Bill Lee, jumped on the opportunity. Unfortunately, after receiving a couple of shipments of acid, we learned the customer was having problems using it. Thus, in 1998 Bill and I headed to Venezuela.

We traveled through Miami and arrived in Maracaibo late in the evening. After a taxi ride to our hotel, we settled in for the night. The next morning, we were picked up by the operations superintendent, Carlos, for a ride to the plant. On the way, he needed to stop by the bank to pick up some cash.

Driving to the bank, we found we had to park a block away. I thought Bill and I would just wait in the car, but Carlos told us we needed to come with him for our protection. I was surprised when Carlos pulled out a long steel rod and locked it to the steering wheel. He explained that this would make it impossible for a thief to steer the car. Next, Carlos pulled out a device that he placed on the brake and jacked it up so the brake pedal could not be depressed. He explained that not having the ability to stop the car would cause a thief an additional problem. Finally, he asked a young man leaning against a wall to make sure the car wasn't stolen. He paid him half of the money up front and half when we returned.

Bill and I looked at each other. Apparently, car theft was a problem. When we inquired about it, we were told there were gangs that specialized in auto theft. The vehicles would be quickly driven the 60 miles to the border crossing into Columbia. Once there, they would either be sold directly or dismantled and sold for parts. Car theft wasn't the only problem. Anything that could be packed off was in danger of being stolen.

After picking up cash, Carlos drove us south for a few miles and then headed east onto a six-mile-long bridge that crossed a portion of Lake Maracaibo. Carlos pointed out that the guardrails on the bridge were poorly constructed. He explained that a few weeks earlier, a bus had plowed through the guardrail and landed in the lake. There were no survivors. Maybe having safety standards for equipment and structures wasn't such a bad idea.

After the initial introductions at the plant, we took a tour of the facility. Much of the plant was properly designed, but there were a few shortcomings and mistakes in their operating procedures. We discussed these and suggested some changes in the way they were handling the White Springs acid. However, a big surprise during the visit was the production personnel. The shift foreman and most of the crew were women. Maybe that's why the plant was so well kept.

When I asked the shift foreman about this, she explained that several years ago there was a lot of offshore drilling as Venezuela's oil fields were developed. The men from Maracaibo could earn big bucks working on the drill rigs and clambered for the opportunity to "get rich." Eventually, the Venezuelan oil fields were fully developed and the drill rigs relocated to the Middle East. Unfortunately, the men were used to the high wages and lifestyle so they stayed with the rigs and also moved to the Middle East. As a result, the women could no longer stay at home but had to go to work at jobs normally handled by men. She pointed out that it was also very hard to find a husband. However, they were always looking and were particularly interested in someone that would take them to live in the U.S.

After visiting the plant, we had a leisurely dinner and an enjoyable evening at the hotel. The next morning, Bill and I headed to the airport and got in line to check in for our flight to Miami. In front of us was a haggard-looking gentleman with six large suitcases. When I asked if he had been on an extended vacation, he looked a little amused.

"This definitely hasn't been a vacation," he said. "I arrived in Columbia a week ago to take over a new job for my company, Schlumberger. They'd told me if I'd run the Bogota office for three years, they would give me a big promotion and I could transfer to the location of my choice."

I knew that Schlumberger was a leader in providing support services to the oil and gas industry. "Then why are you headed back home so soon then?"

"When I arrived in Bogota a week ago, I found that the office was in disarray and normal office procedures were not being used. It turned out that several employees were taking kickbacks. I promptly fired them."

"So then what happened?" I asked.

"Yesterday, as I was walking into the office building, someone took a shot at me. The bullet knocked a piece of brick out of the wall just behind my head. I decided that the job could go to hell. I couldn't get a flight from Bogota to Miami yesterday so I jumped on a flight to Maracaibo, spent the night in a hotel, and am on my way to Miami this morning."

Suddenly, my job didn't seem bad at all. None of my headaches had made me worry about my personal safety. After hearing his story, I was glad when I made it back home in one piece.

The mid-1990s had turned out to be an interesting time. Being acquired by PCS and then having White Springs and Arcadian added to the group significantly increased the size of the corporation. Fortunately, PCS had done a good job in helping us feel like part of a family. We continued to have regular meetings with senior management which gave us the opportunity to develop friendships. Luckily, I was able to visit other plants and learned a lot about production technology and handling people. And over time I gradually started to feel more secure in my new position. But I wondered what other adventures the future would hold and what challenges I would have to face. At least I was once again busy enough that I wasn't involved in too many shenanigans.

CHAPTER 30

The Brazilian Distraction

It pays to have friends in high places

Although Texasgulf was primarily a fertilizer company, it was always looking for opportunities to enter other markets. This would help the company survive if there was a major crash in fertilizer sales. In the mid-1990s, an opportunity to enter a new market presented itself in Brazil. The sales group was approached to see if PCS would provide feed grade phosphoric acid to a Brazilian animal feed plant located near Sao Paulo in the town of San Vicente. The plant was owned by the Japanese company, Mitsui, and had been purchasing phosphoric acid from a local supplier. However, the supplier knew Mitsui's options for purchasing acid were limited and jacked up the price to an unreasonable level.

Since the Mitsui facility was an animal feed plant, Fred Stephens got involved in the negotiations. Instead of selling them phosphoric acid, he worked out a deal to buy the plant. However, when he presented it to Tom Wright, Tom rejected it because Elf wasn't interested in expanding the animal feed business.

Years later when PCS took over the company, Fred decided to give it another try. To his surprise, PCS was interested and Fred re-started negotiations with Mitsui. As he neared the completion of the deal, I was asked to accompany Fred to Brazil to make sure there were no problems with the plant and to provide my input. Thus, despite my reluctance, I was once again off on a foreign adventure.

We flew from Raleigh through Miami to Sao Paulo, Brazil. At the airport we were met by Alex Ariosa, a sales agent for PCS in Brazil. Alex had sold PCS's fertilizer in Brazil for years and had proven invaluable to the company due to his contacts with people in high places. As a result, he handled millions of dollars of PCS products annually. Alex arrived at the airport to pick us up in his Jeep Cherokee. As we headed into town, I noticed that the Jeep's windows looked odd.

"Alex, what's going on with your windows?" I asked. "They seem to have a strange tint."

"That's because the windows are bulletproof," Alex said. "In fact, special panels have been added to the doors and floor to make the whole vehicle bulletproof."

"Why did you do that?"

"Sao Paulo has a serious problem with carjacking and kidnappings. Americans are at particular risk because they stand out in a crowd and their companies will often pay ransom to the kidnappers to get their employees back."

I was glad Alex had insisted on driving us. I doubted PCS would pay much to get me back. Since we were worn out from our travels, Alex dropped us off at the hotel so we could rest up.

The next morning, I joined Fred and Alex for breakfast before we headed out to visit the San Vicente plant. Leaving the hotel, we first went past large, high-rise buildings and first-class office buildings. But as we approached the edge of town, things changed dramatically. We began to pass mile after mile of small, shabby huts. They appeared to be constructed from packing crates and miscellaneous junk. Typically, there would be one water spigot sticking out of the ground with three or four huts surrounding it. The ditch on the side of the road was used as a latrine. There were millions of very poor people living like this in the outskirts of Sao Paulo. Although I had heard about the situation, it was still astonishing to actually see the miserable conditions these people had to endure. No wonder there was so much trouble with crime and kidnapping in Brazil.

With the city behind us, we crossed several broad, shallow lakes. We then came to a place overlooking San Vicente and the ocean. The view was spectacular. We were a little over 2,400 feet above the city and could see the steep hillside, city, and ocean below. There were big fluffy clouds hanging around the edge of the cliff. The road wound down the steep slope for six miles before reaching the bottom. From there we headed south about seven miles to the plant. Except for the outskirts of Sao Paulo, the drive was scenic.

Upon arrival, we met with the management team and then toured the plant. The plant was using technology similar to that used in our Dical plants, but the equipment was undersized, inefficient, and in some cases needed repair. I was surprised to learn that San Vicente only sold bagged product to the customers. In the U.S. most shipments were bulk. Next, we toured the port facilities where we would unload phosphoric acid shipped from the United States. We found that the needed facilities were available for our use. While near the ocean, we had a late lunch before heading back to Sao Paulo.

The next day, we hoped to finalize negotiations. Fred, Alex, and I met the Mitsui contingent at their hotel with Fred handling the negotiations for PCS. I was surprised to learn that a Mr. Suzuki would lead the Mitsui contingent. It was almost like they were using Japanese names I was familiar with. The negotiations were slow and tortuous. Finally, after several breaks for side discussions, a tentative agreement was reached at 8:00 p.m. on Friday evening. The detailed agreement would still need to be written up and formally accepted by both sides, but Fred had achieved his goal for this trip. We shook hands and parted ways.

As we climbed into Alex's Jeep, I was glad the day was over and looked forward to going to bed. However, as we left the parking lot, Alex headed in an unexpected direction.

"Where are we going, Alex?" I asked.

"I think that reaching an agreement with Mitsui is cause for a celebration."

"Alex, I'm tired and just want to go to bed."

"This will just be a quick stop. We need to have a drink to celebrate."

I reluctantly agreed since I didn't have any choice. Alex told us he was heading to a nightclub called the Café Foto. After a short drive, we pulled into a parking lot next to a large, four-story building. Being 8:15 p.m. on a Friday night, there was a large line of men stretching down the side of the building waiting to get in. Apparently, the Café Foto was a popular place. Thinking that I might get Alex to head to the hotel, I said, "I'm pretty tired and don't really want to spend the night standing in line."

"Not to worry," Alex said.

As we came to a stop near the front door, a young man appeared out of the darkness and ran up to the Jeep.

"Can I park your car, Mr. Ariosa?" he said.

Apparently, Alex had been here before. Alex handed him the keys and we climbed out. Several of the men in line yelled at us in Portuguese as we walked up to the attendant at the door. He unclipped the rope and let us through.

"It is good to see you again, Mr. Ariosa. Step right in," he said.

We stepped through the door where we were met by a gentleman in a suit.

"Mr. Ariosa, I am glad you have decided to pay us a visit. I am sure we can find a place for you."

After my eyes adjusted to the light, I scanned my surroundings. There was a bar on our end of the club and a live band next to a dance floor some distance away on the opposite side. Tables were located between the bar and dance floor. A stairway led up to the next level where there were additional tables. It was not clear what was above the second floor.

We were waiting just inside the club, when the doorman caught the attention of a large man on the other side of the room. As the man walked over, he loomed larger and larger as he approached. When he stopped next to us, I was astounded to see that my head only reached to the middle of his chest. Being nearly 7 feet tall, he was the tallest man I'd ever met with arms as large as my legs. Although he introduced himself, we couldn't understand his name.

So we just called him Lurch after the butler in the old *Addams Family* sitcom.

The doorman whispered to Lurch for a few seconds. Lurch nodded and walked over to a table near the dance floor and talked to the two men seated at the table. Apparently, Lurch didn't like their response. He suddenly reached out and grabbed them by their necks, jerked them out of their chairs, and dragged them across the room. When he reached a fire exit, he kicked the door open, tossed them out into the alley, and slammed the door. I was impressed. I definitely didn't want to aggravate Lurch.

After the men were removed, a waiter darted over to the table, cleaned it off, and covered it with a white linen tablecloth. Next, he placed a bottle of Johnnie Walker Black Label whiskey on the table with three glasses. The doorman then turned to Alex.

"Your table is ready, Mr. Ariosa."

We walked over and sat down. As we unwound while we talked, I looked around the room. There were a lot of men in the club. A few were in their twenties or thirties, but most were older. The men wore slacks and some had on sport coats. The women, on the other hand, stood out. They were generally between 18 and 26 years of age. Some were dressed in elegant gowns, while others were dressed like punk rockers or had on miniskirts. Regardless of how they were dressed, they were all extremely attractive.

"Alex, what's going on with the women?"

"They are here for companionship. If you find someone that you just want to talk to, it will cost you a couple of drinks. If you're interested in more intimate contact, it will cost a little more. If you would like someone to keep you company for the night, it will cost two or three hundred dollars depending on the girl. But don't worry about the cost—I can put it on my expense report."

No good could come from this. Alex was insistent that I at least talk to the girls and I insisted that I could get in enough trouble without his help.

When I awoke the next morning, I had a headache but no companion.

Since Fred had achieved his objective, it was time to head home. Alex came by the hotel to pick us up for the ride to the airport. For once, I had made an overseas tip and hadn't gotten myself in any trouble.

A few months after returning to the U.S., I made a trip to the White Springs facility in Florida to talk with Jerry Chia. Jerry was a technical expert in feed phosphate production, and I wanted Jerry's opinion about the proposed changes to the San Vicente plant. I was in the process of showing Jerry pictures of the pug mill when he stopped me. Squinting at one of the pictures he pointed to a man and said, "Who's that?"

I looked at the picture for a few seconds and said, "That's Ronaldo Toguchi, the production manager."

"You need to fire him."

This surprised me. How could you decide to fire someone based on their picture?

"What do you mean I need to fire him?"

"He is Japanese, isn't he?"

"Well, yes. But how can you tell?"

"I can tell. I am Chinese. My family moved here from Taiwan. However, my ancestors are from Nanking. Based on what they did to my family there, all Japanese are my sworn enemy."

I remembered reading that during World War II, the Japanese had brutalized Nanking. The invading Japanese army had killed about 200,000 Chinese civilians and raped 20,000 women and girls. It was one of history's more disgusting incidents.

"But that wasn't Ronaldo; he's not more than forty years old. In fact, it wasn't his father either. Ronaldo said that his family immigrated to Brazil in 1907."

"That doesn't matter. He's Japanese. He can't be trusted. PCS should not have such a filthy person on its payroll."

No matter how long I argued with Jerry, I couldn't persuade him. Eventually, I changed the subject and in the following months was careful not to let the topic come up again. But the incident surprised me. I knew from experience that there were groups in the United States that were very prejudiced. However, I didn't realize that this was a serious problem between groups of people in other parts of the world.

It took a few months to get the deal written up and finalized. A party was held in Sao Paulo for the official signing and payment for the plant. A few months after that, I made a trip to San Vicente to continue work on upgrading the plant. One morning, I was in the upstairs conference room meeting with Sonny, the plant manager, and some of his key people. We were sitting around the conference table discussing the plant modifications in detail to make sure we hadn't overlooked anything. Suddenly, the receptionist barged in. She had a look of panic in her eyes and called Sonny over for a private discussion.

"We've got trouble," Sonny said. "A contingent of the local army is here to shut us down."

I looked out the window and was startled to see about twenty soldiers spreading out in the plant. We hurried downstairs and found the officer in charge. He looked at us for a few seconds then spoke in broken English.

"You do not have proper permits to operate," said the officer. "We shut you down and lock gate. Will watch plant until you have permits. Maybe take four or five months."

Sonny and I looked at each other. "We'd better call Alex," I said, "and see if he can help."

We placed a call to Alex and explained the situation. He said he would look into it and get back to us. In the meantime, we were told absolutely not to leave the property. Alex said that they would likely try to pack off anything of value. We then called Fred Stephens and some of the other PCS management personnel to bring them up to speed.

Late in the afternoon, the officer barged back in the office.

"You pack now," he said. "Time to go."

I said, "What do you mean it's time to go?"

"We in charge now. We guard plant make sure no one enters."

We stepped outside and looked around. All the employees were being herded past the office and through the front gate. We walked back in the office.

"I'm not sure we can stall much longer," Sonny said. "We will be lucky if they don't start removing equipment tonight. I think we're screwed."

The commander had a smug expression on his face as they

waited to escort us off the property. As we stood there, the phone rang. The receptionist answered it and then said it was for the commander. The commander picked up the phone. As he talked, his eyes got wider and he started to look uneasy. Finally, he hung up and walked over to us.

"Very sorry," he said. "Big mistake. We go now. Very sorry. We leave quick."

With that, he dashed out the door and barked out orders to his men. They looked disconcerted and then quickly assembled and climbed in their trucks and drove off. At the same time Sonny's phone rang. It was Alex on the line. He said that he had a discrete discussion with a couple of high-ranking government officials. There should be no further trouble. If there was, just let him know and he would make sure they were very sorry for their actions.

On another trip to Brazil, a companion and I were asked to visit the Cajati phosphate facility owned by the Brazilian company, Serrana. The Cajati facility mined phosphate ore from a large open pit mine and used it to produce various types of phosphoric acid. PCS was considering purchasing the facility to further expand into the growing Brazilian fertilizer market.

The mine was located about 120 miles southwest of Sao Paulo. However, the available roads meant that the trip would take five or six hours each way. In addition, there were not any reasonable accommodations near the mine. I mentioned my lack of enthusiasm to Fred Stephens and suggested that it might be hard to fit the trip into my schedule. He said he would look into other arrangements. When he called back later, he said Serrana would pick me up in their helicopter at the Sao Paulo domestic airport. We would leave at 9:00 a.m. and I could expect to be back by 4:00 p.m. My efforts to avoid another adventure had failed.

It was clear and sunny in Sao Paulo on the day of the trip to Cajati. A car picked me and my cohorts up at the hotel and transported us to the airport where my fellow travelers were waiting. The helicopter was much larger than expected and held eight passengers plus the pilot and co-pilot. We climbed aboard and were asked to put on headphones equipped with microphones for the trip. This seemed strange, but after they started the engine it made more sense. When the rotor got up to speed the noise was horrific. The headphones deadened the noise and allowed us to talk.

Takeoff was a little different than expected. Instead of going straight up, we had to pretend we were a plane. Thus, we lifted off and then taxied along about 10 feet above the ground until we reached the runway. The helicopter then headed down the runway and gradually gained altitude. As we climbed, we had a spectacular view of downtown Sao Paulo. The size of the city was very impressive. The pilots pointed out Sao Paulo's landmarks as we headed southwest toward Cajati.

After ten minutes, we passed over the edge of Sao Paulo and flew over an immense area of trees and vegetation. It was green as far as we could see in every direction. In places there were farms and other agriculture. Occasionally, we passed over a road or a small village. However, there were no large cities or towns. After another 30 minutes we passed over low-lying clouds. They appeared to extend all the way to the ground.

I asked the pilot, "Are the clouds going to cause us a problem?"

"No. We have a satellite navigational system. We can still find our way."

We traveled over the clouds for another 20 minutes, then started to slow down. Soon we were hovering in one place. Then the helicopter began to slowly descend into the clouds.

"Are you sure this is safe?" I asked. "How far above the ground do we need to come out of the clouds?"

"We have a large landing area so with our navigation system, we can land even if the clouds go right to the surface."

I didn't feel very good about this. If the navigational system was even slightly in error we were putting our lives in danger. I knew it was easy for a pilot to get disoriented in fog and crash. It happened all the time. But despite my concerns we continued downward in the clouds. It was hard to tell if we were descending or moving in some other direction. After what seemed like an eternity, the ground appeared just before we touched down. I heaved a sigh of relief.

My travel companions as we prepare to leave Cajati, Brazil

Getting out of the helicopter, it was surprising how small our landing area was, only about half as big as a city block. I had expected that we would land at an airport. Instead, there wasn't much around other than a road leading up to the flat area where we landed. After the rotor stopped, a couple of cars pulled up and we piled in. On the edge of our landing area was a couple of light poles. It was fortunate that we hadn't clipped one of them.

We took a short drive down the hillside to the open pit mine and processing facility. The plant was fairly modern and produced several phosphate products. However, the visit was interesting in other ways. My curiosity was aroused when we were forbidden entry into a couple of areas. I'd never had this happen before. They claimed to be doing top secret activities of some sort in these places. My suspicion was that they were making purified phosphoric acid using patented technology but were not paying any royalties.

After we completed our tour, we headed back to the helicopter. I was happy to see that the clouds had dissipated. The flight back to Sao Paulo was uneventful.

Although we continued to try to expand into Brazil, overall it was unsuccessful. It was difficult to be competitive without having a low-cost phosphoric acid production facility inside the country. Shipping acid all the way from North America and bringing it through a port was expensive and left us vulnerable. After several years, the San Vicente facility was sold and we had to be content shipping finished feed phosphate products into the country. It generated a little income but not what we'd hoped for.

From a business perspective, I learned a lot from this venture. From the beginning it was apparent that having a local businessman like Alex Ariosa was critical to being successful when doing business in another country. Without his connections and knowledge, it would have been a disaster. He was able to help us understand how business was conducted in Brazil and how to take care of problems. It was also clear that more time should have been spent at the beginning to understand the sensitivity of our economics to factors outside our control. By not doing so, we didn't realize our chances for long-term success were slim. Fortunately for Fred and me, the actual cash spent was not too large. The biggest cost was the time wasted when other opportunities might have been discovered and developed.

From a personal perspective, I learned something about cultures and life in other countries. Although I had heard about the difficult life for the poor in Brazil, to actually see it had been shocking. With no money, it was nearly impossible for the children born into this situation to get any kind of education or decent job. I was also surprised by the hard feelings that existed between some Chinese and Japanese. To me, World War II was in the distant past. I also found it interesting that women earning money by doing favors for men were not looked down upon. They were doing what they needed to do to go to college, feed their families, and improve their situation. It was just another way to work and make money.

CHAPTER 31

The End of Raleigh

Be careful who you tease; they might get revenge

The Brazilian adventure had shown me there was more to running a company than engineering. It was also a good idea to pay attention to politics, particularly company politics. This caused me to start thinking about who would replace our CEO, Chuck Childers. Rumor had it that he planned to retire in 1999. I assumed he would be replaced by an engineer since all of the CEOs that had led the company during my professional career had been engineers. This made sense—at least to me since we were selling commodities. Generally, all of the customers paid about the same price for what they purchased regardless of the supplier. This meant that in order to survive, you needed to be a low-cost producer. It was important that the CEO understood the details of manufacturing and what ideas for reducing costs or expanding production made sense.

Unfortunately, the most likely candidate, Tom Wright, was also preparing to retire. This meant that there weren't any production people with the experience necessary to take over as CEO. The mystery of who would fill the job was finally solved in June 1998, when Bill Doyle was appointed to fill the position of president and chief operating officer. Bill had previously been the president of the sales division. It was clear that the board's intent was to give Bill some operating experience before making him CEO. The presidents of the potash, phosphate, and nitrogen divisions now reported to Bill.

With no operating experience, Bill was keenly interested in learning about the production facilities, particularly the phosphate and nitrogen operations. He had been around potash long enough to already know quite a bit about those facilities. And so, in the fall of 1998, Bill commandeered the corporate jet to tour PCS's phosphate and nitrogen plants. I was apprehensive when I learned that I was to accompany Bill Doyle and the head of the Nitrogen Division, Jim Dietz, on the tour. This seemed like a good opportunity for me to screw up and get into serious trouble, particularly since our first stop was a feed phosphate plant located near Davenport, Iowa. Davenport hadn't been under my supervision very long and had occasionally had trouble with housekeeping and safety.

After arriving and introducing the office staff, the plant manager, Jack Sullivan, led us on a tour of the plant. I heaved a sigh of relief that the troops had cleaned up the plant and Jack did a good job explaining operations as we walked along. After the tour, we had an all-employee meeting in the conference room. The employees voiced their concerns about the feed phosphate business in general and the Davenport plant's future in particular. Bill evaded the questions. He did, however, stress the importance of safety. There would be no tolerance of unsafe procedures or managers that took shortcuts at the expense of safety. If they did, it was implied that their employment would be in jeopardy.

I heaved a sigh of relief when we finally departed. The tour had gone well and, fortunately, there hadn't been any safety problems. The next visit was to the Clinton, Iowa, ammonia facility. I was surprised when I learned we would use the jet to make the 40-mile trip. Traveling with senior management had its perks. Upon arrival at the plant, we suited up in coveralls and received a safety orientation about how to get away from anhydrous ammonia in case there was a release. Apparently, it was very nasty stuff.

As we toured the facility, Bill Doyle and the plant manager,

June, walked a little ahead of the rest of the group. It seemed that June wanted to have a private conversation with Bill. Unfortunately, as we toured the ammonium nitrate plant there had been some spillage. In places, hard, white, BB-like material was scattered along the steel deck. When Jim Dietz stepped on some, his right foot went out from under him. His hard hat flew off and he barely saved himself from a serious fall by grabbing a steel column. When the excitement stopped, Jim was hanging onto the column about halfway to the floor with both feet in front of him on the BBs. I rushed over and helped him stand up. He had wrenched his back a little and was in pain. Jim quickly looked at the group ahead. Since Bill had stressed safety at Davenport, Jim was relieved to see Bill was still walking along with June. Apparently, the plant noise had masked the commotion during the accident.

A little later in the tour, while Bill and I were looking at the ammonia converter, Jim pulled the plant manager aside. After a heated, one-sided discussion, June left for a few minutes to talk with the shift foreman. I suspected Jim was not happy about skating on BBs and made sure there would be an immediate improvement in housekeeping.

Later that afternoon, we had a meeting with the Clinton staff. Partway through the meeting, Bill Doyle brought up the importance of first impressions.

"It is important that people visiting Clinton feel that this is a first-class facility," Bill said. "Unfortunately, when we visited today the entryway smelled like cigarette smoke."

Of all the things in the plant to worry about, I was surprised that cigarette smoke was a top concern.

"It was more like we were going into a bar instead of a top-notch production facility," Bill continued. "You need to find somewhere else to have a cigarette."

Several people looked at each other. Finally, the accounting supervisor, Dwayne, spoke up, "There really isn't anywhere else to smoke since it was banned from the office."

I sat up and started to pay attention. Bill Doyle had instituted the ban on smoking in the company's office buildings. It didn't seem like a smart move to complain about the smoking ban in a large meeting with Bill. Particularly when Bill was our new boss.

"Possibly you can smoke outside on the back side of the building," Bill said.

"But in the winter it's cold and the wind's blowing."

Bill was starting to look irritated. "Surely you can find a sheltered place somewhere outside to smoke."

"We've looked around; the only place we could find is in the entryway."

"But that isn't acceptable. The smoke is trapped there since there's no ventilation. You need to find somewhere else to smoke."

"But I'm telling you there isn't any place else. Maybe you have a suggestion as to where we can smoke," Dwayne said.

"I think that you can smoke all you want as you stand on the other side of the street looking for a new job. I don't think we need anyone on the payroll that isn't smart enough to solve this problem."

Dwayne had flunked the IQ test.

As we continued the tour of the plants over the next few days there were, fortunately, no other significant incidents. I started to relax. The feed plants had passed inspection and none of my troops said anything stupid in the employee meetings. However, there would be additional meetings in the coming months where we could get into trouble. One incident that I observed occurred at a quarterly meeting held at the corporate office in Saskatoon.

At the meeting, we each got to provide senior management an update on our area of responsibility and any problems we were experiencing. It also helped us to learn about other areas of the company.

When Bill Doyle was made the COO, Gary Carlson was promoted to be the President of Sales. Gary had aspirations of moving up in the company. At a break during one of the quarterly meetings, Bill got up to see if there were any messages. While he was gone, Gary struck up a conversation with Chuck Childers. Since Chuck was sitting down, Gary sat down next to him in Bill Doyle's seat. Gary was trying to sell Chuck on some scheme he had hatched up.

After a few minutes, Bill walked back into the room. It was apparent that he was annoyed that he couldn't sit down. After about five minutes, Bill announced that it was time for the meeting to resume and that we should all return to our seats. We all sat down in our seats except for Gary who ignored Bill and kept talking with Chuck. A pissed-off looking Bill stood there next to Gary.

Bill announced again that it was time to start. Gary again ignored him and kept sitting there talking to Chuck. After a few more minutes, Bill told Gary he needed to get out of his seat so that the meeting could continue. Gary stood up so that Bill could sit down, but still stood next to Chuck to continue his conversation with him. Finally, Bill told Gary to immediately return to his seat. Gary finally moved out of Bill's seat and the meeting resumed. I suspected that had been foolish on Gary's part. It turned out I was right. Coincidently, Gary didn't survive the year.

During the summer of 1999, the CEO, Chuck Childers, announced his retirement. A few months later, an invitation arrived inviting me and Betty to a restricted viewing of *This Is Your Life*, starring Chuck Childers. The viewing was to be in Chicago. Attendees were to wear formal attire. Apparently, this was not going to be the typical retirement party.

The Raleigh contingent flew to Chicago the morning of the party and stayed at the downtown Marriott Hotel just off of Michigan Avenue. I was a little anxious being in downtown Chicago. I had only been there once before and had nearly been mugged. As the time for the viewing neared, we put on our tuxedos and took a cab to the Drake Hotel—the site of the party.

The Drake Hotel is something of a Chicago landmark. The hotel's architecture was patterned after the Italian Renaissance when it opened in 1920. Located at the north end of the Michigan Avenue, many important visitors such as Winston Churchill, Eleanor Roosevelt, Hubert Hoover, and Dwight D. Eisenhower had stayed there. Historically, the Drake Hotel was the place to hold an event if you wanted it to be noticed.

Driving up Michigan Avenue, we passed many elegant buildings and shops including the towering John Hancock Center. As the cab pulled up to the Drake, the doorman rushed over to open our door. Inside, we were directed to the coatroom and then our meeting place. We were being treated like royalty. I wasn't used to it.

A bar had been set up in a large room next to the ball room. On the walls were posters of famous movies such as *The Wizard of Oz* and *Casablanca*. However, we were surprised to find Chuck Childers' image superimposed over the images on the movie posters. We weren't in Kansas anymore.

As we lounged around, more guests continued to arrive. Many were people that I had met in Arizona or at the quarterly meetings. Looking at the posters, we speculated on what would befall us in the main ballroom. After about an hour, the doors were finally opened. A raised stage could be seen on the left end of the room equipped with a podium and large movie screen. Our round dinner tables were arranged on the main floor below the stage and set up with fine linen and silverware. Behind each plate was a nametag in a silver frame which designated our seating assignment. Each guest also received a small crystal ball.

After introducing ourselves, we sat down and made small talk while we waited for the event to start. When everyone was seated, we were welcomed by the VP of Public Relations. She spoke about Chuck's illustrious career and how fortunate PCS was to have Chuck as the CEO. A movie had been made to celebrate the occasion, which we would watch during dinner. We chatted as we ate the salads. We had expected to have a dinner and a few speakers. No one expected that there would be a 60-minute movie.

After the salad course, the lights dimmed and the movie started. The first part of the movie showed black and white pictures of Chuck Childers accompanied by a narration of his early childhood. After about eight minutes, I was surprised when the movie stopped and a voice said, "I remember playing hooky from grade school to go fishing with Chuck."

"Is that you, Bill?" asked Chuck. A gentleman walked out from behind the curtain and shook hands with Chuck. During the next fifteen minutes, Bill told us about their escapades during their youth. This went on throughout the evening all patterned after the old TV show, *This is Your Life.*

Chuck finally wrapped up the meeting with a speech and we headed back to the hotel at about 1:30 a.m. It had been a long night, but it signified the changing of the guard. After a little over a year as the chief operating officer, Bill Doyle was now the CEO of the company.

Since Bill lived in Chicago and enjoyed the area, one of his first acts was to announce the closure of the Raleigh, North Carolina, and Memphis, Tennessee, offices. The functions handled by these offices would now be taken care of at a new office located in Northbrook, Illinois, about 10 minutes from Bill's house. In Raleigh, the announcement was devastating. Only about 18 of the approximately 110 people would be moving. The rest would join the ranks of the unemployed; most of whom had worked for the company for twenty or more years. The people in the Raleigh office were like family. We enjoyed each other's company and had lunch together. Although sometimes we argued, at the end of the day we were still friends and watched out for each other. Now the family was being ripped apart. Fortunately for me, they still needed someone to look after the feed plants and I was given the opportunity to transfer to Northbrook. I had very conflicted emotions about this. On the one hand, I was glad to have the opportunity to keep my job. On the other hand, I really didn't want to relocate again, particularly since my kids had graduated from high school and most of them lived near us in Raleigh.

As I thought about quitting, I wasn't enthusiastic about looking for a job when I was almost 50 years old. Thus, a move to Chicago seemed like a reasonable option. My wife, Betty, was of the opinion we should stay close to the kids as long as we could. However, there was no likelihood of me finding a job in mineral processing in Raleigh. To stay in the area would probably require me accepting a much lower-paying job which didn't seem like a good idea as retirement approached. Thinking that Betty would eventually come to her senses, the transfer to Northbrook was accepted.

To help us get started with the relocation, PCS arranged for all of us to visit Northbrook in February of 2000. The timing of the trip was not helpful in my efforts to convince Betty of the benefits of the move. February is not a fun time in Northern Illinois. Not surprisingly, it was very cold and snowy during the visit. At one point we were taken on a bus tour of nearby neighborhoods to look at housing. It was something of a shock to find all of the houses viewed during the tour were in excess of $500,000 while similar houses in Raleigh were only selling for about $200,000. Betty made sure to point this out to me.

At the end of the visit, the group was gathered in a large conference room for a presentation on relocating. Afterward, we were given the opportunity to ask questions. Someone toward the front of the room asked, "Will there be any adjustment in salary for the difference in the cost of living?"

The room was quiet for several seconds, then the president of Human Resources said, "Living expenses in Chicago are not any higher than in Raleigh or Memphis. Thus, there is no reason for a salary adjustment."

Jim Heppel, the VP of HR for the phosphate group leaned over and said, "If he will lie about that, he will lie about anything."

I reported to work in Northbrook the first week of July in 2000. At the time, I hadn't purchased a house and initially lived in a nearby hotel. However, after a couple of months I moved in with an accountant, Joe Safrit, who had purchased a townhouse and rented me a room. His wife had not yet made the transition so it was often just the two of us. We didn't see much of each other during the day but would sometimes eat together in the evening.

One evening, we were cooking hamburgers on the grill located on the second story deck. The neighbor's deck was adjacent to Joe's. I was assigned to cook the burgers while Joe was in the house getting the other stuff ready.

While I was standing by the grill, the lady next door stepped out on the deck. "How are you doing?" I asked her.

"I am doing well. How about you?"

"I am doing pretty good, just unwinding while I cook a couple of hamburgers."

"Ah, if you don't mind me asking, I haven't seen you around and am curious who you are?"

The way she asked the question and the tone in her voice bothered me for some reason.

"I'm Clark. I am friends with Joe and we're living here together."

The color drained out of her face. For some reason, the fact that this appeared to upset her seemed like an opportunity for a practical joke.

"You don't have a problem with that, do you?"

"Ah, no. No, I guess I don't have a problem."

"That's good because I wouldn't want to cause any problems for Joe."

"Ah, no. No problems here. I have to go."

With that she headed into the house. At the same time, Joe came barreling out of the kitchen.

"What the hell did you tell her that for?" Joe asked.

"I didn't lie. We're friends and I am rooming with you."

"Yeah, but I bet she thinks we're sharing the bedroom. I'm not sure any good is going to come from this."

"She just needed to have her horizons broadened," I said. "People shouldn't be so judgmental about what adults do."

"Easy for you to say. You're only going to be living here for a few months. What's she going to think, or say, when my wife shows up?"

Several days later, Joe came into my office. "You've done it now, hot shot. When I was leaving for work this morning I ran into my neighbor. She had her two sons and was heading for her car. She asked who I was and I told her that I was her neighbor. She didn't say another word but just quickly herded the boys into her car and took off."

I offered to talk to his neighbor but Joe flatly refused. Months later he reported that when he met others in his complex, they would just shake their heads as he passed by. It was a different world in Chicago in the year 2000.

The Northbrook office building was completed just before we moved in. It was a spacious six-story building made of red stone with lots of windows. The ground floor contained a cafeteria, parking garage, and fitness center. I was lucky to be assigned a large corner office on the fifth floor. Just outside my office was an open area divided into cubicles for the various secretaries, including Laura, who was the secretary for the safety department. She was a spunky Russian who had a talent for getting into mischief. Laura was single and in her late twenties. I would often tease Laura as I stood in my doorway or as I walked past her desk. But she tended to hold her own in any encounter. There were a wide range of topics that would get her fired up. I particularly liked to tease her about whether she had actually done any work while spending the day on the phone arranging her next date.

One morning, while walking to my office, I passed a group of secretaries clustered around Laura's desk. Laura was saying something about waiting for the rest of the group to arrive before making a big announcement. She told me that I might want to stick around to hear it, but I just waved and sat down at my desk.

After a few minutes, I stepped out of my office to pick up a memo from the printer. Even more secretaries were clustered around Laura's desk. As soon as she saw me she started to speak. "I am glad everyone is here. I wanted to let you all know that I am pregnant."

There were several squeals of delight and comments about how happy they were for her. Laura then looked at me, and with a big smile said, "And the other thing you should know is that Clark is the father. Clark, I told you that you needed to be careful, now look what you've gone and done."

The secretaries gasped as they looked at me wide-eyed. I stood there immobile as I tried to come up with a response. My mouth was moving but nothing was coming out. Laura, however, wasn't done with me.

"I told you it would be all fun and games until you got me pregnant. Now it's time to pay up. I have the doctor's bills right here."

Some of the secretaries just stood and looked at me. Others scampered off to their desks trying to avoid my gaze. I was eventually able to mutter something about not knowing what she was talking about. Even to me, it didn't sound convincing. I finally headed back to the safety of my office.

Later that day, I asked the head of HR whether I could file a sexual harassment complaint. He listened to my concerns and then laughed me out of his office. He said nobody in their right mind would believe Laura couldn't find somebody more interesting than me. After that, as I passed Laura's desk she would ask for child support, but I would just keep walking.

I had finally found someone that was in my league in carrying out practical jokes. I wondered whether Joe Safrit had put her up to it for revenge for my comments to his neighbor. But in the end, it did have the effect of easing tensions and helping us to begin to feel like a family.

CHAPTER 32

The Aurora DFP Fiasco

Sometimes you have to work hard to really screw up

In the late 1990s, I had to deal with a problem created by Dave Edmiston 16 years earlier: Saltville. In 1983, the company wanted to diversify into DFP, a phosphate supplement used by the poultry industry. Normally such a plant would be built near its source of raw materials to minimize freight costs. However, Dave found he could reduce construction costs by retrofitting an old lime kiln located in Saltville, Virginia. In addition to the low price for the facility, the Commonwealth of Virginia would reimburse the company up to $10 million to encourage the use of the idle plant. Although the retrofitted plant would be 360 miles from its source of raw materials, Dave wasn't worried. He was only responsible for getting the plant built as cheaply as possible. The operations group would be responsible for operating the plant at a profit.

Unfortunately, as the VP of Feed Phosphate Operations in 1999, the plant was now my responsibility. And, although Dale Jensen and his team were doing a good job running the facility, its location was becoming a serious problem. The cost to ship raw materials 360 miles to Saltville was getting out of control. The railroad knew we had limited options and was pushing up the rail rates. Since we were also at the mercy of the local landfill to take

the scrubber waste, its fee also escalated. This made Saltville a
high-cost producer that could not survive a price war. Plus, if the
landfill operator made good on his threat to quit taking the scrubber's waste, it would force the plant's closure.

After worrying about Saltville's drawbacks for a few years,
I decided to form a team to evaluate the possibility of building
a new DFP plant at Aurora. This would not only eliminate the
freight on raw materials and landfill costs, it would also allow the
new plant to take advantage of the latest technology. I appointed
Dale Jensen, the manager of Saltville, to head up the team since
he had a good understanding of DFP technology and would be
my first choice to manage the new facility. Tim Honeycutt, his
general superintendent, would also be on the team. The next two
members of the team came from the phosphate facility in White
Springs, Florida. Jerry Chia was originally from Taiwan and Dr.
Bhaskar Bandyopadhyay, known as Dr. Bandy, was from India.
They both had extensive experience in alternate ways of producing
DFP which would assure that we evaluated all possible options. I
planned to monitor and help the team as necessary.

One of the first items on the team's agenda was to determine
whether a rotary kiln was the best technology to use in the new
plant. Fortunately, a company named Fuller had a facility located
near Allentown, Pennsylvania, that could test the various options.
The team planned to meet there to monitor the tests. I decided to
tag along.

On the day I arrived at the Allentown airport, I was surprised
to find that the other members of the team had landed just 15
minutes ahead of me. After collecting our luggage, we lined up at
the Hertz counter to get rental cars with Dr. Bandy at the head of
the line.

"Since we're all going to the same place," I said, "why don't
we ride with Dr. Bandy?"

"I've only reserved a compact car," Dr. Bandy said. "Vern
Lloyd won't let us rent anything larger."

I was surprised by this. I'd never heard of the company forcing
anyone to use a compact car. However, I knew that Dr. Bandy's
boss had a reputation for being a miser.

"Well, it's cheaper if we share a car rather than rent three of them," I said. "Just get a full-size car and we'll all ride together. It'll give us a chance to talk."

"That might make sense to you, but Vern is going to want to know why I'm spending an extra $25 per day."

"Just rent the damn car. If Vern doesn't like it, have him give me a call."

Thus, Bandy reluctantly rented the larger car and, unfortunately, became the designated driver.

The next morning, we climbed in the rental car and Dr. Bandy drove us to the Fuller facility. He seemed to be nervous and made a few driving mistakes which we were happy to point out to him. At the end of our first day, the five of us loaded in the car for the trip to the hotel. As Bandy exited Fuller's parking lot, he made a left turn into oncoming traffic on a one-way street. After dodging a couple of cars on the three-lane road, we were forced to stop at an intersection by a phalanx of cars that faced us. They were waiting for the traffic light to turn green. It looked like Custer's Last Stand. Fortunately, when the light turned green, they didn't move. This allowed us to make a quick right turn onto a side street where we pulled over to the side of the road. Over Dr. Bandy's protests, but by popular demand, I drove the car during the rest of the trip. Maybe Dr. Bandy's driver training in India hadn't prepared him to chauffeur us around in the United States.

Luckily, the rest of the trip went well. Fuller confirmed that a rotary kiln was the best option for Aurora. I was glad to hear that since it meant we already had experienced operators to run the new plant.

Next, the team retained Mustang Engineering in Tampa to develop a preliminary cost estimate for the project. Mustang was chosen since they were near several large phosphate facilities in Florida and had a lot of experience with this type of technology. They estimated the new plant would cost $40 million. Finally, the team got my old boss, Fred Stephens, to provide an estimate of the sales tons and price for the DFP he could sell from the new plant. Based on this, the economic evaluation estimated PCS would make a 19 percent return on investment. That was good enough to convince the company to go ahead with the project.

When I received formal approval, I turned Dale loose to build the plant. Jerry Chai and Dr. Bandy went back to their old jobs, but I added Don Maneval from Aurora to the team to help out. He would be able to integrate the new plant into the Aurora complex. I was confident Dale and his team could handle the project and turned my attention to other projects. Unfortunately, that's when things started to unravel.

One of the first problems was inadvertently created by Fred Stephens. My current boss, Tom Regan, came by my office one day to let me know Fred had worked out a deal to buy DFP from Coronet at a price below Saltville's production costs. Coronet was a Florida DFP producer owned by the Japanese. Tom then said, "That will let us shut down Saltville early and save the company some money."

This would be a mistake.

"Tom, I don't think buying DFP is such a good idea," I said. "If we shut down Saltville now, we'll lose the key personnel needed to quickly get the new plant running."

Tom thought about it for a few seconds. "I think you're over-reacting. All we need is a few key personnel. As long as we keep Dale, Tim, and some of the shift foremen, we should be in good shape."

"We're already going to have trouble keeping the shift foremen. They grew up in the mountains of Virginia and love it there. It's going to be hard to get them to move to the heat and humidity of North Carolina."

"You worry too much. Everything will be fine. Besides, Fred's already signed the deal to buy the product, so get used to it."

I hoped he was right, but I wasn't convinced.

Surprisingly, the first to abandon ship was Tim Honeycutt, Saltville's general superintendent. I learned about it on a Monday morning when Dale called.

"Tim had a little problem this morning and quit," Dale said.

"What kind of problem?" I asked.

Dale explained that since Tim was afraid of flying he had been driving back and forth from Saltville to Mustang Engineering in Tampa. Tim would head to Florida on a Monday, stay in Tampa for ten days, then make the 11-hour drive back home to Virginia. We all knew he was getting tired of this routine.

"Tim finally decided to try and fly from the Tri-Cities airport to Tampa," Dale continued. "He borrowed some of his wife's prescription anxiety pills, took a couple, and got on the plane."

"Oh, shit. How did that go?"

"Not too good. When the plane taxied to the end of the runway, Tim lost it. He jumped out of his seat and tried to open the door to get off. The flight attendants pounced on him and held him down until they got back to the terminal. That's when security took over and escorted him off the plane. Tim called a little later to tell me what happened and that he quit."

I was not happy about the news. Things were not going well. A few months later, Dale called to tell me that since the Saltville employees would start work at Aurora before the new DFP plant was in operation, Aurora wouldn't have much for them to do. Despite this, Aurora would put them on the payroll but only at minimum wage until the new plant started up. The Saltville employees said they'd rather stay in the mountains and look for work than spend a couple of years at Aurora at minimum wage.

I told Dale that I'd call Aurora and see if I could get it straightened out. I spoke with both the plant manager and the head of HR but neither would budge. Now I was really getting stressed up. The only employee from Saltville left to help on the project was Dale. Unfortunately, a few months later, Dale called to let me know that he too was quitting.

"I don't really want to run the new plant without someone with DFP experience helping out," he said. "As you know, bringing a new DFP plant online is tough. Instead of trying to do that, I've decided to go back to school and become a lawyer."

My worst fears had been realized. There was no one except me working on the project with any DFP experience. And, I hadn't been involved in the details of operating Saltville since Dale became manager ten years earlier. I would have to dedicate nearly 100 percent of my time to try to save the project. Regrettably, the engineering was still in the early stages. Don Maneval stepped up and tried to help with the plant design as much as he could. But without DFP experience, he didn't know which items were critical. I knew some of the information but not as much as Dale or Tim.

This project is doomed and I'm screwed!

Don and I carried on the best we could for the next three years. The initial cost estimate of $40 million was soon increased to $53 million to cover unexpected modifications to Aurora's infrastructure. Unfortunately, the final cost for the project came in at $63 million due to modifications required by senior management and improvements to increase plant reliability.

Touring the Aurora DFP plant with (left to right) my former wife, Betty, my daughter, Leslee, my father, Howard, and my son, Sam

Despite the major cost overrun, the CEO, Bill Doyle, decided it would be appropriate to have a dedication ceremony for the DFP plant in July 2002. Aurora arranged for a large, circus-sized tent to be erected on the west side of the kiln. Local dignitaries were invited to attend. Bill and the senior management team would fly down on the corporate jet and land on the runway next to Aurora's admin building. I was able to hitch a ride with them on the jet.

The main event was supposed to be the dedication ceremony scheduled for 1:00 p.m. It turned out the main event occurred at 11:00 a.m. As the Aurora management team waited near the runway to greet our flight, they suddenly heard a strange noise. Looking up, they saw a jet plane dive into the Pamlico River. A few seconds later, they spotted a parachute with a person hanging below, slowly float down and splash into the river. Remembering the plane crash that wiped out Texasgulf's management team in 1981, they worried that history had repeated itself.

"It looks like someone got out of the plane!" yelled Aurora's maintenance superintendent.

"Maybe they only had a parachute for Bill Doyle," said Bill Cooper, the plant manager. "In any case, we better rescue whoever's in the river."

The maintenance superintendent and an assistant ran to the company dock, jumped into a power boat and headed toward the parachute. In a few minutes, they returned with the sole survivor, the pilot of a Harrier Jet from the Marine base at Cherry Point. The plane had engine trouble, so the pilot abandoned it over the Pamlico to minimize the chance of hurting someone on the ground.

Those of us in the corporate jet had no idea about all the excitement going on until we prepared to land at Aurora. Our pilots didn't know what to think when they saw a helicopter in the middle of Aurora's runway. They got on their radio and found out the Marine base had sent out the helicopter when the heard their jet had problems. When the helicopter arrived, it found the pilot had already been fished out of the river, so they landed on the runway to pick him up.

With all of the unexpected excitement, the rest of the day was somewhat anticlimactic. As scheduled, at 1:00 p.m., Bill Doyle and several local dignitaries spoke about the benefits of the project. Next, the VIPs were divided into groups and taken on a tour of the new facility. As I was leading my group along, I came upon an embarrassing surprise.

During the engineering phase, I had insisted that the kiln be sufficiently elevated so that the red-hot clinker would be discharged above ground level. Otherwise, the clinker would discharge into a pit where a drag conveyer would be required to lift it back to the surface. If the drag conveyor failed, the red-hot clinker would fill the pit and roast the crew sent to clean up the mess. The engineering firm listened and developed a preliminary design with the kiln raised so that any spillage could be cleaned up using a front-end loader. But raising the kiln and other equipment 15 feet would cost an additional $15 million. This seemed like a lot of money to spend to keep someone from doing a miserable job a few times a year. I reluctantly agreed to stay with the original design.

Now, as I took guests on a tour of the new facility, the pit at the discharge of the kiln sported a new sign in large letters: "Huff's Hole." My guests had a few snide remarks and questions about the designation.

Touring the Aurora DFP plant with (left to right) my daughter-in-law, Crystal, my son, Jon, my daughter, Julie, and my mother, Dorothy

A couple of months after the dedication, we began to bring the kiln into production. Without any knowledgeable operators it was difficult, expensive, and time consuming. There was a lot of experimentation required to find the correct formulation for the feed and the proper kiln temperature for processing it. This situation was further aggravated by problems in Aurora's phosphate mine. As the mine progressed into a different part of the ore body, the chemical analysis and mineralogy of the phosphate rock shifted. This meant that the feed formulation had to be adjusted which required even more experimentation. I spent many days and nights in the control room trying to help. But since no one had much experience producing DFP, it was a nightmare—a nightmare that went on for months.

After we finally got the plant running at decent levels, I still had to make trips to Aurora to help with problems. Often, I'd need to participate in discussions to sort out what was going wrong. The discussions were usually held in the DFP plant's conference room which, like everything else at Aurora, was located within a tall security fence. To enter the Aurora complex, it was necessary to stop at the guard station, park, and go inside to get a visitor's pass. Normally, if Aurora knew someone was coming for a visit, the visitor's name was put on a list provided to the guards in advance. Sometimes, however, they would forget.

One morning I arrived at the guard station and walked inside to get my pass. I was already in a bad mood. I'd had to travel to Aurora on short notice due to serious problems with the new plant. And now, I had a sinus headache and was going to be late for the meeting. I waited impatiently for my turn to get a visitor's pass. Finally, I stepped up to the counter and gave the guard my name and told him I was headed to a meeting at the DFP plant.

The guard looked at his clipboard. "Mr. Huff, I don't see you on the list. I know they're having a big meeting somewhere so it will probably take a couple of hours to get approval for your pass."

"That's probably the meeting I'm supposed to attend. You need to give them a call so I can get to the meeting. I'm already late."

"I can't do that right now. I am busy handling the daily report and processing other requests for passes. I'll give them a call when I have time. What did you say you were doing here?"

By now I was pissed off and not in the mood to argue further.

"I'm from the corporate office in Northbrook. I'm here to fire the plant manager and am making a list of the others I need to fire. What did you say your name was?" I took out a pen and notepad and looked at him.

"There is no reason to get upset, Mr. Huff. Just go right on in. I'm sorry for any inconvenience. Just drive right on in."

With that, he quickly handed me a pass. I walked out to my car and headed to the plant to join the meeting. A while later during a break, Bill Cooper wandered in and said he needed to have a private conversation with me. When we stepped outside I could see he was upset.

"What the hell did you tell the guard?" Bill asked. "Everyone's talking about you coming to Aurora to fire me."

"I was just late for the meeting and the guard was being a pain in the ass. I thought by telling him I was here to fire you it would speed things up, which it did."

"Dammit, Clark. It's going to take me a week to get things settled down."

"I'm sorry to hear that, Bill, but if my name had been on the visitor list, none of this would've happened."

This proved to be another case where a shenanigan helped solve a problem. After this, as soon as I walked in the guard station and identified myself, I was handed a pass and sent on my way. And oddly enough, I heard a few months later that Bill Cooper was actually fired.

Gradually, I was able to disengage myself from the DFP project. Other projects came up that needed my attention. But years later, as I look back at the Aurora DFP project, I can't believe what a disaster I created. On a personal level, building the plant had been like torture. With no Saltville personnel to assist, I'd had to spend most of three years helping with the design, construction, and startup of the plant. It seemed like a never-ending nightmare. But for the company, it had proven to be worse. A few years after the plant started up, the market for DFP slumped. An enzyme was discovered making more of the phosphate in grain available to poultry. This meant that the birds required less supplemental phosphate and, thus, less DFP. To make matters worse, the Russians and others had excess DFP that they began to export to the United States at prices lower than Aurora's production cost. The net result was that Aurora's DFP plant was shut down.

So in the end, if we had just kept operating Saltville we would have saved the $63 million invested in the new plant. Saltville would have likely been able to continue to operate at a modest profit for an additional four or five years. Don Maneval and I, along with the dozens of other people involved in the Aurora DFP project, could have spent our time doing something useful for the company. My biggest mistake was not making sure to include critical people in discussions about the project. I should have made sure the sales group, along with my boss and key people at Aurora, were involved. Having their input would have helped avoid a lot of mistakes and saved the company a lot of money.

Thanking back on this, it was the worst fiasco of my professional career. But the thing that aggravates me even more is that the whole mess could have been avoided if Dave Edmiston had located the DFP plant at Aurora in the first place. In achieving his goal of building the plant for minimum cost, he created a major headache for me and the company. Plus, I didn't need his help to look stupid.

CHAPTER 33

Learning to Play Monopoly

Ignoring warning signs means you flunked the IQ test

I was glad when the Aurora DFP fiasco was finally over. It felt good to unwind at home for a change. Fortunately, the other plants in my group did a good job taking care of themselves in my absence. As I was catching up on my work, I'd still occasionally reflect back on the terrible job I'd done on the DFP project. I'd screwed up people's lives and cost the company a lot of money. Thus, I was astonished in early 2004 when I was promoted to VP of Capital for the Phosphate Division. This seemed crazy. After I had screwed up a major capital project, I was promoted to look after the capital projects for a whole division. Maybe they thought I had learned from my mistakes and was now a genius.

The promotion came about when my friend, Guy Whitaker, retired from the job. He decided he didn't want to spend another winter in Illinois and moved back to North Carolina. I hated to see him go but was glad to get the new job. The VP of Capital was responsible for looking after non-routine capital expenditures which included evaluating projects to determine whether they made economic sense and monitoring the execution of projects to make sure they were done properly. By now, I knew quite a bit about financial analysis because of all the projects I'd submitted during the past 30 years. I had done the financial and risk analysis on all of these projects and had argued with the financial group over details. And based on the shenanigans I'd tried, I knew what to look out for. The capital budget for the plants was typically about $80 million, but sometimes there would be a large project which could drive up annual spending to $200 million or more. Although looking after such large amounts of money made me nervous, I was excited to have a job that invited me to take risks and compete with other companies.

I have always been very competitive. As a boy I loved to play games, particularly Monopoly. Many kids wouldn't play with me after a few games because I nearly always won, especially if I was the banker. Now I had the chance to play an adult version of Monopoly. And the best part was I was using someone else's money. I was anxious for the game to begin.

One of my first large projects was related to a byproduct produced at the Aurora, North Carolina, facility. When phosphoric acid is concentrated by boiling off the water, the fluorine also comes off as hydrofluorosilicic acid or HFSA. HFSA can then be sold to water treatment facilities for fluoridating drinking water.

In 2004, a company that made silicon wafers for the computer industry, MEMC, approached PCS. They wanted us to build a plant to convert the HFSA to silicon tetrafluoride or STF. They would then buy the STF and ship it to their plant in Texas to produce silicon wafers.

Initially, PCS had little interest in producing STF since it was entirely different than any other product we manufactured. However, since MEMC had to have STF, this put us in a strong negotiating position. Plus, this would further diversify the company.

Negotiations with MEMC continued through the summer with meetings every few weeks. We visited the MEMC facilities and they visited Aurora, but most of the negotiations were held in the Northbrook office. Negotiations were a little one-sided since they desperately needed an STF source and PCS didn't really need to get the business. The plant was expected to cost $132 million and PCS would have to put up the money. This meant that PCS needed to have language that assured the recovery of their investment plus a tidy profit on the deal. As a result, negotiations dragged on for quite a while. If the price was too high, MEMC would be out of business, but if it was too low PCS didn't want to take the risk. I was glad things didn't proceed too fast. I had never been involved in these types of negotiations nor looked after a project this large. I needed time to feel my way along.

Fortunately, I had several PCS people helping with the negotiations, including one of the PCS lawyers, Karin Torain. She took the time to explain things to me and diligently looked after PCS's interests. After 14 months of negotiations, in May of 2006 we reached a verbal agreement. Karin forwarded MEMC a copy of the contract which they verbally approved. The MEMC contingent planned to travel to Chicago early Monday morning for a formal signing ceremony followed by lunch. They would then leave Monday afternoon to fly back to St. Louis. I was excited to finally have the contract completed except for the signatures. I headed home Friday afternoon looking forward to a peaceful weekend.

Unfortunately, my restful weekend was disrupted Saturday afternoon when I developed an excruciating pain on the right side of my lower abdomen. I was reluctant to go to the emergency room since I was afraid they'd want to keep me and I'd miss the Monday morning signing. Much to my relief, late Saturday night, the pain suddenly went away. I felt fine Sunday morning and throughout the day. However, Sunday night the pain returned. It hurt bad enough that I was about to concede and go to the hospital but then it suddenly subsided again. I couldn't figure out what was going on but hoped it would leave me alone until after the Monday signing.

I was relieved Monday morning when the pain hadn't returned. Although I didn't have an appetite and felt kind of nauseated, I figured I could tough it out. At the office, as I was checking to make sure everything was ready for the signing, I started to feel a little dizzy. Soon, the sweat started to roll off of my forehead. I called the doctor to see if I could run by and get some medication before the meeting. I was told in no uncertain terms to go to the hospital.

I reluctantly headed home to pick up Betty and drove to the

hospital. By then I was becoming very dizzy which, to my wife's dismay, was not improving my driving.

During the check-in at the hospital, the lady at the front desk asked for my insurance card. While I was fumbling in my wallet, she said, "You don't look too good." She then picked up her phone. "I need a nurse out front immediately."

In a few seconds, a nurse appeared. She took my temperature and blood pressure. She then called out, "I need a gurney right now!"

"Don't you need my insurance information?"

"Your wife can take care of that. You're in trouble. We need to get you in back so a doctor can immediately check you out."

They rolled me back into the emergency room. I changed into a white gown while waiting for the doctor. He came in and poked at me. The pain was mainly in my right, lower abdomen.

"You have acute appendicitis," he said. "Normally, we would run an MRI, but it is critical we get you into surgery right now. We'll remove your appendix laparoscopically. You will just have three small incisions and should only have to stay in the hospital for a couple of nights."

Ah, shit. I'd still hoped to be at the office for the signing. That event was slipping away. At least I wouldn't be out of commission too long.

In a few minutes, an orderly came by and wheeled me into the operating room. Sometime later, I gradually woke up in a room. Betty was standing by the end of the bed talking with the surgeon. I was still somewhat disoriented. After a few minutes I lifted the blanket to look at my bandages. Instead of three small incisions, I had two small ones and one very large gash.

I asked the doctor, "What happened? Did your scalpel slip?"

He shook his head at me. "If you'd come to the hospital when you were first in pain, you would have had three small incisions and a short stay in the hospital." Before I could respond, he continued. "However, since you were hardheaded, you screwed around until your appendix ruptured. We had to make a large incision so we could wash out your abdomen."

"So, when can I go home?" I asked.

"You're probably going to need to be in the hospital for at least seven days while you get IV medications to fight the infection and morphine to control the pain."

Despite what he said, I really didn't feel too bad. After he and Betty left the room, I decided I'd better check to see how the MEMC contract signing had gone. I gave Karin Torain a call. She said that the whole thing had fallen apart. Without me there to explain the contract, the PCS CEO, Bill Doyle, wouldn't agree to some of the wording. The discussions had turned ugly and MEMC had headed back to St. Louis without even staying for lunch.

I was concerned that the relationship with MEMC had degenerated and I wanted to fix things. I started to give Karin instructions on how to best deal with the problems until I got back in the office. After several minutes, Karin broke into the conversation.

"Clark, are you all right? Where are you?"

"Ah, I'm at Lake Forest Hospital," I said. "They had to remove my appendix but I feel fine."

"Are you on drugs?"

"They are giving me morphine for the pain. Why do you ask?"

"Dammit, Clark! I just spent five minutes taking detailed notes about some nude women walking through the forest alongside a tiger. Call me when you're off the drugs, you dumbass." With that, she slammed the phone down.

I began to realize morphine could do more than ease the pain. I really wasn't feeling too bad and thought that my mental processes were just fine. I was glad I hadn't said anything worse. Or maybe I had and she was too embarrassed to tell me.

After a couple of days, I told the doctor I was feeling good and ready to go home. I was able to get out of bed and walk up and down the halls without any problems. He told me that he would take me off the morphine and come back in the afternoon to see how I was doing. It turned out that without the morphine I wasn't doing well. In the afternoon the pain in my stomach was terrible. Walking down the hallway was out of the question. It was three more days before they released me. If I'd just gone to the hospital on Saturday instead of acting stupid, the appendix fiasco would have been a relatively minor nuisance.

After I got back in the office, I was able to talk to the CEO and ease his concerns. Fortunately, we were able to get the contract with MEMC signed a few weeks later. Shortly thereafter, construction was underway. The plant was completed in a little over a year and fell within budget. The new facility operated well and generated a good income stream. A few years later when we evaluated the project, we found it had generated a 30 percent return on the investment. The project had been a great success. On top of that, the next time there was a downturn in phosphate prices the MEMC project was mainly responsible for Aurora's positive cash flow for the year.

The project taught me a lot. I learned about negotiating large contracts and then getting the right people to build the plant. Based on what I'd learned on the DFP project, I included Aurora personnel in the initial discussions. This gave them a vested interest in making sure the project was successful. For this reason, they were much more helpful in solving problems. I also learned that it's not a good idea to talk too much while you're on drugs. You might say something that you'll regret.

CHAPTER 34

Adventures in China

Everyone doesn't look at things the same way

I was surprised one morning in early 2005 when my boss, Tom Regan, told me I would be making a trip to China—PCS owned 22 percent of the Chinese company, Sinofert, that was considering expanding into the feed phosphate business. I would be accompanied by my old friend Steve Auman and Dandan Xiang from the Saskatoon sales office. Dandan was a native of China with black hair, a slender build, and a tendency to poke fun at me. Since she spoke the language and understood the culture, she would act as our interpreter while keeping Steve and me out of trouble. Based on our past shenanigans, she would have her hands full.

In preparing for the trip, we decided to take along some presents to hand out to the dignitaries we would meet. Steve and I were in the storage room rummaging through golf shirts and hats when Dandan happened to walk by.

"What are you guys up to?" she asked.

"We're sorting out gifts to hand out during our China trip," I said.

"Those green golf hats won't do. You need to find something else to hand out."

"What's the problem with the hats?"

"We will be going to the interior of China. These areas are isolated from outsiders and still have their old customs."

"So, what does that have to do with the hats?"

"Well, if someone's wife is messing around, it would shame him if you told him to his face. Instead, they just leave a green hat on his desk or chair to let him know he has a problem at home. They will wonder what you guys have in mind if you show up and start handing out green hats."

That might have proven embarrassing.

The first leg of the trip was to Beijing. Much to my surprise, there was a nonstop flight from Chicago. After the 14-hour flight, Steve, Dandan, and I were tired and ready for bed. We were met at the Beijing airport by the rest of our entourage. Sean was with Sinofert and made all the arrangements for our travel in China and would escort us. Connie was a sales agent for PCS in China and she was familiar with the Chinese feed phosphate business.

As we left the airport and headed into town, I began to appreciate the immensity of the city. With a population of 20 million, Beijing had about twice as many people as the whole state of Illinois. Initially, we mostly passed industrial buildings, but these soon were replaced by office buildings and apartment complexes. As we traveled towards the center of town, traffic soon picked up and began to impede our progress. There were people meandering around everywhere and I started to see McDonald's cafés and signs in English. It was clearly an international city.

As we continued deeper into Beijing, the smog and dust increased significantly. The wind from the northwest carried dust into the city from the Gobi Desert. The smog from the cars and smoke from the power plants added to the problem. Many of the people in the street wore surgical masks to reduce their exposure.

After spending the night in Beijing, we flew to Guiyang to visit the Kailin phosphate mines and related facilities. Our flight was on a Chinese airline that treated men and women differently. Steve, Sean, and I were seated in first class. Dandan had a first class ticket but was forced to sit in coach with Connie. She was not happy. Apparently, her time in North America had raised her expectations. After we landed in Guiyang and picked up our bags, we rode in a van for the 36-mile trip to the Kailin mine site.

Guiyang was 1,100 miles southwest of Beijing and seldom had visitors from the West. There were no American restaurants or English signs. Everything was written in Chinese. As we left the city on our way to the mine, China's efforts to upgrade the infrastructure were apparent. In some places, the road was a brand-new, multi-lane asphalt highway. Traffic was able to move along at a brisk pace. But after a few miles, the highway ended and we were diverted onto an ancient cobblestone road. Then travel slowed to a crawl. Semi-trucks and autos were intermingled with horse-drawn wagons and people on bikes. The traffic was squeezed together on the very narrow road which made it difficult to pass. After what seemed like forever, we would be back on a new section of the road and speeding along again for a few miles. Then the whole process repeated itself.

After the long and bumpy ride, we finally started to climb up a hill leading to the mine site. Partway up the hill, we unexpectedly pulled up to a white, nondescript building.

"Why are we stopping?" I asked.

Sean looked up from his notebook. "They've made arrangements for us to have lunch at a local restaurant."

"Can't we wait to have lunch? It's early in the day and I would like to see the mine."

Dandan spoke up. "If you don't stop for lunch, it would indicate that you think the restaurant isn't up to your standards. They would feel bad that you didn't appreciate the arrangements they've made. They've spent a lot of time planning the visit."

"I guess we'd better eat."

It was good we had Dandan along to explain the quirks of the culture.

We piled into the restaurant and were led upstairs to a private room. Our host and a couple of his employees were waiting for us. Introductions were made and then we were seated at a large round table. The host spoke to Dandan in Chinese for a few moments and then she turned to us. She explained that as part of the lunch they would like to honor us with a few drinks of a local beverage called baijiu that had a little kick to it. Again, it would shame them if we didn't drink it. I explained that, for "religious reasons," I didn't drink alcohol. Dandan said that they would respect that and I was let off the hook. The rest of the group needed to have at least one drink so as not to offend them. Fortunately, my cohorts were up to the task and made up for my shortfall.

In the center of the table was a disk where the food could be rotated around like a Lazy Susan so that each of us could take what we wanted. Although we had plates, there was no silverware. It looked like I was going to have to learn how to use chopsticks. Dandan took it upon herself to give me a lesson. The entrées were brought out one at a time so we could "ooh" and "ah" over them as they were placed on the Lazy Susan. As I looked at the first entrée, I didn't recognize what it was.

"What's that?" I asked.

"Those are deep fried scorpions."

I put a few on my plate. They weren't too bad, kind of like shrimp. I also took some rice and some fried vegetables of an unknown variety. "What's that?" I asked as another plate was paraded out.

"Those are millipedes that have been cooked in oil. You should take some. They're considered a delicacy and you'll offend the host if you don't try one."

"I think the host will be less offended if I don't. Otherwise, I will likely throw up on the floor."

The quick lunch ended up taking two hours. By the time we left, most of the group was staggering a little as we made our way to the van. Once onboard, we headed up the winding road to an office building where we were led to a conference room. Those of us who were still functional listened to a detailed review of the ore body and phosphate mines. There were actually six mines operating in the region located on the side of a ridge where the ore zone had been exposed by erosion.

After the presentation, we piled back into the van for a short drive to one of the mine portals. There, we saw a conveyor belt carrying rock from the mine come out of the portal and dump the rock onto a large pile. Various types of mobile equipment traveled in and out of other portals located along the ore zone.

Our tour guide and his assistants spent a half hour explaining the details of the mining technique. At the end of a short question and answer session, they thanked us for coming and started to walk away.

"When are we going to take the underground tour?" I asked.

It seemed crazy to me to travel all this way and not actually see inside the mine.

The group stopped and had a discussion in Chinese for a few seconds.

"We have never had a Westerner ask to go underground in one of our mines. They think it is too dangerous."

I doubted the mine would be any more dangerous than the Burgin.

"Would we be safe if we went up to the mine face?" I asked.

They discussed this for a few more seconds. "There shouldn't be any problems. After all, this isn't a coal mine. However, you might get a little dirty."

"After traveling all this way, I'd really like to see the mine in operation."

The host looked at his assistants for a few seconds, shrugged his shoulders and said, "You should be able to follow us into the mine in your van."

After giving me a hostile glare, my companions reluctantly climbed in the van and we headed into the mine. I was glad to get a chance to go underground and learn about the geology and their mining methods. The mine face was located in an underground cavern where there was a lot of activity. Some miners were drilling holes for the explosives while others were removing rock that had been previously blasted down. It was dusty and very noisy. Dump trucks, supply trucks, and a jumbo drill passed by so we had to be careful not to get run over. In places, the ceiling was covered with wire mesh that looked like chain-link fencing. Apparently, a section of the roof was trying to fall into the entry. To prevent this, it was held in place by large bolts installed in holes drilled in the roof.

Looking around, I said to the mine manager, "It looks like everyone is in a hurry. I'm surprised that they don't run over each other."

"We sometimes have accidents where someone is bumped and gets banged up a little. It usually isn't too serious. However, it is important that we hurry. The ore zone is not very strong. It usually only stays open for a few hours and then collapses. It is a disaster to be here when it caves in so the miners try to be quick."

My old Saltville buddy Steve said, "I think we have seen everything of interest. Let's get the hell out of here."

With that, we jumped back in the van and headed out of the mine. My traveling companions suggested that I make the next trip underground alone.

From Guiyang we traveled southwest to Kunming. We were told that although it was only a 270-mile trip, the roads and traffic made travel by car very tedious. Thus, we boarded a plane and flew. The next day we visited the Three Circles mine and chemical plant. Expecting that they would be using obsolete technology and equipment, I was shocked to find that the facility was state of the art. In many ways it surpassed most North American phosphate operations. I was beginning to realize that the image of China portrayed on American TV might be highly biased. There were certainly areas where antiquated technology was used, but there were also places using leading edge technology.

The safety standards, by contrast, were more relaxed than expected. Workers were not wearing hard hats, safety shoes, or safety glasses. Although much of the equipment was manufactured in China, it was identical to equipment manufactured in the U.S. Upon closer inspection, I found that the pumps all had the same serial number and the manufacturer's name was missing. It looked like a Chinese firm had made a mold of a U.S. pump casing and was casting duplicates in a local foundry. When I asked our guide, he just smiled and shrugged his shoulders.

Back at the motel, I quickly showered and prepared for dinner. As I started to leave the room, I noted the excellent job the maid was doing. Any time I left, she would hurry in and freshen up the room. I thought that she deserved a tip and left twenty dollars on the counter with a note reading, "For The Maid." I suspected that she couldn't read English but thought she would get the idea.

As I was standing in the hotel lobby waiting for the van to take us to dinner, the hotel manager stepped out of his office. Looking around he walked up to our group. "Is there a Mr. Huff here?" he asked.

"I'm Clark Huff. What can I do for you?"

"You left money in your room for the maid."

"Ah, yes. She was doing a good job so I left her a tip."

"You can't do that. We seldom see Westerners in this part of China, so the people here are not used to your customs. No one here tips."

"She is doing a great job and the twenty dollars will probably mean a lot to her."

"It would. Unfortunately, it will likely cause her serious trouble. When she takes the money home, her husband will want to know why she got it. He won't understand tipping. He will think that she was performing other services and will likely beat her. Besides, if you are looking for companionship, we can arrange for someone much better looking and more proficient. We will just add her cost to your bill. But you need to go get the money from your room and take it with you."

"Ah, no companion is necessary. I'll go get the money."

Another lesson on how different things can be in a foreign country. Things that would have been absolutely taboo in the Mormon Utah where I grew up are perfectly acceptable in other places.

After the education about tipping, a van picked us up and carried us to the restaurant for dinner. The plant manager had arranged for a private room. He brought along five people to mingle with our group. The Chinese were very conscious of status. They perceived that I was the highest-ranking member of the group so I was seated next to the plant manager. Steve Auman was seated on the other side of the manager. Much to Dandan's dismay, they perceived that she, being a woman, was there to carry our bags. She was seated at the far end of the table. She was not happy.

Although women in the U.S. were sometimes discriminated against in 2005, it was much worse in China.

As dinner progressed, we discussed things we had seen during the plant tour. The technology implemented in the facility had really impressed us and it clearly surpassed any of the PCS facilities. On the other hand, safety seemed to be a lower concern. The manager said that finding workers was not a problem. They were standing in line hoping for a chance to get a job. If a worker was seriously injured on the job, the records would show that he was terminated the preceding day.

The biggest concern for the manager was to make sure that the plant did not cause an international incident. An international incident could have serious repercussions.

"My predecessor was not very lucky," the manager said. "One evening, the containment dike for the waste water from the chemical plant broke. The water ran into the river and caused a major fish kill along the river in China and all the way down to Laos. It made headlines in the international news."

This would certainly be a problem.

"A few weeks after the whole thing died down, a couple of men showed up at the manager's house one evening. They took him for a ride. He hasn't been seen since then. I received a call the next morning letting me know I was the new plant manager. Based on what happened to my predecessor, I have observers stationed every 100 feet along the dike with strict orders to call me immediately if they observe anything unusual."

That seemed like money well spent. Particularly since it was the company's money.

Toward the end of dinner, the manager asked what we would like to do for the rest of the evening. I told him that we would find a quiet place to relax while we compared notes. He said that he'd make arrangements for us at an exclusive place. I said that the hotel bar would be fine and that he needn't bother but he insisted. He called over one of his assistants and told him to take care of it.

As we prepared to leave, the manager said that the van would take us back to the hotel to freshen up before we went to relax. This seemed unusual and I suggested that we really didn't need to freshen up. He looked a little confused but insisted that we swing by the hotel first.

After a quick visit to our rooms, the group gradually assembled in the hotel lobby. The van driver and his assistant were surprised when Dandan showed up. In English, they explained that it would be inappropriate for her to accompany our group. She told them that it was her job to watch after us so she was coming along. They said she needed to stay behind. She told them that she was going and climbed in the van. Apparently, she didn't want to be snubbed again.

Steve Auman (on left) and me comparing notes in the Chinese brothel

The rest of us climbed in the van and headed into town. After about 30 minutes, we pulled up to a marble-faced, high-rise building. Inside, we took the elevator to the fourth floor. As I got off the elevator, I looked around and saw we were in a large, two-story high room. There was a wide, sweeping staircase going from our level up to the next. I was intrigued to see a very beautiful woman in a long, revealing dress on each side of the steps. Standing at the door to the elevator was a woman that spoke English.

"As you climb the stairs to the room reserved for you, please select the lady you would like to spend the evening with. You will find appropriately equipped bedrooms off of the central room where you will be served drinks and can amuse yourself in other ways."

I looked at Dandan. "What the hell kind of a place is this?"

"You know what it is."

"What are we supposed to do? We can't spend the night here with these girls. We need to get back to the hotel."

"You can't do that. They will think that your actions show you don't believe the girls are up to your standards and will be offended."

Apparently, the Chinese took pride in everything and could be easily offended.

Dandan continued. "You'll need to go up to the room for a few hours. You don't need to do anything with the girls, just act like you're enjoying yourself."

Thus, up to the room we went for a few drinks while we compared engineering and other notes. When the girls came in to serve drinks, they would scowl at Dandan and make heated comments in Chinese. They apparently thought she was hurting their business. Dandan responded with a nasty tone in her voice that usually provoked a heated discussion. She deserved serious hazardous duty pay.

After a couple of hours, we collected our notes and headed back to the hotel. It was good that we had Dandan there to get us out of trouble.

The rest of the trip went well. We eventually made it back to Beijing. We toured the city and paid our respects to Chairman Mao. Apparently, foreigners that wanted to do business in Beijing needed to "pay their respects" to show we weren't snubbing the government. We also managed to have dinner at the restaurant that first served Peking Duck. Needless to say, we all ordered it. However, Dandan chided us for not being more adventurous in our selection of hors d'oeuvres. She, on the other hand, ate all kinds of strange things.

The next day we boarded the flight back to Chicago. On the way to the airport, Dandan said that she wasn't feeling well. As it turned out, her adventurous dining seriously upset her digestive system. She spent most of the 13-hour flight home sitting in the plane's restroom. When preparing to land, they had to coax her off of the toilet, although she said she was perfectly willing to take her chances without a seatbelt.

Unfortunately, we never expanded into phosphate production in China. We just couldn't find any synergies that would give us an advantage. But, we were still interested in doing something in China. As China's economy continued to improve, the potential opportunity was enormous.

In May of 2008, we made another trip to China to investigate their leading-edge technology in the use of coal to produce ammonia. On this trip, we had a larger PCS contingent that included that chief operating officer, myself, and four others, including Dandan. Once again, she was given the task of keeping us out of trouble. We flew non-stop from Chicago to Beijing and checked into a hotel to catch up on our sleep.

The next morning, we were bused to a coal-fired ammonia plant near Jinan. Unfortunately, just before we arrived, they had a bad accident. When we inquired as to how bad the accident was, they said it wasn't too bad. They had only needed two ambulances. As we had learned during our first trip to China, an accident requiring more than two ambulances might elicit world attention and result in a change of plant management. We found out later that they had stuffed four people into each ambulance.

China Travel Group (L to R)—Dandan, me, Keith Wilson, John Kowalczyk, Jim Dietz, Richard Holder and John Godber (not shown)

Due to the mishap, we had a very limited tour of the facility and then caught a plane to our next stop—Kunming. There we visited another facility using state-of-the-art ammonia technology. Again, we were very impressed. That night we were entertained in a private box at a dinner theater. The show highlighted dances from the various cultures making up China. As with my previous trip, I was having trouble adjusting to the Chinese food. The further we got from Beijing, the stranger the cuisine became. Thus, I was surprised when they brought out a very tasty, pink-colored soup. It had little pieces of meat in it that we couldn't make out.

I spoke to our interpreter, "The soup tastes good. What is it?"

After speaking to the waiter, our interpreter said, "The best explanation is that it is the essence of female frog soup."

We looked closer at our bowls for a few seconds and then set down our spoons.

One of my travel companions, John, said, "Clark, if you have any more questions about our dinner, don't ask. The less we know the happier we will all be."

That sounded like sage advice.

As we finished our visit of China, we returned to Beijing for our flight home. However, we arrived a couple of days early and decided to take the opportunity to visit some of the tourist attractions.

The Forbidden City was very interesting. As we toured, one of our party, Richard, received a lot of attention. Richard was originally an engineer from Trinidad. He was relatively tall, good looking, and had dark skin. As we toured the attractions, Richard stood out in the crowd. Apparently, they didn't see many men like him. One day, we visited the Great Wall. As we were walking along, Richard let out a yell.

"What happened, Richard?" I asked.

"That Chinese girl just grabbed my groin. She stood close to me like she was looking at something on the wall and when I was momentarily distracted, she reached out and grabbed me."

"Then what happened?"

"She took off with her friends but as she was leaving she was telling them something in a hushed voice and giggling."

Although we were interested in learning about Chinese

ammonia plants, it looked like some of the Chinese were interested
in learning about Richard.

We returned from China very impressed with their technology. Unfortunately, we were not able to use the technology in the
United States. As it turned out, the United States started using
fracking to produce cheap natural gas. An ammonia plant using
cheap natural gas provides better economics than coal and has less
of an environmental impact.

The trips to China were educational in ways I had not anticipated. There seemed to be little relationship between what I saw
on the nightly news and what I observed in China. Although they
generally lagged behind the United States in technology, they were
catching up and, in some areas, had surpassed us. I also learned
that things normally considered taboo in the United States were
acceptable in China. My travels around the world were helping to
broaden my horizons and significantly reduce my prejudices. And I
once again found the value of having someone like Dandan along
on the trips to keep us out of trouble.

CHAPTER 35

The Russian Excursion

Rubbing elbows with the big boys

I really enjoyed being the VP of Capital and Technology. It was the best job I could imagine; I spent hundreds of millions of dollars on all kinds of interesting projects like building a new sulfuric acid plant, upgrading a large power plant, and purchasing dump trucks capable of hauling 300 tons each. I was very disappointed when they wouldn't let me drive one of the dump trucks. As the company looked for opportunities to expand, I got to visit other parts of the world such as Israel, South America, Europe, and China. Since the United States and Russia were at odds with each other, I was surprised to learn in August of 2011 that the company was looking at an opportunity in Russia. As part of the evaluation, the chief financial officer, Wayne Brownlee, and the chief operating officer, Dave Delaney, and I would visit the former Soviet Union.

I was very apprehensive about making a trip to Russia. Although the Cold War was over, the evening news still carried stories about various conflicts between the United States and Russia, as well as stories about people disappearing for mysterious reasons. This seemed like an opportunity for trouble. Despite my misgivings, Dave and I were to fly from Chicago through Frankfurt, Germany, and meet with Wayne in Moscow.

I checked my bags at Chicago's O'Hare Airport and caught up with Dave at our gate. While we were talking, they announced that our flight would be delayed 30 minutes due to mechanical problems. Unfortunately, the 30 minutes turned into two and a half hours. I was frustrated and worried that we would arrive in Frankfurt too late to catch our flight to Moscow. Not a good way to start an international trip.

After waiting anxiously to board the plane, we finally got on and took our seats. Unlike my first international flight to Israel when I was crammed into coach, I now got to fly in business class. I had a much larger seat that could be made into a bed and I also received free meals and drinks. But despite the nice accommodations, I sat and worried about what we were going to do in Frankfurt. I suspected we would have to spend the night and catch an early flight to Moscow the next morning. This would mess up our schedule for the tour of the Russian facilities.

As the eight-hour flight came to an end, we finally landed in Frankfurt. I could feel my chest tighten as our plane meandered around the airport before finally pulling up to its gate. To add to the stress, our flight to Moscow would depart on the opposite side of the airport. Dave and I were screwed. I couldn't see how we were going to make our connection. Our flight would leave in five minutes and it would take at least 20 minutes to make our way to our gate.

When our plane parked and the door opened, Dave and I rushed to get off. As I stepped onto the jet bridge, I was startled to see a gentleman standing there holding a sign reading "Dave-PCS." Dave identified himself and we were quickly escorted down the jet bridge's external stairs and then climbed into a waiting car. The driver took off and raced past parked planes and other obstacles to reach the gate for our next flight. We jumped out of the car and ran up the external stairs of the jet bridge next to our plane. At the top, our escort used his access card to open the door and we walked in and stepped aboard our waiting plane. As a flight attendant guided us to our seats, she said they had been waiting for us and were glad we'd finally made it. I heaved a sigh of relief as I sat down and my heartbeat returned to normal. They immediately closed the jet's door and we were on our way to Moscow. Apparently, there were significant advantages when traveling with the COO.

The preferential treatment continued when we reached Moscow. As we exited the plane, a gentleman met us and escorted us past the lines of people waiting to clear customs. After walking down a long hallway, we entered a private lounge and sat down at a table where a waiter immediately took our drink order. Our escort then gathered up our passports and baggage claim tags and hurried out the door. While Dave and I waited, we sipped our drinks and discussed miscellaneous company business. About 30 minutes later, our chaperone and a helper came back with our bags and guided us through the airport to a limo for the trip to the hotel.

I was impressed when I found that our hosts made reservations for us at the Ritz Carlton across from Red Square. I had a suite of rooms that included an office and sitting room. I found out later that my room cost almost a thousand dollars a day. I was glad someone else was picking up the tab. From the lounge on top of the hotel, we had an excellent view of Moscow and Red Square— certainly different than the Israeli trip in 1975. There, I checked into a small motel room with a non-functioning air conditioner and ended up sharing my room with a few hundred mosquitoes. It hadn't been much fun.

After breakfast the next morning, a limo picked us up for the ride to a small airport on the edge of Moscow. We boarded a private jet in preparation for the 240-mile flight straight north to Cherepovets. On the plane we were met by Ivan, the president of the company, along with Igor and Alexi who were Ivan's assistants, plus four aides. We weren't introduced to the aides and it was not clear what they did. Although we were dressed somewhat casually, the aides were dressed in suits and just kept to themselves. It seemed strange that they stayed near the group but didn't seem to be paying any attention to what was being said.

After the introductions, we took our seats and the jet took off. Traveling in the Russian corporate jet was a little different than what I was used to. When traveling on our company plane, we all sat together in the same compartment. But here, a wall with a doorway divided the cabin into two compartments, kind of like first class and coach. We, along with Ivan and his assistants, traveled in the front compartment. The aides and some other people sat in the rear compartment. Another surprise was the young and attractive blonde-haired flight attendant who served us drinks and snacks during the flight. I'd never seen this on our company plane. Maybe traveling in Russia wasn't so bad after all.

Upon landing in Cherepovets, the group was divided between four cars and we headed south toward town. The first 15 minutes of the drive took us across a flat countryside covered by green fields intermingled with trees. Then the scenery abruptly changed to manufacturing plants and warehouses for the last three miles. Many of the buildings looked like they needed repairs or were abandoned while others appeared to be in good shape. When we arrived, Ivan took us on a tour of the phosphate chemical plant where the phosphate concentrate was converted into phosphoric acid and other products. We also toured a very modern nitrogen complex that produced ammonia. As with my visit to China, I was surprised by their technology. I had expected to find that they used technology similar to what we used 30 years ago. Instead, their instrumentation, computers, and equipment were equal and in some cases more advanced than ours. Everything appeared to be well maintained and the work areas were spotless. Ivan explained that not all plants were up to this standard but some were. They had started modernizing their facilities in order to compete with the Western world.

After touring their facilities, I expected we would head to the hotel to freshen up before going to dinner. Instead, Ivan explained that there were no appropriate hotels in the area so we would stay at a lodge owned by his company. After a 45-minute drive into a heavily forested rural area, we pulled up to the two-story lodge situated near a small river on a well-kept estate. We picked up our bags and walked inside where Ivan handed us the keys to our rooms.

"When you get to your room," Ivan said, "you will find a robe in your closet. Take off all your clothes, put on your robe, and we will meet in the lobby in 15 minutes for banyan."

Dave, Wayne, and I exchanged curious looks with each other.

"Ah, what is banyan?" I asked.

"It is kind of like a sauna. Nothing to worry about. Just an opportunity to relax."

I was nervous about this opportunity to "relax." I remembered our opportunity to "relax" in China had landed us in a brothel. I didn't want to disappoint the girls again.

I went to my room, took off all my clothes and put on the bath robe. I then nervously headed back to the lobby to wait for the others. After the group assembled, we walked down a short hallway to a room with a small swimming pool full of ice-cold water. There, we hung our robes on a rack and strode naked into the adjacent room containing the steam sauna. On the left side of the sauna were several wooden benches for us to sit while being steamed. I felt very self-conscious sitting naked on wooden benches with two senior PCS officials, plus our host and his assistants. I didn't dare let my eyes wander and just stared straight ahead. I also wondered what it would have been like if we had brought along one of our lady executives.

On the right side of the sauna was a three-foot-high table made of thick cedar planks. After we had been steamed for a while, Ivan asked me to move to the table and lay face down. My uneasiness and heart rate jumped up a notch as I lay down naked on the table. Ivan then pulled a long, maple branch out of a pot of warm water and started whacking my back with it.

What had I gotten myself into?

"This helps your body release the toxins from deep in your tissue," Ivan said. "Roll over on your back so I can get the other side."

I was even more nervous about this.

"Okay," I said, "but be careful what you whack."

After I had been steamed and whacked, I walked out of the sauna nude and jumped into the pool. The water was about five feet deep and ice cold. However, I was so hot from the sauna that the cold water felt good, at least for a few minutes. When I had sufficiently cooled down, I climbed out and headed back to the sauna for more steaming and whacking.

That night at dinner I asked Ivan, "Is banyan something you

do when you have a group of naïve Westerners visiting? You get them to take off their clothes and then steam them, whack them, and have them jump into a pool of freezing water?"

Ivan laughed. "No. This is something we adopted from Finland during the Soviet era. We found that it was a good way to have an open discussion about sensitive topics without fear of being recorded. It's hard to conceal a recorder when you're naked."

That made sense.

"Although the Soviet era ended," Ivan said, "we still find it useful if we want to have delicate business discussions that might not be completely legal in some countries."

I thought about adopting this for negotiations in the United States. We might come to an agreement quicker if we were all sitting around naked with no one taking notes.

While we discussed the "pampering," I thought I'd ask about other activities I'd heard about.

"How about some of the other diversions?" I asked. "In the movies they always portray Russian meetings as involving heavy drinking and evenings with sexy women."

Ivan said, "The CEO told us that such activities are no longer acceptable. He felt it diminished our image in the international community. Thus, we have no female servants or maids at the lodge and will only have a glass or two of wine at night during meals."

I was surprised. So far the trip had been nothing like I'd expected based on what I'd seen on TV. Although the customs were a little different than ours, generally the people appeared to be friendly and looked out for each other. It seemed that the way countries like Russia were portrayed in the news was too simplistic and highly biased.

Ivan continued. "The CEO also told us that we had to quit smoking if we wanted to keep our jobs."

"That must have been an unexpected change."

"It was. There were many of us that weren't very happy about that change."

Since we were building friendly rapport, I asked Ivan about the "aides."

The CEO thought about it a few seconds then said, "That's a different matter. Igor's father is an oligarch and is very wealthy. This puts Igor at risk of being kidnapped and held for ransom. The aides tag along to make sure that doesn't happen. Those briefcases they carry around contain serious firepower."

It might not be a good idea to offend Igor's "aides."

The next morning, we climbed back aboard the private jet and headed to Kirovsk which is a little over 600 miles north of Cherepovets. It is located on the Kola Peninsula about 50 miles north of the Arctic Circle. As we neared our destination, I grabbed my armrests when I spotted two Russian fighter planes with serious missiles under their wings pull alongside our plane.

"What's that about?" I asked. It seemed like my Russian nightmare might be coming true.

"That isn't anything to worry about," Ivan said. "There is a Russian submarine base about eighty miles away. The jets are just escorting us to be sure we don't stray from our flight plan and take pictures of the base."

I hoped our pilot knew where he was going.

About 30 minutes later, we landed at an airstrip located in the heavily wooded foothills of a large mountain. As I got off the plane I was unexpectedly hit by the cold air. Although it was August, the air temperature was only 38 degrees Fahrenheit. Being in the middle of the summer, I hadn't thought to bring a coat. The mine we were going to visit was in the mountains north of the airport and was reached via a scenic drive that looped up a heavily forested valley toward a dome-shaped mountain. Before we came to the mine, we passed through the town of Kirovsk where the buildings were mostly made of concrete. The workers and other people in the area lived in apartments. Ivan said the apartments and stores were all interlinked by large tunnels which allowed the residents to go visiting or shopping in the winter without having to venture outside.

Upon arrival at the mine site, we walked in the office building and were greeted by the manager and escorted to a conference room. There we received an orientation concerning the phosphate deposit's geology and the mining system used to extract the ore.

Next, we put on coveralls and work coats, and drove up to an overlook where we could view one of the old mine pits. Open pit mines were initially used to recover the phosphate ore. Based on the size of the pits, they had moved a lot of rock over the years. However, as the pits got deeper, they had to get wider, which meant they had to mine barren rock on the sides of the vertical ore vein. Eventually, this made the open pit mine uneconomic. The Russians now used underground mining to recover the ore which minimized the amount of waste rock that had to be removed.

After viewing the mine pit, we climbed back into our transport and headed underground. Unlike the other underground mines I'd visited, we didn't access this one by dropping down a shaft. Instead, we just drove down into a valley and then into a tunnel on the side of the mountain. It was a little like a highway tunnel except we had to pass through ventilation doors and the road twisted around a lot. After about 20 minutes, we finally pulled up to a mine face. We were approximately 2,400 feet below the top of the mountain.

After a brief review of the mine, the tour guide and I got into a long discussion of the details of their mining methods. Because of the time I'd spent working in the Burgin mine in my youth, I was very interested in all aspects of their mining method. I asked

Our group at the overlook inspecting the old Russian mine pit

about the pattern of holes that they drilled and the sequence of detonation. I was also curious about the type of explosives and blasting caps they used. After about 15 minutes of listening to my questions, Wayne had had enough.

"Clark," Wayne said, "I didn't like it when we went through the portal and started the drive underground. Sitting here 2,400 feet below the surface with water dripping on me and explosives nearby isn't helping me feel any better. If you have any more goddamn questions, you can ask them while we're sitting in the conference room drinking coffee."

With that, Wayne climbed back in the transport. I decided it would be a good idea for me to shut up and climb in with him.

The underground workings of the Russian mine with the bucket of a front end loader coming out of a side entry

After exiting the mine, we finished our discussions in the conference room and then headed for our next destination—the refinery. Our caravan drove back down the mountain on the winding highway. Once we got off the mountain, we navigated to the east around its flank toward the beneficiation plant. As usual, the lead car of the caravan contained two of the "aides." The executive team and we guests were split up between the next two cars. The final car bringing up the rear contained two more aides. This helped to assure that Igor was adequately protected. As we were driving along a straight stretch of highway, a car unexpectedly came racing up from behind, passed two of our cars, and then forced its way into the middle of our group. Immediately, the rear car of "aides" raced up and pulled alongside the intruder. The intruder was then forced off the pavement and skidded around as it went down the shoulder of the road plowing through brush before coming to an abrupt stop.

The whole thing was over before I had a chance to be scared. We didn't know whether this was a kidnapping attempt or just some locals annoyed by our caravan. If they were locals, they might be a little more cautious about who they messed with in the future.

During the tour of the beneficiation plant, I was once again impressed with the modern equipment and technology the Russians used. I wished we had brought along someone from our Aurora phosphate mine to take notes and consider changes to that facility. After touring the plant we headed back to the airport, flew to Moscow, and settled into our rooms at the Ritz Carlton.

The next morning, I felt sad that I was heading back to the United States. I would have liked to have stayed a couple of more days and toured Moscow. I doubted I would get another chance since it didn't appear likely that a partnership would provide an advantage to either company. But during the trip I had learned a lot about a competitor and to not underestimate the capabilities of foreign companies.

As I flew back home, I compared this trip to the one I'd made to Israel in 1975. Even though I was once again experiencing a different culture, I now found it interesting rather than daunting. At the time I traveled to Israel I avoided foreign food if I could. But after decades of foreign travel, I was much more tolerant and often enjoyed trying something new. I was also much more relaxed as I traveled and worried less than I did on my first trip.

Unfortunately, the trip to Russia was the last major adventure of my business career. Surprisingly, although the company name and owners had changed, I'd spent 39 years working with mostly the same people. As I thought about it during my last months at work, I realized I really enjoyed my job. The people I worked with were like family. It was fun being around them and working on projects together. This was important since I had to spend such a large percentage of my waking hours at work. It would have been miserable to spend that much time with people I didn't like or doing a job I hated. I knew that it was going to be very difficult to leave all this behind. And it was.

Stupidity in Action: Lessons in Leadership Learned the Hard Way

Sitting in the parking lot at the end of my last day of work, could I really be the boy that instigated BB gun wars, poisoned his siblings, and eventually blew myself up? After the long path I've taken and lessons learned from my stupidity, should I really give up the best job I've ever had and leave behind some of my best friends? But I feel I owe it to my parents to help them in their time of need. After all, they had helped me survive my childhood and learn important lessons. My father encouraged me to experiment and figure out how things worked. My mother's impatience resulted in my exile to the mink ranch where I learned about being an adult at a very young age.

I was also fortunate to have Mr. Bachman, Mr. Small, and Mr. Bartholomew as my teachers in high school. They helped me realize I was smarter than I thought and provided glowing recommendations to the University of Utah for me. As I pursued my professional career, my wife, Betty, did an excellent job raising our kids and looking after the household. Without all the time and effort she put in, I wouldn't have been free to excel in my profession. And as I reminisce, I remember how lucky I was to have had Rudy Higgins as an early boss. He taught me a lot about listening calmly to opposing ideas and to not take offense when someone disagreed with me. By encouraging people to speak up I would sometimes gain critical ideas and information. I was also fortunate to have had Tom Wright, Fred Stephens, and Tom Reagan tolerate my stupidity and help me learn how to be an effective company executive.

While reflecting back on my life and career, I thought of some of the most critical lessons.

DON'T REACT WHEN YOU'RE MAD—I learned what happened when I got mad and restrained my mother—nine summers on the mink ranch. Conversely, I saw how AK Gentry stepped in for me with the longshoremen in Long Beach, California. Instead of arguing with them, he got the workers to voluntarily unload the rail cars by providing a couple of cases of beer which saved the company tens of thousands of dollars.

THINK ABOUT THE CONSEQUENCES IF YOU GET CAUGHT— My life would have been entirely different if I'd been arrested for such things as forging driver's licenses in high school or dynamiting the badger hole. I was very lucky that I lived at a time and place where I could get away with such stupid things until I finally learned not to do them.

FIGURE OUT WHY THINGS WORK—Understanding how math and science work rather than just memorizing facts was the key to excelling in high school, college, and work. Explaining this process to my buddy Sheldon in high school helped him pass algebra and graduate. If something made sense to me, I could remember and use the information forever.

IF SOMETHING DOESN'T FEEL RIGHT, STEP BACK AND THINK ABOUT IT—In the Burgin mine I would have been crushed by a roof fall if I hadn't paid attention to my premonition. By not paying attention to my premonition about the water inflow in the Patience Lake potash mine, I almost had the company invest in a disaster.

FIND A JOB YOU ENJOY—It was not fun working in the

summer heat on the mink ranch at minimum wage. This seemed like torture, but it provided me the motivation to find a job I liked—engineering—that granted me a decent salary. It was a good decision. I enjoyed what I was doing my whole career and particularly enjoyed being the VP of Capital and Technology.

JUST BECAUSE YOU'RE THE BOSS, YOU DON'T KNOW EVERYTHING—In the Burgin mine the foreman wouldn't listen to the workers and, as a result, often made mistakes. On the other hand, when I listened to the maintenance foreman at Moab and let him do his job, the department ran smoothly and efficiently. Listening to the kiln operators at Saltville provided insight as to why the kiln was not producing product. My job was primarily to sort out the good ideas from the bad. The more input I got, the easier it was to make a good decision.

NEVER FEUD WITH PEOPLE—Getting into a nine-month-long emotional battle with Rudy Higgins before he was transferred to Moab and made plant manager was stupid. He was just providing his thoughts about what was going wrong. Fortunately, when he was made manager he didn't hold a grudge against me and did a lot to help me further my career. On the other hand, feuding with Ken Kutz meant that I had to make a last-minute trip from Canada to Argentina to resolve a trivial problem. Not a smart thing to do.

MAKE YOUR DEPARTMENT LIKE YOUR FAMILY—Everyone in the group will enjoy work and do a better job if they feel like part of an extended family. It's good to occasionally have lunch together, joke with each other, and have casual conversations. Sometimes a shenanigan will relieve the tension while getting the point across. I had learned this at the mink ranch and tried to foster this type of atmosphere at Moab and throughout my career. Fortunately, some of my bosses like Rudy Higgins, Fred Stephens, and Tom Regan also encouraged this attitude which made work much more enjoyable.

BE CAREFUL WHO YOU PISS OFF—Needlessly aggravating Bob Forest at Saltville and Tom Wright on multiple occasions almost got me fired several times. It's better to pay attention to others' feelings. It was not a good idea to point out Tom's mistakes in meetings. I should have been more sensitive to what would upset him and talked with him in private if there was a problem.

WHEN YOU'RE THE BOSS, YOU'RE THE BOSS—As Tom Wright pointed out after the silo collapse, take charge of the area you're responsible for. This includes projects started before you're made boss. This will help make sure nothing falls through the cracks and that you do a better job.

PROMOTE THE MOST CAPABLE PEOPLE—As Dr. Fogarty pointed out, don't promote people just because they suck up to the boss. It is important to promote the most capable people. Having the wrong managers at Saltville and Weeping Water during their early years cost the company a lot of money and resulted in product quality problems. As I retired, this problem was becoming rampant in the company as salesmen were promoted to senior positions in operations and several incompetent "suck-ups" were promoted. This contributed to the demise of the company.

INVOLVE ALL DEPARTMENTS ON MAJOR PROJECTS—The Aurora DFP fiasco would have been avoided if sales and senior management had understood the details of the project. Conversely, having everyone involved in my next major project—to provide the raw material to MEMC for use in the production of silicon computer chips—resulted in a success.

GET APPROPRIATE HELP WHEN WORKING IN A FOREIGN COUNTRY—Alex Ariosa was indispensable while we were doing business in Brazil and his contacts saved us a lot of headaches. When we were considering new business in China, Dandan did an excellent job explaining the culture and keeping us out of trouble. It is a good practice to remember that other cultures look at things differently and that what is acceptable in one may not be in another.

Although I wasn't very bright as a kid, over the years my dumb actions provided the opportunity to learn these valuable lessons. Regrettably, I still have a lot to learn. But I was fortunate that the early lessons happened in a small farming town 70 years ago. Otherwise, my stupidity would have resulted in my arrest and my life would have been much different. In writing this book I hoped to not only provide some entertainment, but also help someone learn these lessons without duplicating my stupidity. I wish someone had sat down and explained them to me early in my life. I could have avoided some very dangerous and expensive mistakes. But, on the other hand, knowing me, I wouldn't have learned anyway without suffering the consequences of my own stupid actions.

Acknowledgements

During my career I gradually developed the reputation for being a storyteller. The stories were often about dumb things I had done and the consequences of my actions. Toward the end of my career I would occasionally be asked to tell an impromptu story during an executive dinner. As retirement approached, several of my coworkers along with my high school friends, encouraged me to write down my stories. They said they found them both entertaining and educational. I would like to thank my work companions, Clark Bailey and Steve Bass, along with my high school friends, Marty Cole, Sheldon Orton, and Kevin Swenson, for providing the boost needed to get me started on writing this book.

As I began, I found my written stories were nothing like the oral stories I had told. Instead, they were like an engineering report with lots of detailed technology that detracted from the main narrative. Fortunately, I was able to retain Abby Derkson to help improve my writing skills. She was straightforward in explaining what I was doing wrong and which areas of my writing needed to be improved. It was like having a private tutor teach me how to develop creative nonfiction. I was lucky to have someone with her patience to help me. She probably should have received hazardous duty pay. At the same time, my administrative assistant at work, Kristi DeGroot, read the early stories and corrected my English mistakes all on her own time.

I would also like to express my appreciation to Alice Osborn for her help in editing and refining the stories. She not only corrected my spelling and English mistakes, but her guidance and experience made the book much more interesting to read. She provided valuable insight into which point of view and what narrative elements would be interesting to the general audience. Alice was also extremely helpful in explaining the process for preparing the book for publication and providing contacts for proofreading and formatting. Alice's vast knowledge of writing and her list of contacts, combined with her encouragement, helped me push forward to complete the book and is much appreciated.

When the book was nearing completion I was fortunate to have my former boss, Fred Stephens, review some of the stories related to my job. It was very helpful in bringing out the nuances related to the events contained within these pages. It was also very helpful to have my brother Stan review some of the stories from my youth. He remembered vividly how close I had come to doing us both in. In addition, my high school friends Sheldon and Kevin helped me sort out the particulars of my teenage years. All of these people's contributions are much valued.

I would like to express my gratitude to Michelle Argyle for her excellent job in designing the book's cover and in formatting the interior for publication. She was also extremely helpful in getting the book to the publisher and explaining how the book distribution system worked.

Finally, I would like to thank my family for their patience, encouragement, and support. My kids offered ideas and suggestions for certain sections of the book. Betty Huff offered encouragement and corrected some of the details, as did my aunt Louis Westwood and niece Olivia Huff. Their help and encouragement is also treasured.

About the Author

Clark Huff believes he was extremely fortunate to grow up in Spanish Fork, Utah; a small town that would tolerate an adventurous but disobedient boy and help him to learn from his mistakes. He quickly found that his favorite recreation was hunting, fishing, and skiing. He attended the University of Utah on a scholarship and graduated with a degree in metallurgical engineering. Clark began his career as an associate engineer at a mineral production facility located in Moab, Utah. Although he continued to pull pranks and make mistakes, he learned from them and eventually gained a reputation for solving difficult problems. Besides Moab, he has lived in North Carolina, Nebraska, and Illinois, as he advanced in the company to finally become the Vice President of Capital and Technology. During his career, he traveled throughout the world. Clark retired in 2012, but occasionally does consulting work. He spends much of his free time enjoying the outdoors, often with his children and grandchildren. Clark currently lives in a quiet town right outside Raleigh, North Carolina.

Made in the USA
Columbia, SC
16 July 2021